LESSONS FROM POLLYANNA:

Using her Glad Game to grow spiritually & have more joy in your life!

Autumn Macarthur

ABOUT THE AUTHOR

Autumn Macarthur is a USA Today bestselling Australian author of Christian romance and devotionals living near London with her very English husband (aka The Cat Magnet) and an increasing number of spoiled rescue cats. She also lives with a pesky neurological condition that makes life unpredictable and challenging!

She loves writing deeply emotional stories to make you smile and remind you how big and wide and deep God's love and forgiveness can be.

When she's not busy herding that growing family of cats, she can be found blogging at http://faithhopeandheartwarming.com, on Goodreads, and on Facebook as Autumn Macarthur.

Stay up to date with her book news and get a free ebook – sign up for her mailing list at https://www.subscribepage.com/LFPsubscribers

She'd love to hear from you!

Faith, hope, & heartwarming –
inspirational romance to make you smile.

Lessons from Pollyanna

Using her Glad Game to grow spiritually & have more joy in your life!

AUTUMN MACARTHUR

ORIGINAL STORY BY
ELEANOR H. PORTER

First Print Edition, January 2017

ISBN-13: 9781520429847

Published by Faith, Hope, & Heartwarming
http://faithhopeandheartwarming.com

CONTENTS

Chapter 1: Miss Polly……………………………………………….... 1

Chapter 2: Old Tom and Nancy……………………………………... 6

Chapter 3: The Coming of Pollyanna………………………………. 11

Chapter 4: The Little Attic Room…………………………………… 18

Chapter 5: The Game……………………………………………….. 25

Chapter 6: A Question of Duty……………………………………... 31

Chapter 7: Pollyanna and Punishments…………………………….. 38

Chapter 8: Pollyanna Pays a Visit…………………………………... 44

Chapter 9: Which Tells of the Man………………………………… 53

Chapter 10: A Surprise for Mrs. Snow……..…………………….... 58

Chapter 11: Introducing Jimmy……………………………………… 67

Chapter 12: Before the Ladies' Aid…………………………….….. 75

Chapter 13: In Pendleton Woods…………………………………… 80

Chapter 14: Just a Matter of Jelly…………………………………... 86

Chapter 15: Dr. Chilton……………………………………………… 92

Chapter 16: A Red Rose and a Lace Shawl………………………… 100

Chapter 17: "Just Like a Book"……………………………………… 108

Chapter 18: Prisms…………………………………………………… 114

Chapter 19: Which is Somewhat Surprising………………………… 120

Chapter 20: Which is More Surprising……………………………... 125

Chapter 21: A Question Answered…………………………………… 131

Chapter 22: Sermons and Woodboxes……………………………… 136

Chapter 23: An Accident…………………………………………….. 144

Chapter 24: John Pendleton………………………………………… 150

Chapter 25: A Waiting Game………………………………………… 157

Chapter 26: A Door Ajar……………………………………………. 163

Chapter 27: Two Visits………………………………………………. 167

Chapter 28: The Game and Its Players……………………………… 174

Chapter 29: Through An Open Window…………………………….. 183

Chapter 30: Jimmy Takes the Helm………………………………... 189

Chapter 31: A New Uncle…………………………………………… 193

Chapter 30: Which is a Letter from Pollyanna……………………… 196

Conclusion & How to play the Glad Game…………………………. 200

Book group discussion questions…………………………………….. 204

How to have a personal relationship with Jesus…………………….. 205

INTRODUCTION

God wants us to live in joy.

We can be sure of that, because He tells us so, often! Pollyanna's father reminded her there are 800 rejoicing verses. My search in the New International Version on the words joy, rejoice, glad, happy, happiness, and praise actually gave nearly a thousand results. That's a lot of praise and rejoicing!

If we follow Jesus, we *should* have joy. R.C. Sproul says, "Over and over again in the pages of the New Testament, the idea of joy is communicated as an imperative, as an obligation. Based on the biblical teaching, I would go so far as to say that it is the Christian's duty, his moral obligation, to be joyful."

But that doesn't mean it's easy. Most of us experience fleeting moments of happiness. Maybe sometimes, amazingly, even days, weeks, or months of it. But we're not in the habit of joy. Inevitably, something will happen to knock us out of our joy.

One of the reasons the book and film of *Pollyanna* is so beloved is the emphasis on gladness. Cynics see Pollyanna as deluded and unrealistic, so much so that The American Heritage Dictionary defines "Pollyanna" as "a person regarded as being foolishly or blindly optimistic." It's become a criticism to call someone a Pollyanna.

In fact, the book is far from deluded or blind to the faults of people and the world. The author is gently satirical, contrasting Pollyanna's optimistic and literal-minded interpretation of what she sees and hears with people's actual intentions. Pollyanna does see things that aren't how she hoped, she is fearful, she grieves. But she also looks for the best in everything, the blessing to be grateful for.

"People have thought that Pollyanna chirped that she was 'glad' at everything... I have never believed that we ought to deny discomfort and pain and evil; I have merely thought that it is far better to 'greet the unknown with a cheer'," said the author Eleanor H. Porter, defending herself and the book against criticism. "Pollyanna did not pretend that everything was sugar-coated goodness.... Pollyanna was positively determined to find the good in every situation."

The truth is, we don't live in a good world filled with good people who always do the right thing. Neither did Pollyanna. We live in a fallen broken world, with fallen broken people. Bad things happen, things we don't want and don't understand. We make mistakes. Wishing it was different doesn't make it so.

Faith in God is what lifts hope we can make the best of things from blind optimism to a true spiritual practice. Trusting that He has a plan and a purpose to bring good out of all that happens to us makes it possible to feel true confidence in the present and the future, and know a real and lasting joy, no matter what happens. As John Piper says, "Hope that is really known and treasured has a huge and decisive effect on our present values and choices and actions."

When I read Pollyanna as a child, I enjoyed the story, but never guessed how much spiritual truth was hidden within it until I re-read it as an adult. There's so much we can learn from this story! Though on the surface it's a children's story, it reads as if much of it is targeted at Christian women. As the story was initially serialized in a Christian women's magazine, they would have been the main readers, at least initially. God has a message for us with this story, even now, over a hundred years after it was written.

We're designed to feel joy. God programmed it into our very DNA as He created us. Too often, the hurts and challenges of life can stop us feeling that joy, but God's will is for us to rediscover it and to revel in it!

> *Rejoice always, pray continually, give thanks in all circumstances;*
> *for this is God's will for you in Christ Jesus.*
> 1 Thessalonians 5:16-18 (NIV)

We need to choose joy, not just once but again and again and again. Choosing joy is one of the biggest ways we can show our faith and trust in God. It means truly believing that He can and will bring our highest good from everything that happens, even our own wrong choices.

When I started on this project, I was pretty much the last person you'd think God would call to write a book on growing a more joyful life! After a year of challenges, I was downright miserable, despite my apparent faith. I'd struggled to accept a new long-term health issue, one that thankfully won't kill me but does make life way more difficult than I like and has meant I can't see any way to fulfill so many dreams. I'd achieved far less than I wanted to do with my writing, chronically behind schedule despite working as hard as I could. I felt I'd failed as a wife, often annoyed and impatient with my doubly disabled husband. I regretted so many mistakes and wrong choices I'd made in my life. Oh, I posted plenty of pretty faith-filled memes to Twitter and Facebook. I prayed and read my Bible every day.

But all that hid the ugly truth: I wasn't feeling any joy or love. I wasn't writing, because how could I write joyful triumphant stories of love and overcoming when I wasn't feeling it?

For years, I didn't own any clothing in grey, thinking it was a non-color, dull, lifeless, joyless. Or black, a mourning color. They look beautiful on some people, but not me. I always wore autumn colors, warm browns, vibrant teal and turquoise, bright leaf greens and rich sea blues.

But almost all the clothes I bought in the past year are grey. Most days, you'll find me wearing grey. I realized, I'd gone into mourning for the old me, the me and all the hopes and dreams that died when I got ill. Last time I did that was years ago, after my fifth miscarriage. I looked in my wardrobe one day about six months after losing baby Rose, and realized everything was black. I hadn't planned it like that, it just happened.

So the idea of choosing joy was about the furthest thing from my mind. I think if someone suggested it to me as an option for getting out of the hole I was in, I would have screamed at them — *How can I possible choose joy, when my life has fallen apart?*

The story I'd been working on, oddly enough, featured a disabled hero, angry with God and everyone around him. The heroine was very much a Pollyanna, always looking on the bright side, despite her own life challenges. Naturally, she drives the hero nuts, in a good way! But only when God nudged me to read Pollyanna again to get some insight for her character (and okay, I admit, I was procrastinating writing that story,too!), did I realize that my bubbly, bouncy, always-happy heroine hid her own anger with God. Only when she admitted that to herself, admitted she couldn't forgive God for all the many things that hadn't worked out the way she'd hoped and prayed, could she drop the false front and find true joy.

Like Pollyanna, both those story characters (The Real Thing, releasing December 2017) and I had to learn that God wants us to live in joy, but that feeling the joy and gladness He intends for us is our choice. We need to grieve, we need to feel sorrow and anger when things feel like they're going wrong, and then we need to move past that, handing those feelings to God, and trusting Him to take care of our present and our future. Joy and bitterness can't live together in the same heart, as Miss Polly finds in *Pollyanna*.

> *The Holy Spirit produces a different kind of fruit: unconditional love, joy, peace, patience,*
> *kindheartedness, goodness, faithfulness, gentleness, and self-control.*
> Galatians 5:22-23 VOICE

Joy is not negotiable! It's a fruit of the Spirit. Not a gift given only a few but something we all should demonstrate in our lives.

So we start by opening our hearts to God on to His Spirit. Being honest with Him and ourselves about what we really feel and the mistakes we've made. We ask Him to forgive us, and to help us trust that despite the things that have gone wrong in our lives, He does intend our highest good. We need to make the conscious choice to look for the blessing and to 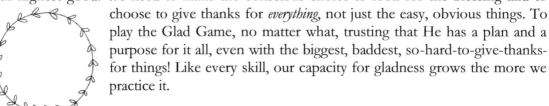 choose to give thanks for *everything*, not just the easy, obvious things. To play the Glad Game, no matter what, trusting that He has a plan and a purpose for it all, even with the biggest, baddest, so-hard-to-give-thanks-for things! Like every skill, our capacity for gladness grows the more we practice it.

The God who brings the dead to life and turns water into wine can also mend our broken places and transform our hurts into joy, if we let Him. That joy can be wild and exuberant and overwhelming, shouting praise to God with our arms in the air. Or at more challenging times, it may be quiet and stubborn and persistent, a candle flame in the dark that can't be extinguished. What it always is, is real.

Right here in the midst of all that seems wrong with our lives and the world, God is ready and waiting for us to ask Him in, waiting for us to play His version of the Glad Game. There is always a reason to be glad. Let's look for it, find it, and be thankful.

We throw open our doors to God
and discover at the same moment that he has already thrown open his door to us.
We find ourselves standing where we always hoped we might stand—out in the wide open spaces of
God's grace and glory, standing tall and shouting our praise.
Romans 5:2 MSG

HOW TO USE THIS BOOK

This book can be read two ways. Simply enjoy the story of *Pollyanna*, or also dig deeper into the spiritual truths hidden in the story with the devotional and questions for personal or group study. Each chapter of the story has its own devotional, with a quote from the book, questions to think about, and relevant Bible verses. Take the time to ponder and ideally journal your answers for the questions in each one.

To get the most from the devotional and journal questions, don't rush. You'll find doing one entry a day or even slowly working through just one a week is plenty! You'll get more from the process by slowing down and allowing the questions to sink deeper into your heart and mind.

Some of the suggestions look deceptively simple but may open up a lot of thoughts and emotions, so give yourself all the time you need to process that and take it to God.

As you start each section, ask God to show you what He wants you to see today. You can simply read the questions and ask that God gives you insight as the day goes by. You may be surprised what answers surface!

Or written journaling is a wonderful way to get in touch with your thoughts and feelings, and to discern God's guidance. I've made a matching journal, to accompany this book, with plenty of space to write your thoughts and responses. Or you can write anywhere that feels comfortable for you, a notebook, loose paper, a file on your phone or laptop. Write as much or as little as feels right to you. Some days that may be just a few lines, other days a topic may particularly resonate with you and you'll want to write far more.

As you write, listen for God's still small voice speaking in your heart and mind, and measure what you hear against what you know of God from His Word. Over time, you get better at hearing it, and knowing you can trust it. There are no right or wrong answers. It's very likely that as you read thoughtfully, you'll see other truths in the chapter beside those I discuss. But don't push it if you're not getting a lot some days. You may find that you ask the questions in the journal session, and the answers come later.

It's worth going back to look at those questions you wrote very little on, maybe a few weeks or months later. Ponder the questions prayerfully. If you look at the questions and your answers and feel a sense of peace, it could be that you have no issue in that area. That's great! But if you look at the questions and want to turn the page as fast as possible, it could be that's the exact topic God is asking you to look at more closely. It's not easy, but try to be willing to go with that. Ask God to guide you and support you.

If a question touches on something you find an especially sensitive issue, it's wisest not to force yourself to push through pain. You don't have to deal with it alone. Pray, seeking support first from God and then from someone you trust—a friend, a family member, or your pastor. Some of the questions go deep. Sometimes we need to let go of old deep hurts to be able to feel the joy God has waiting for us.

My prayer for you as you journal your way through the story is that you will find joy. True joy, not a superficial false front, going through the motions of being glad, but a soul-deep heart-felt joy no circumstance can shake.

God intends for us to live our lives gladly and joyfully. He created us for joy.

With His help, let's open our hearts and minds to living with joy, trust, and gratitude every day, no matter what we face in our lives.

Autumn♡

PS: If you're not sure you have a personal relationship with Jesus, or if you're a seeker wanting to know more about what it means to be a Christ-follower, you might find the chapter on page 202 is a good place to start.

CHAPTER 1:
MISS POLLY

Miss Polly Harrington entered her kitchen a little hurriedly this June morning. Miss Polly did not usually make hurried movements; she specially prided herself on her repose of manner. But to-day she was hurrying — actually hurrying.

Nancy, washing dishes at the sink, looked up in surprise. Nancy had been working in Miss Polly's kitchen only two months, but already she knew that her mistress did not usually hurry.

"Nancy!"

"Yes, ma'am." Nancy answered cheerfully, but she still continued wiping the pitcher in her hand.

"Nancy," — Miss Polly's voice was very stern now — "when I'm talking to you, I wish you to stop your work and listen to what I have to say."

Nancy flushed miserably. She set the pitcher down at once, with the cloth still about it, thereby nearly tipping it over — which did not add to her composure.

"Yes, ma'am; I will, ma'am," she stammered, righting the pitcher, and turning hastily. "I was only keepin' on with my work 'cause you specially told me this mornin' ter hurry with my dishes, ye know."

Her mistress frowned.

"That will do, Nancy. I did not ask for explanations. I asked for your attention."

"Yes, ma'am." Nancy stifled a sigh. She was wondering if ever in any way she could please this woman. Nancy had never "worked out" before; but a sick mother suddenly widowed and left with three younger children besides Nancy herself, had forced the girl into doing something toward their support, and she had been so pleased when she found a place in the kitchen of the great house on the hill — Nancy had come from "The Corners," six miles away, and she knew Miss Polly Harrington only as the mistress of the old Harrington homestead, and one of the wealthiest residents of the town. That was two months before. She knew Miss Polly now as a stern, severe-faced woman who frowned if a knife clattered to the floor, or if a door banged — but who never thought to smile even when knives and doors were still.

"When you've finished your morning work, Nancy," Miss Polly was saying now, "you may clear the little room at the head of the stairs in the attic, and make up the cot bed. Sweep the room and clean it, of course, after you clear out the trunks and boxes."

"Yes, ma'am. And where shall I put the things, please, that I take out?"

"In the front attic." Miss Polly hesitated, then went on: "I suppose I may as well tell you now, Nancy. My niece, Miss Pollyanna Whittier, is coming to live with me. She is eleven years old, and will sleep in that room."

"A little girl — coming here, Miss Harrington? Oh, won't that be nice!" cried Nancy, thinking of the sunshine her own little sisters made in the home at "The Corners."

"Nice? Well, that isn't exactly the word I should use," rejoined Miss Polly, stiffly. "However, I intend to make the best of it, of course. I am a good woman, I hope; and I know my duty."

Nancy colored hotly.

"Of course, ma'am; it was only that I thought a little girl here might — might brighten things up for you," she faltered.

"Thank you," rejoined the lady, dryly. "I can't say, however, that I see any immediate need for that."

"But, of course, you — you'd want her, your sister's child," ventured Nancy, vaguely feeling that somehow she must prepare a welcome for this lonely little stranger.

Miss Polly lifted her chin haughtily.

"Well, really, Nancy, just because I happened to have a sister who was silly enough to marry and bring unnecessary children into a world that was already quite full enough, I can't see how I should particularly *want* to have the care of them myself. However, as I said before, I hope I know my duty. See that you clean the corners, Nancy," she finished sharply, as she left the room.

"Yes, ma'am," sighed Nancy, picking up the half-dried pitcher — now so cold it must be rinsed again.

In her own room, Miss Polly took out once more the letter which she had received two days before from the far-away Western town, and which had been so unpleasant a surprise to her. The letter was addressed to Miss Polly Harrington, Beldingsville, Vermont; and it read as follows:

Dear Madam: — I regret to inform you that the Rev. John Whittier died two weeks ago, leaving one child, a girl eleven years old. He left practically nothing else save a few books; for, as you doubtless know, he was the pastor of this small mission church, and had a very meager salary.

I believe he was your deceased sister's husband, but he gave me to understand the families were not on the best of terms. He thought, however, that for your sister's sake you might wish to take the child and bring her up among her own people in the East. Hence I am writing to you.

The little girl will be all ready to start by the time you get this letter; and if you can take her, we would appreciate it very much if you would write that she might come at once, as there is a man and his wife here who are going East very soon, and they would take her with them to Boston, and put her on the Beldingsville train. Of course you would be notified what day and train to expect Pollyanna on.

Hoping to hear favorably from you soon, I remain,

Respectfully yours,

Jeremiah O. White.

With a frown Miss Polly folded the letter and tucked it into its envelope. She had answered it the day before, and she had said she would take the child, of course. She hoped she knew her duty well enough for that! — disagreeable as the task would be.

As she sat now, with the letter in her hands, her thoughts went back to her sister, Jennie, who had been this child's mother, and to the time when Jennie, as a girl of twenty, had insisted upon marrying the young minister, in spite of her family's remonstrances. There had been a man of wealth who had wanted her — and the family had much preferred him to the minister; but Jennie had not. The man of wealth had more years, as well as more money, to his credit, while the minister had only a young head full of youth's ideals and enthusiasm, and a heart full of love.

Jennie had preferred these — quite naturally, perhaps; so she had married the minister, and had gone south with him as a home missionary's wife.

The break had come then. Miss Polly remembered it well, though she had been but a girl of fifteen, the youngest, at the time. The family had had little more to do with the missionary's wife. To be sure, Jennie herself had written, for a time, and had named her last baby "Pollyanna" for her two sisters, Polly and Anna — the other babies had all died. This had been the last time that Jennie had written; and in a few years there had come the news of her death, told in a short, but heart-broken little note from the minister himself, dated at a little town in the West.

Meanwhile, time had not stood still for the occupants of the great house on the hill. Miss Polly, looking out at the far-reaching valley below, thought of the changes those twenty-five years had brought to her.

She was forty now, and quite alone in the world. Father, mother, sisters — all were dead. For years, now, she had been sole mistress of the house and of the thousands left her by her father. There were people who had openly pitied her lonely life, and who had urged her to have some friend or companion to live with her; but she had not welcomed either their sympathy or their advice. She was not lonely, she said. She liked being by herself. She preferred quiet. But now —

Miss Polly rose with frowning face and closely-shut lips. She was glad, of course, that she was a good woman, and that she not only knew her duty, but had sufficient strength of character to perform it.

But — POLLYANNA! — what a ridiculous name!

CHAPTER 1
DEVOTIONAL & JOURNAL

"She was glad, of course, that she was a good woman, and that she not only knew her duty, but had sufficient strength of character to perform it."

Miss Polly, a middle-aged single woman, reluctantly takes responsibility for her orphaned niece. Are Miss Polly's words and behavior as she prepares for Pollyanna's arrival those of a truly "good woman"? Why or why not?

Does Miss Polly show any signs of faith in God in this chapter, or only faith in herself?

It's easy to fall into self-sufficiency, the trap of thinking we're strong enough to do whatever we need to do without calling on God's help. Nearly all of us do sometimes, and some of us do all the time! We may even have been taught it's a good thing to do. We live in a society that values being strong and appearing to have it all together. But the secret truth we live with and do our best to hide is our knowledge we're not so strong or so good. Many of us live with a constant struggle to appear to be good enough, and to make sure our secret weakness isn't seen by anyone else.

For most of my life I felt I could do it on my own, and I wanted to. I prided myself on my strength, my endurance, my capacity to DIY. I was brought up to be willing to have a go at doing just about anything, from climbing a cliff to moving across the world on my own to renovating a house unassisted. I was used to seeing myself as strong, and I didn't want to have to rely on anyone for anything. As a nurse, my life-long job had been helping others. I was also caregiver to my disabled husband, so accustomed to being the strong one in our marriage, too.

But my relationship with God was on the shallow side. I didn't pray, really pray from the depths of my heart, all that often. I didn't ask His help unless it was an emergency. I wasn't letting God be God. I called Him Lord, but I wasn't surrendering to Him and giving Him Lordship over my life.

Then things went wrong. Suddenly, my strength disappeared. I couldn't even walk to the bathroom by myself! A disabling and long-term untreatable illness made me face just how limited my own abilities are, and how easily shattered my belief I could do it all myself was.

Thankfully, God is there for us. He created us to live in reliance on his strength, not our own.

"I am the vine, and you are the branches.
If you stay joined to me, and I to you, you will produce plenty of fruit.
But separated from me you won't be able to do anything.
John 15:5 ERV

This is a great way to look at how things should be for us with God. He is the trunk and roots, the source of all the rest of the plant, giving us nourishment and support. We are the branches, visible in the world, producing fruit. We can get to look at the fruit we produce, and start thinking we're doing it on our own.

But as much of the plant is underground and invisible as shows above the surface. Cut off a branch, and it doesn't affect the rest of the plant too much. The roots stay strong. But it *does* affect the branch. Separated from the trunk and the roots, the branch can't feed or support itself. It stops producing fruit. It withers and dies.

Separated from Him, we can do nothing. It's a tough lesson to learn, in our self-reliant world. It took a long, painful struggle, but having to admit I can't do it on my own and that I need help, I've drawn so much closer to God (and my husband too!).

The change is like the difference between a friend you have nice easy chats with on FB now and then; and the friend you talk to every day about everything, no secrets, the one you know you can ask to come over and help you when you really need help. I know I need God. I know I need help. I don't have to pretend to be strong all the time any more. Even if I recover from this illness and become physically more able to do for myself, I won't forget this lesson. I want to live the life God intends for me, the life He created me for!

What challenges have been caused in your life by relying on your own strength, the way Miss Polly does?

How can doing the right thing for the wrong reason cause problems?

How can you do things differently in the future, with God's help?

Lord, help me to know that You will always be there to support and strengthen me when I need you. Help me to call on You and draw on Your strength instead of relying on myself. Please help me to trust that You keep Your promises, so even if I don't feel You are with me, I know and believe You are. Thank You!

CHAPTER TWO:
OLD TOM AND NANCY

In the little attic room Nancy swept and scrubbed vigorously, paying particular attention to the corners. There were times, indeed, when the vigor she put into her work was more of a relief to her feelings than it was an ardor to efface dirt — Nancy, in spite of her frightened submission to her mistress, was no saint.

"I — just — wish — I could — dig — out the corners — of — her — soul!" she muttered jerkily, punctuating her words with murderous jabs of her pointed cleaning-stick. "There's plenty of 'em needs cleanin' all right, all right! The idea of stickin' that blessed child 'way off up here in this hot little room — with no fire in the winter, too, and all this big house ter pick and choose from! Unnecessary children, indeed! Humph!" snapped Nancy, wringing her rag so hard her fingers ached from the strain; "I guess it ain't CHILDREN what is MOST unnecessary just now, just now!"

For some time she worked in silence; then, her task finished, she looked about the bare little room in plain disgust.

"Well, it's done — my part, anyhow," she sighed. "There ain't no dirt here — and there's mighty little else. Poor little soul! — a pretty place this is ter put a homesick, lonesome child into!" she finished, going out and closing the door with a bang, "Oh!" she ejaculated, biting her lip. Then, doggedly: "Well, I don't care. I hope she did hear the bang, — I do, I do!"

In the garden that afternoon, Nancy found a few minutes in which to interview Old Tom, who had pulled the weeds and shovelled the paths about the place for uncounted years.

"Mr. Tom," began Nancy, throwing a quick glance over her shoulder to make sure she was unobserved; "did you know a little girl was comin' here ter live with Miss Polly?"

"A — what?" demanded the old man, straightening his bent back with difficulty.

"A little girl — to live with Miss Polly."

"Go on with yer jokin'," scoffed unbelieving Tom. "Why don't ye tell me the sun is a-goin' ter set in the east termorrer?"

"But it's true. She told me so herself," maintained Nancy. "It's her niece; and she's eleven years old."

The man's jaw fell.

"Sho! — I wonder, now," he muttered; then a tender light came into his faded eyes. "It ain't — but it must be — Miss Jennie's little gal! There wasn't none of the rest of 'em married. Why, Nancy, it must be Miss Jennie's little gal. Glory be ter praise! ter think of my old eyes a-seein' this!"

"Who was Miss Jennie?"

"She was an angel straight out of Heaven," breathed the man, fervently; "but the old master and missus knew her as their oldest daughter. She was twenty when she married and went away from here long years ago. Her babies all died, I heard, except the last one; and that must be the one what's a-comin'."

"She's eleven years old."

"Yes, she might be," nodded the old man.

"And she's goin' ter sleep in the attic — more shame ter HER!" scolded Nancy, with another glance over her shoulder toward the house behind her.

Old Tom frowned. The next moment a curious smile curved his lips.

"I'm a-wonderin' what Miss Polly will do with a child in the house," he said.

"Humph! Well, I'm a-wonderin' what a child will do with Miss Polly in the house!" snapped Nancy.

The old man laughed.

"I'm afraid you ain't fond of Miss Polly," he grinned.

"As if ever anybody could be fond of her!" scorned Nancy.

Old Tom smiled oddly. He stooped and began to work again.

"I guess maybe you didn't know about Miss Polly's love affair," he said slowly.

"Love affair — HER! No! — and I guess nobody else didn't, neither."

"Oh, yes they did," nodded the old man. "And the feller's livin' ter-day — right in this town, too."

"Who is he?"

"I ain't a-tellin' that. It ain't fit that I should." The old man drew himself erect. In his dim blue eyes, as he faced the house, there was the loyal servant's honest pride in the family he has served and loved for long years.

"But it don't seem possible — her and a lover," still maintained Nancy.

Old Tom shook his head.

"You didn't know Miss Polly as I did," he argued. "She used ter be real handsome — and she would be now, if she'd let herself be."

"Handsome! Miss Polly!"

"Yes. If she'd just let that tight hair of hern all out loose and careless-like, as it used ter be, and wear the sort of bunnits with posies in 'em, and the kind o' dresses all lace and white things — you'd see she'd be handsome! Miss Polly ain't old, Nancy."

"Ain't she, though? Well, then she's got an awfully good imitation of it — she has, she has!" sniffed Nancy.

"Yes, I know. It begun then — at the time of the trouble with her lover," nodded Old Tom; "and it seems as if she'd been feedin' on wormwood an' thistles ever since — she's that bitter an' prickly ter deal with."

"I should say she was," declared Nancy, indignantly. "There's no pleasin' her, nohow, no matter how you try! I wouldn't stay if 'twa'n't for the wages and the folks at home what's needin' 'em. But some day — some day I shall jest b'ile over; and when I do, of course it'll be good-by Nancy for me. It will, it will."

Old Tom shook his head.

"I know. I've felt it. It's nart'ral — but 'tain't best, child; 'tain't best. Take my word for it, 'tain't best." And again he bent his old head to the work before him.

"Nancy!" called a sharp voice.

"Y-yes, ma'am," stammered Nancy; and hurried toward the house.

CHAPTER 2
DEVOTIONAL & JOURNAL

"...it seems as if she'd been feedin' on wormwood an' thistles ever since—she's that bitter an' prickly ter deal with."

Miss Polly has become old before her time and withdrawn from society after a broken romance. Old Tom describes her as eating wormwood, a bitter herb with many medicinal uses, but potentially addictive and even poisonous when misused. Bitterness is the same. It can start with simple anger over a hurt or wrong done to us, but if we choose to dwell on the hurt, to embrace anger and remain unforgiving, the seeds of bitterness and resentment are sown.

Bitterness is described in the Bible many times as a "root", and just like weeds in the garden, a root may grow under the ground for a long time before we see the plant. Left to grow, these feelings can poison and damage every aspect of our lives, from our health, our relationships, to our sense of connection with God. Over time, our hearts become hardened, unloving, and unforgiving. It may be obvious, like Miss Polly putting her orphaned niece in an attic room because she couldn't forgive her beloved sister for leaving the family. Or it may be subtle – people we can't love or forgive, hurts we dwell on, anger with God for allowing certain things to happen, or anger with ourselves. It can show as self-sufficiency, insisting on our ability to do it on our own, needing no one, not even God's help.

When we have the root of bitterness hidden in our heart, not only does it become hard for us to love others or God, we can't let love in. We can't feel joy. We can't feel glad for anything. And bitter people aren't pleasant to be around!

It can be easy to see bitterness in others, but we may not recognize our own potential for bitterness, as our anger can feel justified. I've struggled with bitterness for many years, directed both toward God, and toward people close to me. It started as grief, first over a series of miscarriages, then over remaining childless.

Healthy grief goes through a series of stages. Not every time, and not always in order, but most often, as people recover from a loss, they'll go through denial, anger, bargaining, sadness and finally acceptance. I certainly experienced a lot of trying to cut bargains with God! Then, when the longer for baby still didn't arrive, I got angry with God, and stayed angry. I couldn't forgive God for what seemed so unfair.

I also couldn't forgive my husband. After my seventh miscarriage, seeing how upset it was, he insisted we stop trying, for my sake. My anger and bitterness was like poison for our marriage. I became hypercritical, so easily irritated. Every little thing he did wrong was magnified. A small complaint would quickly escalate into a huge, vicious argument.

Like weeds taking over a garden, our marriage turned into a loveless wasteland producing no good fruit, just more seeds of bitterness. Every argument, every angry word spoken, became another resentment added to the list. We we're living like husband and wife. More like reluctant room-mates, who couldn't wait to get away from each other.

Banish bitterness, rage and anger, shouting and slander, and any and all malicious thoughts
—these are poison. Instead, be kind and compassionate.
Graciously forgive one another just as God has forgiven you...
Ephesians 4:31,32 VOICE

As God drew me back to Him, I felt His loving forgiveness, freely given in grace. And He showed me I needed to show the same love in my own life, and extend the same grace to my husband He did to me. I need to focus on Him, instead of my anger over the past, and my expectations that my husband should change to be the way I wanted him to be.

I'm still not a perfect wife. It's true what they say about red-heads and temper, and even though the red is now mixed with grey, my fiery temper remains. But I don't use that as an excuse not to be the woman God calls me to be. If I want a loving marriage, I need to love. I need to let go of bitterness, and embrace the joy God has waiting for me. And embrace my husband more, too!

Have you seen examples of bitterness warping a person's character?

Are there any areas in your life where bitterness has taken root?

How does that affect your relationships with others?

How does it affect your relationship with God?

How does it affect your capacity for joy?

Lord, please help me to be willing to look honestly at my heart and mind and see how anger, resentment, or bitterness might affect me. Help me to see that holding onto these things poisons my joy, and harms me far more than it harms whoever I'm angry with. I know that You can heal those hurts and soften my heart. Help me to trust that You will work in my heart, helping me to forgive, making me new, and reviving my capacity to feel the joy You intend for me. Thank you!

CHAPTER THREE:
THE COMING OF POLLYANNA

In due time came the telegram announcing that Pollyanna would arrive in Beldingsville the next day, the twenty-fifth of June, at four o'clock. Miss Polly read the telegram, frowned, then climbed the stairs to the attic room. She still frowned as she looked about her.

The room contained a small bed, neatly made, two straight-backed chairs, a washstand, a bureau — without any mirror — and a small table. There were no drapery curtains at the dormer windows, no pictures on the wall. All day the sun had been pouring down upon the roof, and the little room was like an oven for heat. As there were no screens, the windows had not been raised. A big fly was buzzing angrily at one of them now, up and down, up and down, trying to get out.

Miss Polly killed the fly, swept it through the window (raising the sash an inch for the purpose), straightened a chair, frowned again, and left the room.

"Nancy," she said a few minutes later, at the kitchen door, "I found a fly up-stairs in Miss Pollyanna's room. The window must have been raised at some time. I have ordered screens, but until they come I shall expect you to see that the windows remain closed. My niece will arrive to-morrow at four o'clock. I desire you to meet her at the station. Timothy will take the open buggy and drive you over. The telegram says 'light hair, red-checked gingham dress, and straw hat.' That is all I know, but I think it is sufficient for your purpose."

"Yes, ma'am; but — you — "

Miss Polly evidently read the pause aright, for she frowned and said crisply:

"No, I shall not go. It is not necessary that I should, I think. That is all." And she turned away — Miss Polly's arrangements for the comfort of her niece, Pollyanna, were complete.

In the kitchen, Nancy sent her flatiron with a vicious dig across the dish-towel she was ironing.

"'Light hair, red-checked gingham dress, and straw hat' — all she knows, indeed! Well, I'd be ashamed ter own it up, that I would, I would — and her my onliest niece what was a-comin' from 'way across the continent!"

Promptly at twenty minutes to four the next afternoon Timothy and Nancy drove off in the open buggy to meet the expected guest. Timothy was Old Tom's son. It was sometimes said in the town that if Old Tom was Miss Polly's right-hand man, Timothy was her left.

Timothy was a good-natured youth, and a good-looking one, as well. Short as had been Nancy's stay at the house, the two were already good friends. To-day, however, Nancy was too full of her mission to be her usual talkative self; and almost in silence she took the drive to the station and alighted to wait for the train.

Over and over in her mind she was saying it "light hair, red-checked dress, straw hat." Over and over again she was wondering just what sort of child this Pollyanna was, anyway.

"I hope for her sake she's quiet and sensible, and don't drop knives nor bang doors," she sighed to Timothy, who had sauntered up to her.

"Well, if she ain't, nobody knows what'll become of the rest of us," grinned Timothy. "Imagine Miss Polly and a NOISY kid! Gorry! there goes the whistle now!"

"Oh, Timothy, I — I think it was mean ter send me," chattered the suddenly frightened Nancy, as she turned and hurried to a point where she could best watch the passengers alight at the little station.

It was not long before Nancy saw her — the slender little girl in the red-checked gingham with two fat braids of flaxen hair hanging down her back. Beneath the straw hat, an eager, freckled little face turned to the right and to the left, plainly searching for some one.

Nancy knew the child at once, but not for some time could she control her shaking knees sufficiently to go to her. The little girl was standing quite by herself when Nancy finally did approach her.

"Are you Miss — Pollyanna?" she faltered. The next moment she found herself half smothered in the clasp of two gingham-clad arms.

"Oh, I'm so glad, GLAD, GLAD to see you," cried an eager voice in her ear. "Of course I'm Pollyanna, and I'm so glad you came to meet me! I hoped you would."

"You — you did?" stammered Nancy, vaguely wondering how Pollyanna could possibly have known her — and wanted her. "You — you did?" she repeated, trying to straighten her hat.

"Oh, yes; and I've been wondering all the way here what you looked like," cried the little girl, dancing on her toes, and sweeping the embarrassed Nancy from head to foot, with her eyes. "And now I know, and I'm glad you look just like you do look."

Nancy was relieved just then to have Timothy come up. Pollyanna's words had been most confusing.

"This is Timothy. Maybe you have a trunk," she stammered.

"Yes, I have," nodded Pollyanna, importantly. "I've got a brand-new one. The Ladies' Aid bought it for me — and wasn't it lovely of them, when they wanted the carpet so? Of course I don't know how much red carpet a trunk could buy, but it ought to buy some, anyhow — much as half an aisle, don't you think? I've got a little thing here in my bag that Mr. Gray said was a check, and that I must give it to you before I could get my trunk. Mr. Gray is Mrs. Gray's husband. They're cousins of Deacon Carr's wife. I came East with them, and they're lovely! And — there, here 'tis," she finished, producing the check after much fumbling in the bag she carried.

Nancy drew a long breath. Instinctively she felt that some one had to draw one — after that speech. Then she stole a glance at Timothy.

Timothy's eyes were studiously turned away.

The three were off at last, with Pollyanna's trunk in behind, and Pollyanna herself snugly ensconced between Nancy and Timothy. During the whole process of getting started, the little girl had kept up an uninterrupted stream of comments and questions, until the somewhat dazed Nancy found herself quite out of breath trying to keep up with her.

"There! Isn't this lovely? Is it far? I hope 'tis — I love to ride," sighed Pollyanna, as the wheels began to turn. "Of course, if 'tisn't far, I sha'n't mind, though, 'cause I'll be glad to get there all the sooner, you know. What a pretty street! I knew 'twas going to be pretty; father told me — "

She stopped with a little choking breath. Nancy, looking at her apprehensively, saw that her small chin was quivering, and that her eyes were full of tears. In a moment, however, she hurried on, with a brave lifting of her head.

"Father told me all about it. He remembered. And — and I ought to have explained before. Mrs. Gray told me to, at once — about this red gingham dress, you know, and why I'm not in black. She said you'd think 'twas queer. But there weren't any black things in the last missionary barrel, only a lady's velvet basque which Deacon Carr's wife said wasn't suitable for me at all; besides, it had white spots — worn, you know — on both elbows, and some other places. Part of the Ladies' Aid wanted to buy me a black dress and hat, but the other part thought the money ought to go toward the red carpet they're trying to get — for the church, you know. Mrs. White said maybe it was just as well, anyway, for she didn't like children in black — that is, I mean, she liked the children, of course, but not the black part."

Pollyanna paused for breath, and Nancy managed to stammer:

"Well, I'm sure it — it'll be all right."

"I'm glad you feel that way. I do, too," nodded Pollyanna, again with that choking little breath. "Of course, 'twould have been a good deal harder to be glad in black — "

"Glad!" gasped Nancy, surprised into an interruption.

"Yes — that father's gone to Heaven to be with mother and the rest of us, you know. He said I must be glad. But it's been pretty hard to — to do it, even in red gingham, because I — I wanted him, so; and I couldn't help feeling I OUGHT to have him, specially as mother and the rest have God and all the angels, while I didn't have anybody but the Ladies' Aid. But now I'm sure it'll be easier because I've got you, Aunt Polly. I'm so glad I've got you!"

Nancy's aching sympathy for the poor little forlornness beside her turned suddenly into shocked terror.

"Oh, but — but you've made an awful mistake, d-dear," she faltered. "I'm only Nancy. I ain't your Aunt Polly, at all!"

"You — you AREN'T?" stammered the little girl, in plain dismay.

"No. I'm only Nancy. I never thought of your takin' me for her. We — we ain't a bit alike we ain't, we ain't!"

Timothy chuckled softly; but Nancy was too disturbed to answer the merry flash from his eyes.

"But who ARE you?" questioned Pollyanna. "You don't look a bit like a Ladies' Aider!"

Timothy laughed outright this time.

"I'm Nancy, the hired girl. I do all the work except the washin' an' hard ironin'. Mis' Durgin does that."

"But there IS an Aunt Polly?" demanded the child, anxiously.

"You bet your life there is," cut in Timothy.

Pollyanna relaxed visibly.

"Oh, that's all right, then." There was a moment's silence, then she went on brightly: "And do you know? I'm glad, after all, that she didn't come to meet me; because now I've got HER still coming, and I've got you besides."

Nancy flushed. Timothy turned to her with a quizzical smile.

"I call that a pretty slick compliment," he said. "Why don't you thank the little lady?"

"I — I was thinkin' about — Miss Polly," faltered Nancy.

Pollyanna sighed contentedly.

"I was, too. I'm so interested in her. You know she's all the aunt I've got, and I didn't know I had her for ever so long. Then father told me. He said she lived in a lovely great big house 'way on top of a hill."

"She does. You can see it now," said Nancy. "It's that big white one with the green blinds, 'way ahead."

"Oh, how pretty! — and what a lot of trees and grass all around it! I never saw such a lot of green grass, seems so, all at once. Is my Aunt Polly rich, Nancy?"

"Yes, Miss."

"I'm so glad. It must be perfectly lovely to have lots of money. I never knew any one that did have, only the Whites — they're some rich. They have carpets in every room and ice-cream Sundays. Does Aunt Polly have ice-cream Sundays?"

Nancy shook her head. Her lips twitched. She threw a merry look into Timothy's eyes.

"No, Miss. Your aunt don't like ice-cream, I guess; leastways I never saw it on her table."

Pollyanna's face fell.

"Oh, doesn't she? I'm so sorry! I don't see how she can help liking ice-cream. But — anyhow, I can be kinder glad about that, 'cause the ice-cream you don't eat can't make your stomach ache like Mrs. White's did — that is, I ate hers, you know, lots of it. Maybe Aunt Polly has got the carpets, though."

"Yes, she's got the carpets."

"In every room?"

"Well, in almost every room," answered Nancy, frowning suddenly at the thought of that bare little attic room where there was no carpet.

"Oh, I'm so glad," exulted Pollyanna. "I love carpets. We didn't have any, only two little rugs that came in a missionary barrel, and one of those had ink spots on it. Mrs. White had pictures, too, perfectly beautiful ones of roses and little girls kneeling and a kitty and some lambs and a lion — not together, you know — the lambs and the lion. Oh, of course the Bible says they will sometime, but they haven't yet — that is, I mean Mrs. White's haven't. Don't you just love pictures?"

"I — I don't know," answered Nancy in a half-stifled voice.

"I do. We didn't have any pictures. They don't come in the barrels much, you know. There did two come once, though. But one was so good father sold it to get money to buy me some shoes with; and the other was so bad it fell to pieces just as soon as we hung it up. Glass — it broke, you know. And I cried. But I'm glad now we didn't have any of those nice things, 'cause I shall like Aunt Polly's all the better — not being used to 'em, you see. Just as it is when the PRETTY hair-ribbons come in the barrels after a lot of faded-out brown ones. My! but isn't this a perfectly beautiful house?" she broke off fervently, as they turned into the wide driveway.

It was when Timothy was unloading the trunk that Nancy found an opportunity to mutter low in his ear:

"Don't you never say nothin' ter me again about leavin', Timothy Durgin. You couldn't HIRE me ter leave!"

"Leave! I should say not," grinned the youth. "You couldn't drag me away. It'll be more fun here now, with that kid 'round, than movin'-picture shows, every day!"

"Fun! — fun!" repeated Nancy, indignantly, "I guess it'll be somethin' more than fun for that blessed child — when them two tries ter live tergether; and I guess she'll be a-needin' some rock ter fly to for refuge. Well, I'm a-goin' ter be that rock, Timothy; I am, I am!" she vowed, as she turned and led Pollyanna up the broad steps.

CHAPTER 3
DEVOTIONAL &JOURNAL

Almost as soon as she meets Pollyanna, Nancy sees the gap between Pollyanna's hopes and the reality of what Miss Polly is providing. She decides to be the girl's *"rock ter fly to for refuge"*.

The Lord is my Rock, my fortress, my place of safety.
He is my God, the Rock I run to for protection.
He is my shield; by his power I am saved. He is my hiding place high in the hills.
Psalm 18:2 ERV

Loneliness is one of the most hurtful emotions, tapping into a soul-deep fear: I am all alone. But it can feel hard sometimes to make connections with other people. I spent much of my life feeling painfully lonely. I didn't believe I deserved love, and so it seemed impossible anyone could truly care for me. Crippling shyness and fear of rejection stopped me reaching out to people. I retreated into a world of books, instead of trying to make contact with people. Yet I desperately longed to be loved.

Come close to the one true God, and He will draw close to you.
Wash your hands; you have dirtied them in sin. Cleanse your heart, because your mind is split down the middle, your love for God on one side and selfish pursuits on the other.
James 4:8 VOICE

God doesn't intend for us to be lonely. He loves His people fiercely, and waits for us to turn to Him. Ultimately, He is enough to meet our needs. But it can take time to develop that level of relationship with Him. And He intends us to live in community with others. He loves us, and He also loves us through other people.

What made the difference for me was drawing nearer to God and deepening my relationship with Him. If we tell God we feel lonely, He can meet us where we are. When we try to pretend we don't need anyone, we block His help. Once I let go of resentment and anger, and stopped blaming other people for my loneliness, I could feel the reality of God's love and forgiveness. I didn't need or want so much from other people, so reaching out and risking rejection felt less scary. At last, I found true friends, and peace of mind.

What does God being your "rock, refuge and hiding place" mean to you?

How do you experience that as a reality in your life? If you're not feeling it, what could you change to make it real?

Is there anyone God might be asking you to be a rock for? What one thing could you do today for that person?

Is there someone in your life you could go to if you needed help? If you can't name anyone, what step could you take today to reach out to someone to change that?
As a start, we have a Facebook group for encouragement and sharing:
https://www.facebook.com/groups/LessonsfromPollyanna

Lord, please, help me to know You as my rock and my refuge, always there for me, always ready to comfort and welcome me. Please, when I feel alone, remind me I need to get right with You first before I can open my heart to anyone else. Help me to get the balance right—admitting when I need help, knowing when I should seek it in some time alone with You, and knowing when I need You to show Your love for me through someone else's presence. Show me the people in my life who care for me, who are willing to there when I need someone. Show me who You would have me be a rock to, and help me to offer that person support when they need it. Open my heart to being Your love in the world. Help me to give as much love as I accept, and to accept as much love as I give. Thank You!

CHAPTER FOUR:
THE LITTLE ATTIC ROOM

Miss Polly Harrington did not rise to meet her niece. She looked up from her book, it is true, as Nancy and the little girl appeared in the sitting-room doorway, and she held out a hand with "duty" written large on every coldly extended finger.

"How do you do, Pollyanna? I — " She had no chance to say more. Pollyanna, had fairly flown across the room and flung herself into her aunt's scandalized, unyielding lap.

"Oh, Aunt Polly, Aunt Polly, I don't know how to be glad enough that you let me come to live with you," she was sobbing. "You don't know how perfectly lovely it is to have you and Nancy and all this after you've had just the Ladies' Aid!"

"Very likely — though I've not had the pleasure of the Ladies' Aid's acquaintance," rejoined Miss Polly, stiffly, trying to unclasp the small, clinging fingers, and turning frowning eyes on Nancy in the doorway. "Nancy, that will do. You may go. Pollyanna, be good enough, please, to stand erect in a proper manner. I don't know yet what you look like."

Pollyanna drew back at once, laughing a little hysterically.

"No, I suppose you don't; but you see I'm not very much to look at, anyway, on account of the freckles. Oh, and I ought to explain about the red gingham and the black velvet basque with white spots on the elbows. I told Nancy how father said — "

"Yes; well, never mind now what your father said," interrupted Miss Polly, crisply. "You had a trunk, I presume?"

"Oh, yes, indeed, Aunt Polly. I've got a beautiful trunk that the Ladies' Aid gave me. I haven't got so very much in it — of my own, I mean. The barrels haven't had many clothes for little girls in them lately; but there were all father's books, and Mrs. White said she thought I ought to have those. You see, father — "

"Pollyanna," interrupted her aunt again, sharply, "there is one thing that might just as well be understood right away at once; and that is, I do not care to have you keep talking of your father to me."

The little girl drew in her breath tremulously.

"Why, Aunt Polly, you — you mean — " She hesitated, and her aunt filled the pause.

"We will go up-stairs to your room. Your trunk is already there, I presume. I told Timothy to take it up — if you had one. You may follow me, Pollyanna."

Without speaking, Pollyanna turned and followed her aunt from the room. Her eyes were brimming with tears, but her chin was bravely high.

"After all, I — I reckon I'm glad she doesn't want me to talk about father," Pollyanna was thinking. "It'll be easier, maybe — if I don't talk about him. Probably, anyhow, that is why she told me not to talk about him." And Pollyanna, convinced anew of her aunt's "kindness," blinked off the tears and looked eagerly about her.

She was on the stairway now. Just ahead, her aunt's black silk skirt rustled luxuriously. Behind her an open door allowed a glimpse of soft-tinted rugs and satin-covered chairs. Beneath her feet a marvellous carpet was like green moss to the tread. On every side the gilt of picture frames or the glint of sunlight through the filmy mesh of lace curtains flashed in her eyes.

"Oh, Aunt Polly, Aunt Polly," breathed the little girl, rapturously; "what a perfectly lovely, lovely house! How awfully glad you must be you're so rich!"

"PollyANNA!" ejaculated her aunt, turning sharply about as she reached the head of the stairs. "I'm surprised at you — making a speech like that to me!"

"Why, Aunt Polly, AREN'T you?" queried Pollyanna, in frank wonder.

"Certainly not, Pollyanna. I hope I could not so far forget myself as to be sinfully proud of any gift the Lord has seen fit to bestow upon me," declared the lady; "certainly not, of RICHES!"

Miss Polly turned and walked down the hall toward the attic stairway door. She was glad, now, that she had put the child in the attic room. Her idea at first had been to get her niece as far away as possible from herself, and at the same time place her where her childish heedlessness would not destroy valuable furnishings. Now — with this evident strain of vanity showing thus early — it was all the more fortunate that the room planned for her was plain and sensible, thought Miss Polly.

Eagerly Pollyanna's small feet pattered behind her aunt. Still more eagerly her big blue eyes tried to look in all directions at once, that no thing of beauty or interest in this wonderful house might be passed unseen. Most eagerly of all her mind turned to the wondrously exciting problem about to be solved: behind which of all these fascinating doors was waiting now her room — the dear, beautiful room full of curtains, rugs, and pictures, that was to be her very own? Then, abruptly, her aunt opened a door and ascended another stairway.

There was little to be seen here. A bare wall rose on either side. At the top of the stairs, wide reaches of shadowy space led to far corners where the roof came almost down to the floor, and where were stacked innumerable trunks and boxes. It was hot and stifling, too.

Unconsciously Pollyanna lifted her head higher — it seemed so hard to breathe. Then she saw that her aunt had thrown open a door at the right.

"There, Pollyanna, here is your room, and your trunk is here, I see. Have you your key?"

Pollyanna nodded dumbly. Her eyes were a little wide and frightened.

Her aunt frowned.

"When I ask a question, Pollyanna, I prefer that you should answer aloud not merely with your head."

"Yes, Aunt Polly."

"Thank you; that is better. I believe you have everything that you need here," she added, glancing at the well-filled towel rack and water pitcher. "I will send Nancy up to help you unpack. Supper is at six o'clock," she finished, as she left the room and swept down-stairs.

For a moment after she had gone Pollyanna stood quite still, looking after her. Then she turned her wide eyes to the bare wall, the bare floor, the bare windows. She turned them last to the little trunk that had stood not so long before in her own little room in the far-away Western home. The next moment she stumbled blindly toward it and fell on her knees at its side, covering her face with her hands.

Nancy found her there when she came up a few minutes later.

"There, there, you poor lamb," she crooned, dropping to the floor and drawing the little girl into her arms. "I was just a-fearin' I'd find you like this, like this."

Pollyanna shook her head.

"But I'm bad and wicked, Nancy — awful wicked," she sobbed. "I just can't make myself understand that God and the angels needed my father more than I did."

"No more they did, neither," declared Nancy, stoutly.

"Oh-h! — NANCY!" The burning horror in Pollyanna's eyes dried the tears.

Nancy gave a shamefaced smile and rubbed her own eyes vigorously.

"There, there, child, I didn't mean it, of course," she cried briskly. "Come, let's have your key and we'll get inside this trunk and take out your dresses in no time, no time."

Somewhat tearfully Pollyanna produced the key.

"There aren't very many there, anyway," she faltered.

"Then they're all the sooner unpacked," declared Nancy.

Pollyanna gave a sudden radiant smile.

"That's so! I can be glad of that, can't I?" she cried.

Nancy stared.

"Why, of — course," she answered a little uncertainly.

Nancy's capable hands made short work of unpacking the books, the patched undergarments, and the few pitifully unattractive dresses.

Pollyanna, smiling bravely now, flew about, hanging the dresses in the closet, stacking the books on the table, and putting away the undergarments in the bureau drawers.

"I'm sure it — it's going to be a very nice room. Don't you think so?" she stammered, after a while.

There was no answer. Nancy was very busy, apparently, with her head in the trunk. Pollyanna, standing at the bureau, gazed a little wistfully at the bare wall above.

"And I can be glad there isn't any looking glass here, too, 'cause where there ISN'T any glass I can't see my freckles."

Nancy made a sudden queer little sound with her mouth — but when Pollyanna turned, her head was in the trunk again. At one of the windows, a few minutes later, Pollyanna gave a glad cry and clapped her hands joyously.

"Oh, Nancy, I hadn't seen this before," she breathed. "Look — 'way off there, with those trees and the houses and that lovely church spire, and the river shining just like silver. Why, Nancy, there doesn't anybody need any pictures with that to look at. Oh, I'm so glad now she let me have this room!"

To Pollyanna's surprise and dismay, Nancy burst into tears. Pollyanna hurriedly crossed to her side.

"Why, Nancy, Nancy — what is it?" she cried; then, fearfully: "This wasn't — YOUR room, was it?"

"My room!" stormed Nancy, hotly, choking back the tears. "If you ain't a little angel straight from Heaven, and if some folks don't eat dirt before — Oh, land! there's her bell!" After which amazing speech, Nancy sprang to her feet, dashed out of the room, and went clattering down the stairs.

Left alone, Pollyanna went back to her "picture," as she mentally designated the beautiful view from the window. After a time she touched the sash tentatively. It seemed as if no longer could she endure the stifling heat. To her joy the sash moved under her fingers. The next moment the window was wide open, and Pollyanna was leaning far out, drinking in the fresh, sweet air.

She ran then to the other window. That, too, soon flew up under her eager hands. A big fly swept past her nose, and buzzed noisily about the room. Then another came, and another; but Pollyanna paid no heed. Pollyanna had made a wonderful discovery — against this window a huge tree flung great branches. To Pollyanna they looked like arms outstretched, inviting her. Suddenly she laughed aloud.

"I believe I can do it," she chuckled. The next moment she had climbed nimbly to the window ledge. From there it was an easy matter to step to the nearest tree-branch. Then, clinging like a monkey, she swung herself from limb to limb until the lowest branch was reached. The drop to the ground was — even for Pollyanna, who was used to climbing trees — a little fearsome. She took it, however, with bated breath, swinging from her strong little arms, and landing on all fours in the soft grass. Then she picked herself up and looked eagerly about her.

She was at the back of the house. Before her lay a garden in which a bent old man was working. Beyond the garden a little path through an open field led up a steep hill, at the top of which a lone pine tree stood on guard beside the huge rock. To Pollyanna, at the moment, there seemed to be just one place in the world worth being in — the top of that big rock.

With a run and a skilful turn, Pollyanna skipped by the bent old man, threaded her way between the orderly rows of green growing things, and — a little out of breath — reached the path that ran through the open field. Then, determinedly, she began to climb. Already, however, she was thinking what a long, long way off that rock must be, when back at the window it had looked so near!

Fifteen minutes later the great clock in the hallway of the Harrington homestead struck six. At precisely the last stroke Nancy sounded the bell for supper.

One, two, three minutes passed. Miss Polly frowned and tapped the floor with her slipper. A little jerkily she rose to her feet, went into the hall, and looked up-stairs, plainly impatient. For a minute she listened intently; then she turned and swept into the dining room.

"Nancy," she said with decision, as soon as the little serving-maid appeared; "my niece is late. No, you need not call her," she added severely, as Nancy made a move toward the hall door. "I told her what time supper was, and now she will have to suffer the consequences. She may as well begin at once to learn to be punctual. When she comes down she may have bread and milk in the kitchen."

"Yes, ma'am." It was well, perhaps, that Miss Polly did not happen to be looking at Nancy's face just then.

At the earliest possible moment after supper, Nancy crept up the back stairs and thence to the attic room.

"Bread and milk, indeed! — and when the poor lamb hain't only just cried herself to sleep," she was muttering fiercely, as she softly pushed open the door. The next moment she gave a frightened cry. "Where are you? Where've you gone? Where HAVE you gone?" she panted, looking in the closet, under the bed, and even in the trunk and down the water pitcher.

Then she flew down-stairs and out to Old Tom in the garden.

"Mr. Tom, Mr. Tom, that blessed child's gone," she wailed. "She's vanished right up into Heaven where she come from, poor lamb — and me told ter give her bread and milk in the kitchen — her what's eatin' angel food this minute, I'll warrant, I'll warrant!"

The old man straightened up.

"Gone? Heaven?" he repeated stupidly, unconsciously sweeping the brilliant sunset sky with his gaze. He stopped, stared a moment intently, then turned with a slow grin. "Well, Nancy, it do look like as if she'd tried ter get as nigh Heaven as she could, and that's a fact," he agreed, pointing with a crooked finger to where, sharply outlined against the reddening sky, a slender, wind-blown figure was poised on top of a huge rock.

"Well, she ain't goin' ter Heaven that way ter-night — not if I has my say," declared Nancy, doggedly. "If the mistress asks, tell her I ain't furgettin' the dishes, but I gone on a stroll," she flung back over her shoulder, as she sped toward the path that led through the open field.

CHAPTER 4
DEVOTIONAL & JOURNAL

"Oh, Aunt Polly, Aunt Polly," breathed the little girl, rapturously; "what a perfectly lovely, lovely house! How awfully glad you must be you're so rich!"

"PollyANNA!" ejaculated her aunt, turning sharply about as she reached the head of the stairs. "I'm surprised at you — making a speech like that to me!"

"Why, Aunt Polly, AREN'T you?" queried Pollyanna, in frank wonder.

"Certainly not, Pollyanna. I hope I could not so far forget myself as to be sinfully proud of any gift the Lord has seen fit to bestow upon me," declared the lady; "certainly not, of RICHES!"

Pollyanna and her aunt have a very different way of looking at enjoying material blessings. Do you think it's a sin to enjoy "any gift the Lord has seen fit to bestow"?

Does Miss Polly show generosity in the way she treats Pollyanna? Which approach to our possessions is likely to make us more or less generous?

How do you think God wants us to feel about His gifts?

Miss Polly is wealthy, but takes no joy in it and gives grudgingly. Pollyanna is poor, yet can find joy in the smallest thing. Money can be a huge issue that affects how much joy we feel. The last few years have been financially challenging in our household, the sort of challenges that can drain joy and strain a marriage. Because my husband has become progressively more disabled by health problems and hasn't been able to work at a job for some years, I'd been the main income earner, working full-time in a high stress job that affected my own health. When I first needed to give up work to care for him, I wasn't concerned. With savings to last a while, the prospect of writing and publishing more books, and confident I could get part-time work, I looked forward to a break from the pressure.

But it didn't quite work out the way I hoped. The extra time to write was a blessing, but didn't replace the lost income. I couldn't get part-time work that would fit with the needs at home. Our savings were almost used up, and my worry level rose as our bank balance dropped... and dropped... and dropped! I prayed frequently, desperately. God's answer stayed the same — not to worry, but to trust that He would take care of our finances and provide all we needed. That level of trust was so scary for me, a new thing I've never done before! I was used to being in control, not being dependent.

> *You can be sure that God will take care of everything you need,*
> *his generosity exceeding even yours in the glory that pours from Jesus.*
> *Our God and Father abounds in glory that just pours out into eternity.*
> Philippians 4:19-20 MSG

Feeling needy and like there's not enough can lead to us wanting to hold on to what we have. A symptom of my fear around money was that I stopped wanting to give. But God wants us to be generous. He wants us to see whatever we have as a gift from Him, to share and give as He has given to us. "Jesus invites us to a life of joyous trust – a way of living in which everything we have we receive as a gift, and everything we have is cared for by God, and everything we have is available to others when it is right and good." (Richard Foster)

God is keeping His promises and providing for us. He doesn't promise wealth, or even comfort in this life, but he does promise to meet our needs, now, and even more in eternity. We live simply and frugally, but we have enough, and enough to give from, too, as I feel led by God to. I notice if I stop giving, the income dries up. When I give more freely, our income increases. Somehow, I don't think that's a coincidence!

It hasn't been easy, but slowly I've come to trust that God will keep His promise. That shift from feeling responsible for everything to relying on Him has brought so much peace and contentment, and a true and deep sense of gratitude.

Is God calling you to trust him more with your finances?

How might that change things?

Dear Lord, I'm grateful for all You have provided me with, whether financial wealth, health, or other blessings. Help me to be willing to give with a generous spirit from what I have, knowing You will bless me abundantly in return. Please help me to feel joy and gratitude for what I have, rather than focusing on what I would like to have but don't. Give me a sense of peace and contentment regardless of whether I am rich or poor in material things, trusting that You will provide for my deepest and truest needs in Your merciful glory and grace. Thank You!

CHAPTER FIVE:
THE GAME

"For the land's sake, Miss Pollyanna, what a scare you did give me," panted Nancy, hurrying up to the big rock, down which Pollyanna had just regretfully slid.

"Scare? Oh, I'm so sorry; but you mustn't, really, ever get scared about me, Nancy. Father and the Ladies' Aid used to do it, too, till they found I always came back all right."

"But I didn't even know you'd went," cried Nancy, tucking the little girl's hand under her arm and hurrying her down the hill. "I didn't see you go, and nobody didn't. I guess you flew right up through the roof; I do, I do."

Pollyanna skipped gleefully.

"I did, 'most — only I flew down instead of up. I came down the tree."

Nancy stopped short.

"You did — what?"

"Came down the tree, outside my window."

"My stars and stockings!" gasped Nancy, hurrying on again. "I'd like ter know what yer aunt would say ter that!"

"Would you? Well, I'll tell her, then, so you can find out," promised the little girl, cheerfully.

"Mercy!" gasped Nancy. "No — no!"

"Why, you don't mean she'd CARE!" cried Pollyanna, plainly disturbed.

"No — er — yes — well, never mind. I — I ain't so very particular about knowin' what she'd say, truly," stammered Nancy, determined to keep one scolding from Pollyanna, if nothing more. "But, say, we better hurry. I've got ter get them dishes done, ye know."

"I'll help," promised Pollyanna, promptly.

"Oh, Miss Pollyanna!" demurred Nancy.

For a moment there was silence. The sky was darkening fast. Pollyanna took a firmer hold of her friend's arm.

"I reckon I'm glad, after all, that you DID get scared — a little, 'cause then you came after me," she shivered.

"Poor little lamb! And you must be hungry, too. I — I'm afraid you'll have ter have bread and milk in the kitchen with me. Yer aunt didn't like it — because you didn't come down ter supper, ye know."

"But I couldn't. I was up here."

"Yes; but — she didn't know that, you see!" observed Nancy, dryly, stifling a chuckle. "I'm sorry about the bread and milk; I am, I am."

"Oh, I'm not. I'm glad."

"Glad! Why?"

"Why, I like bread and milk, and I'd like to eat with you. I don't see any trouble about being glad about that."

"You don't seem ter see any trouble bein' glad about everythin'," retorted Nancy, choking a little over her remembrance of Pollyanna's brave attempts to like the bare little attic room.

Pollyanna laughed softly.

"Well, that's the game, you know, anyway."

"The — GAME?"

"Yes; the 'just being glad' game."

"Whatever in the world are you talkin' about?"

"Why, it's a game. Father told it to me, and it's lovely," rejoined Pollyanna. "We've played it always, ever since I was a little, little girl. I told the Ladies' Aid, and they played it — some of them."

"What is it? I ain't much on games, though."

Pollyanna laughed again, but she sighed, too; and in the gathering twilight her face looked thin and wistful.

"Why, we began it on some crutches that came in a missionary barrel."

"CRUTCHES!"

"Yes. You see I'd wanted a doll, and father had written them so; but when the barrel came the lady wrote that there hadn't any dolls come in, but the little crutches had. So she sent 'em along as they might come in handy for some child, sometime. And that's when we began it."

"Well, I must say I can't see any game about that, about that," declared Nancy, almost irritably.

"Oh, yes; the game was to just find something about everything to be glad about — no matter what 'twas," rejoined Pollyanna, earnestly. "And we began right then — on the crutches."

"Well, goodness me! I can't see anythin' ter be glad about — gettin' a pair of crutches when you wanted a doll!"

Pollyanna clapped her hands.

"There is — there is," she crowed. "But *I* couldn't see it, either, Nancy, at first," she added, with quick honesty. "Father had to tell it to me."

"Well, then, suppose YOU tell ME," almost snapped Nancy.

"Goosey! Why, just be glad because you don't — NEED — 'EM!" exulted Pollyanna, triumphantly. "You see it's just as easy — when you know how!"

"Well, of all the queer doin's!" breathed Nancy, regarding Pollyanna with almost fearful eyes.

"Oh, but it isn't queer — it's lovely," maintained Pollyanna enthusiastically. "And we've played it ever since. And the harder 'tis, the more fun 'tis to get 'em out; only — only sometimes it's almost too hard — like when your father goes to Heaven, and there isn't anybody but a Ladies' Aid left."

"Yes, or when you're put in a snippy little room 'way at the top of the house with nothin' in it," growled Nancy.

Pollyanna sighed.

"That was a hard one, at first," she admitted, "specially when I was so kind of lonesome. I just didn't feel like playing the game, anyway, and I HAD been wanting pretty things, so! Then I happened to think how I hated to see my freckles in the looking-glass, and I saw that lovely picture out the window, too; so then I knew I'd found the things to be glad about. You see, when you're hunting for the glad things, you sort of forget the other kind — like the doll you wanted, you know."

"Humph!" choked Nancy, trying to swallow the lump in her throat.

"Most generally it doesn't take so long," sighed Pollyanna; "and lots of times now I just think of them WITHOUT thinking, you know. I've got so used to playing it. It's a lovely game. F-father and I used to like it so much," she faltered. "I suppose, though, it — it'll be a little harder now, as long as I haven't anybody to play it with. Maybe Aunt Polly will play it, though," she added, as an after-thought.

"My stars and stockings! — HER!" breathed Nancy, behind her teeth. Then, aloud, she said doggedly: "See here, Miss Pollyanna, I ain't sayin' that I'll play it very well, and I ain't sayin' that I know how, anyway; but I'll play it with ye, after a fashion — I just will, I will!"

"Oh, Nancy!" exulted Pollyanna, giving her a rapturous hug. "That'll be splendid! Won't we have fun?"

"Er — maybe," conceded Nancy, in open doubt. "But you mustn't count too much on me, ye know. I never was no case fur games, but I'm a-goin' ter make a most awful old try on this one. You're goin' ter have some one ter play it with, anyhow," she finished, as they entered the kitchen together.

Pollyanna ate her bread and milk with good appetite; then, at Nancy's suggestion, she went into the sitting room, where her aunt sat reading.

Miss Polly looked up coldly.

"Have you had your supper, Pollyanna?"

"Yes, Aunt Polly."

"I'm very sorry, Pollyanna, to have been obliged so soon to send you into the kitchen to eat bread and milk."

"But I was real glad you did it, Aunt Polly. I like bread and milk, and Nancy, too. You mustn't feel bad about that one bit."

Aunt Polly sat suddenly a little more erect in her chair.

"Pollyanna, it's quite time you were in bed. You have had a hard day, and to-morrow we must plan your hours and go over your clothing to see what it is necessary to get for you. Nancy will give you a candle. Be careful how you handle it. Breakfast will be at half-past seven. See that you are down to that. Good-night."

Quite as a matter of course, Pollyanna came straight to her aunt's side and gave her an affectionate hug.

"I've had such a beautiful time, so far," she sighed happily. "I know I'm going to just love living with you but then, I knew I should before I came. Good-night," she called cheerfully, as she ran from the room.

"Well, upon my soul!" ejaculated Miss Polly, half aloud. "What a most extraordinary child!" Then she frowned. "She's 'glad' I punished her, and I 'mustn't feel bad one bit,' and she's going to 'love to live' with me! Well, upon my soul!" ejaculated Miss Polly again, as she took up her book.

Fifteen minutes later, in the attic room, a lonely little girl sobbed into the tightly-clutched sheet:

"I know, father-among-the-angels, I'm not playing the game one bit now — not one bit; but I don't believe even you could find anything to be glad about sleeping all alone 'way off up here in the dark — like this. If only I was near Nancy or Aunt Polly, or even a Ladies' Aider, it would be easier!"

Down-stairs in the kitchen, Nancy, hurrying with her belated work, jabbed her dish-mop into the milk pitcher, and muttered jerkily:

"If playin' a silly-fool game — about bein' glad you've got crutches when you want dolls — is got ter be — my way — o' bein' that rock o' refuge — why, I'm a-goin' ter play it — I am, I am!"

CHAPTER 5
DEVOTIONAL & JOURNAL

"You don't seem ter see any trouble bein' glad about everythin'," retorted Nancy, choking a little over her remembrance of Pollyanna's brave attempts to like the bare little attic room.

Pollyanna laughed softly.

"Well, that's the game, you know, anyway."

"The — GAME?"

"Yes; the 'just being glad' game."

This chapter introduces Pollyanna's Glad Game, her game of looking for the blessing and the things to be glad about in everything that happens to her.

Can you think of things you've experienced that proved to hold unexpected blessings?

How did it feel when you recognized the blessing?

It's easy to be glad and thankful for the good things in our lives. The successes, the celebrations, the gifts. But not everything feels so obviously good! We make mistakes, other people make mistakes, Bad things happen. We have a choice how we respond to that – we can get angry, bitter, and resentful; or we can choose to keep trusting and loving God, allowing Him to work things out. Even Pollyanna admits it's not always so easy – she found it hard to be glad over the ugly attic room at first, and still struggles with her father's death. She cries, alone in her room, the first night at Aunt Polly's house.

But God tells us:

That's why we can be so sure that every detail in our lives of love for God
is worked into something good.
Romans 8:28 MSG

This isn't a promise that only good things will happen to us once we become Christians. I wish! It's a promise that when we choose His way, no matter what happens, God will work it around to being for our ultimate good. I certainly haven't found believing this and living this easy. I spent long painful years of being angry with God over bad things that happened, things I couldn't see any good in and blamed Him for.

It didn't help. I ended up with more problems. Not just the things I was already upset about, but a miserable attitude, damaged relationships with the people around me, and a broken relationship with God. Ouch! Charles Swindoll says "life is 10% what happens to me and 90% how I react to it." All my reaction did was multiply the pain.

Thankfully, I didn't stay stuck there in that escalating spiral of unhappiness. God reached out to me and is slowly healing me, teaching me to trust Him. Teaching me to have an attitude more like Pollyanna, determined to find whatever good she can in every situation — "You see, when you're hunting for the glad things, you sort of forget the other kind…"

Always give thanks to God the Father for everything in the name of our Lord Jesus Christ.
Ephesians 5:20 ERV

God does ask us to be thankful, for everything. Even the tough things, trusting that He can bring good out of them.

Are there things of the "other kind" in your life right now, things you don't like, that feel too hard, that you can't feel glad for? Most of us this side of sainthood have them! Make a list of them, now. You may prefer to use scrap paper for this so you can destroy the list.

Hand the list over to God. Ask Him to bring good from it, and ask His help to see the gift hidden in the challenge. Trust that He will take care of it. Can you let yourself experience that same feeling for these things as you did for the things with the more obvious blessing?

Lord, it's not always easy to be thankful. Some things test me, feel just too hard and too painful for even You to bring good from them. But I'm willing to try. I'm willing to trust that even with these things, you can shape them to Your plan and purpose and use them to bless me. Please show me the gift hidden in these challenges. Help me to open my heart and mind today to seeing Your hand at work in these situations. Help me to feel the peace and joy that comes from trusting You, even if I can't see the reason things have happened as they have. I love You and trust You. I know You are always working to produce good in my life. Thank You!

CHAPTER SIX:
A QUESTION OF DUTY

It was nearly seven o'clock when Pollyanna awoke that first day after her arrival. Her windows faced the south and the west, so she could not see the sun yet; but she could see the hazy blue of the morning sky, and she knew that the day promised to be a fair one.

The little room was cooler now, and the air blew in fresh and sweet. Outside, the birds were twittering joyously, and Pollyanna flew to the window to talk to them. She saw then that down in the garden her aunt was already out among the rosebushes. With rapid fingers, therefore, she made herself ready to join her.

Down the attic stairs sped Pollyanna, leaving both doors wide open. Through the hall, down the next flight, then bang through the front screened-door and around to the garden, she ran.

Aunt Polly, with the bent old man, was leaning over a rose-bush when Pollyanna, gurgling with delight, flung herself upon her.

"Oh, Aunt Polly, Aunt Polly, I reckon I am glad this morning just to be alive!"

"PollyANNA!" remonstrated the lady, sternly, pulling herself as erect as she could with a dragging weight of ninety pounds hanging about her neck. "Is this the usual way you say good morning?"

The little girl dropped to her toes, and danced lightly up and down.

"No, only when I love folks so I just can't help it! I saw you from my window, Aunt Polly, and I got to thinking how you WEREN'T a Ladies' Aider, and you were my really truly aunt; and you looked so good I just had to come down and hug you!"

The bent old man turned his back suddenly. Miss Polly attempted a frown — with not her usual success.

"Pollyanna, you — I Thomas, that will do for this morning. I think you understand — about those rose-bushes," she said stiffly. Then she turned and walked rapidly away.

"Do you always work in the garden, Mr. — Man?" asked Pollyanna, interestedly.

The man turned. His lips were twitching, but his eyes looked blurred as if with tears.

"Yes, Miss. I'm Old Tom, the gardener," he answered. Timidly, but as if impelled by an irresistible force, he reached out a shaking hand and let it rest for a moment on her bright hair. "You are so like your mother, little Miss! I used ter know her when she was even littler than you be. You see, I used ter work in the garden — then."

Pollyanna caught her breath audibly. "You did? And you knew my mother, really — when she was just a little earth angel, and not a Heaven one? Oh, please tell me about her!" And down plumped Pollyanna in the middle of the dirt path by the old man's side.

A bell sounded from the house. The next moment Nancy was seen flying out the back door.

"Miss Pollyanna, that bell means breakfast — mornin's," she panted, pulling the little girl to her feet and hurrying her back to the house; "and other times it means other meals. But it always means that you're ter run like time when ye hear it, no matter where ye be. If ye don't — well, it'll take somethin' smarter'n we be ter find ANYTHIN' ter be glad about in that!" she finished, shooing Pollyanna into the house as she would shoo an unruly chicken into a coop.

Breakfast, for the first five minutes, was a silent meal; then Miss Polly, her disapproving eyes following the airy wings of two flies darting here and there over the table, said sternly:

"Nancy, where did those flies come from?"

"I don't know, ma'am. There wasn't one in the kitchen." Nancy had been too excited to notice Pollyanna's up-flung windows the afternoon before.

"I reckon maybe they're my flies, Aunt Polly," observed Pollyanna, amiably. "There were lots of them this morning having a beautiful time upstairs."

Nancy left the room precipitately, though to do so she had to carry out the hot muffins she had just brought in.

"Yours!" gasped Miss Polly. "What do you mean? Where did they come from?"

"Why, Aunt Polly, they came from out of doors of course, through the windows. I SAW some of them come in."

"You saw them! You mean you raised those windows without any screens?"

"Why, yes. There weren't any screens there, Aunt Polly."

Nancy, at this moment, came in again with the muffins. Her face was grave, but very red.

"Nancy," directed her mistress, sharply, "you may set the muffins down and go at once to Miss Pollyanna's room and shut the windows. Shut the doors, also. Later, when your morning work is done, go through every room with the spatter. See that you make a thorough search."

To her niece she said: "Pollyanna, I have ordered screens for those windows. I knew, of course, that it was my duty to do that. But it seems to me that you have quite forgotten YOUR duty."

"My — duty?" Pollyanna's eyes were wide with wonder.

"Certainly. I know it is warm, but I consider it your duty to keep your windows closed till those screens come. Flies, Pollyanna, are not only unclean and annoying, but very dangerous to health. After breakfast I will give you a little pamphlet on this matter to read."

"To read? Oh, thank you, Aunt Polly. I love to read!"

Miss Polly drew in her breath audibly, then she shut her lips together hard. Pollyanna, seeing her stern face, frowned a little thoughtfully.

"Of course I'm sorry about the duty I forgot, Aunt Polly," she apologized timidly. "I won't raise the windows again."

Her aunt made no reply. She did not speak, indeed, until the meal was over. Then she rose, went to the bookcase in the sitting room, took out a small paper booklet, and crossed the room to her niece's side.

"This is the article I spoke of, Pollyanna. I desire you to go to your room at once and read it. I will be up in half an hour to look over your things."

Pollyanna, her eyes on the illustration of a fly's head, many times magnified, cried joyously: "Oh, thank you, Aunt Polly!" The next moment she skipped merrily from the room, banging the door behind her.

Miss Polly frowned, hesitated, then crossed the room majestically and opened the door; but Pollyanna was already out of sight, clattering up the attic stairs.

Half an hour later when Miss Polly, her face expressing stern duty in every line, climbed those stairs and entered Pollyanna's room, she was greeted with a burst of eager enthusiasm.

"Oh, Aunt Polly, I never saw anything so perfectly lovely and interesting in my life. I'm so glad you gave me that book to read! Why, I didn't suppose flies could carry such a lot of things on their feet, and — "

"That will do," observed Aunt Polly, with dignity. "Pollyanna, you may bring out your clothes now, and I will look them over. What are not suitable for you I shall give to the Sullivans, of course."

With visible reluctance Pollyanna laid down the pamphlet and turned toward the closet.

"I'm afraid you'll think they're worse than the Ladies' Aid did — and THEY said they were shameful," she sighed. "But there were mostly things for boys and older folks in the last two or three barrels; and — did you ever have a missionary barrel, Aunt Polly?"

At her aunt's look of shocked anger, Pollyanna corrected herself at once.

"Why, no, of course you didn't, Aunt Polly!" she hurried on, with a hot blush. "I forgot; rich folks never have to have them. But you see sometimes I kind of forget that you are rich — up here in this room, you know."

Miss Polly's lips parted indignantly, but no words came. Pollyanna, plainly unaware that she had said anything in the least unpleasant, was hurrying on.

"Well, as I was going to say, you can't tell a thing about missionary barrels — except that you won't find in 'em what you think you're going to — even when you think you won't. It was the barrels every time, too, that were hardest to play the game on, for father and — "

Just in time Pollyanna remembered that she was not to talk of her father to her aunt. She dived into her closet then, hurriedly, and brought out all the poor little dresses in both her arms.

"They aren't nice, at all," she choked, "and they'd been black if it hadn't been for the red carpet for the church; but they're all I've got."

With the tips of her fingers Miss Polly turned over the conglomerate garments, so obviously made for anybody but Pollyanna. Next she bestowed frowning attention on the patched undergarments in the bureau drawers.

"I've got the best ones on," confessed Pollyanna, anxiously. "The Ladies' Aid bought me one set straight through all whole. Mrs. Jones — she's the president — told 'em I should have that if they had to clatter down bare aisles themselves the rest of their days. But they won't. Mr. White doesn't like the noise. He's got nerves, his wife says; but he's got money, too, and they expect he'll give a lot toward the carpet — on account of the nerves, you know. I should think he'd be glad that if he did have the nerves he'd got money, too; shouldn't you?"

Miss Polly did not seem to hear. Her scrutiny of the undergarments finished, she turned to Pollyanna somewhat abruptly. "You have been to school, of course, Pollyanna?"

"Oh, yes, Aunt Polly. Besides, fath — I mean, I was taught at home some, too."

Miss Polly frowned.

"Very good. In the fall you will enter school here, of course. Mr. Hall, the principal, will doubtless settle in which grade you belong. Meanwhile, I suppose I ought to hear you read aloud half an hour each day."

"I love to read; but if you don't want to hear me I'd be just glad to read to myself — truly, Aunt Polly. And I wouldn't have to half try to be glad, either, for I like best to read to myself — on account of the big words, you know."

"I don't doubt it," rejoined Miss Polly, grimly. "Have you studied music?"

"Not much. I don't like my music — I like other people's, though. I learned to play on the piano a little. Miss Gray — she plays for church — she taught me. But I'd just as soon let that go as not, Aunt Polly. I'd rather, truly."

"Very likely," observed Aunt Polly, with slightly uplifted eyebrows. "Nevertheless I think it is my duty to see that you are properly instructed in at least the rudiments of music. You sew, of course."

"Yes, ma'am." Pollyanna sighed. "The Ladies' Aid taught me that. But I had an awful time. Mrs. Jones didn't believe in holding your needle like the rest of 'em did on buttonholing, and Mrs. White thought backstitching ought to be taught you before hemming (or else the other way), and Mrs. Harriman didn't believe in putting you on patchwork ever, at all."

"Well, there will be no difficulty of that kind any longer, Pollyanna. I shall teach you sewing myself, of course. You do not know how to cook, I presume."

Pollyanna laughed suddenly.

"They were just beginning to teach me that this summer, but I hadn't got far. They were more divided up on that than they were on the sewing. They were GOING to begin on bread; but there wasn't two of 'em that made it alike, so after arguing it all one sewing-meeting, they decided to take turns at me one forenoon a week — in their own kitchens, you know. I'd only learned chocolate fudge and fig cake, though, when — when I had to stop." Her voice broke.

"Chocolate fudge and fig cake, indeed!" scorned Miss Polly. "I think we can remedy that very soon." She paused in thought for a minute, then went on slowly: "At nine o'clock every morning you will read aloud one half-hour to me. Before that you will use the time to put this room in order. Wednesday and Saturday forenoons, after half-past nine, you will spend with Nancy in the kitchen, learning to cook. Other mornings you will sew with me. That will leave the afternoons for your music. I shall, of course, procure a teacher at once for you," she finished decisively, as she arose from her chair.

Pollyanna cried out in dismay. "Oh, but Aunt Polly, Aunt Polly, you haven't left me any time at all just to — to live."

"To live, child! What do you mean? As if you weren't living all the time!"

"Oh, of course I'd be BREATHING all the time I was doing those things, Aunt Polly, but I wouldn't be living. You breathe all the time you're asleep, but you aren't living. I mean living — doing the things you want to do: playing outdoors, reading (to myself, of course), climbing hills, talking to Mr. Tom in the garden, and Nancy, and finding out all about the houses and the people and everything everywhere all through the perfectly lovely streets I came through yesterday. That's what I call living, Aunt Polly. Just breathing isn't living!"

Miss Polly lifted her head irritably.

"Pollyanna, you ARE the most extraordinary child! You will be allowed a proper amount of playtime, of course. But, surely, it seems to me if I am willing to do my duty in seeing that you have proper care and instruction, YOU ought to be willing to do yours by seeing that that care and instruction are not ungratefully wasted."

Pollyanna looked shocked. "Oh, Aunt Polly, as if I ever could be ungrateful — to YOU! Why, I LOVE YOU — and you aren't even a Ladies' Aider; you're an aunt!"

"Very well; then see that you don't act ungrateful," vouchsafed Miss Polly, as she turned toward the door.

She had gone halfway down the stairs when a small, unsteady voice called after her: "Please, Aunt Polly, you didn't tell me which of my things you wanted to — to give away."

Aunt Polly emitted a tired sigh — a sigh that ascended straight to Pollyanna's ears.

"Oh, I forgot to tell you, Pollyanna. Timothy will drive us into town at half-past one this afternoon. Not one of your garments is fit for my niece to wear. Certainly I should be very far from doing my duty by you if I should let you appear out in any one of them."

Pollyanna sighed now — she believed she was going to hate that word — duty.

"Aunt Polly, please," she called wistfully, "isn't there ANY way you can be glad about all that — duty business?"

"What?" Miss Polly looked up in dazed surprise; then, suddenly, with very red cheeks, she turned and swept angrily down the stairs. "Don't be impertinent, Pollyanna!"

In the hot little attic room Pollyanna dropped herself on to one of the straight-backed chairs. To her, existence loomed ahead one endless round of duty.

"I don't see, really, what there was impertinent about that," she sighed. "I was only asking her if she couldn't tell me something to be glad about in all that duty business."

For several minutes Pollyanna sat in silence, her rueful eyes fixed on the forlorn heap of garments on the bed. Then, slowly, she rose and began to put away the dresses.

"There just isn't anything to be glad about, that I can see," she said aloud; "unless — it's to be glad when the duty's done!" Whereupon she laughed suddenly.

35

CHAPTER 6
DEVOTIONAL & JOURNAL

"Aunt Polly, please," she called wistfully, "isn't there ANY way you can be glad about all that — duty business?"

Miss Polly's attempts to teach Pollyanna her concept of duty don't go quite as she expected! The dictionary definition of duty is something "done from a sense of moral obligation rather than for pleasure". This certainly seems to be Miss Polly's view about doing what she considers to be right.

Pollyanna makes a clear distinction between the things Aunt Polly wants her to do, and the things she wants to do.

"Oh, but Aunt Polly, Aunt Polly, you haven't left me any time at all just to — to live."

"To live, child! What do you mean? As if you weren't living all the time!"

"Oh, of course I'd be BREATHING all the time I was doing those things, Aunt Polly, but I wouldn't be living. You breathe all the time you're asleep, but you aren't living. I mean living — doing the things you want to do..."

Do you agree that doing our duty can't be enjoyable?

What do you do because you *have* to, rather than because you want to?

How does that feel?

I have to confess – I give the word "duty" negative implications, too, just like Miss Polly tells Pollyanna. Many of us use duty to mean a burden, a joyless routine, an obligation we do grudgingly, only because we have to. I definitely don't feel any sense of excitement, passion, joy, or fulfillment when I think of doing my duty.

Yet duty has a purpose, a very necessary one. A sense of wanting to do our duty or to obey God can be all that keeps us going through tough times. I've dragged myself to work only because it's my to do what I'm paid for. I've driven away from the house after arguing with my husband, and only commitment to my marriage vow has brought me back, not love. I've read my Bible chapters for the day so I can tick that off my list, but haven't allowed God's word to sink into my mind and heart. It if wasn't for duty, I might have quit my job. If it wasn't for duty, I might have ended my marriage. If it wasn't for duty, I might have drifted away from God. Only that sense of obligation to do what I didn't want to do, with gritted teeth if necessary, carried me through.

But I want doing my duty to be so much more than doing what I feel I must with a bad attitude. Like the writers of these psalms, I want to delight in doing God's will. I want to find joy in doing my duty, out of love for the Lord and love for other people.

"I delight to do Your will, O my God, And Your law is within my heart."
Psalm 40:8 NKJV
But those who do right should be glad and should rejoice before God;
they should be happy and glad.
Psalm 68:3 NCV

I'm not there yet, a long way off! But I'm willing for God to teach me. I want all I do to be done from love, as a service to God, or to other people. And I want to feel joy in that, not splitting things off into work and play, or duty and fun, but to find delight in it all, to see it all as serving God.

Which of the things you do make you feel most joyfully alive?

Is this something you believe God approves of? If so, how can you do if more often?

What difference would it make in your life if you could feel the same way about the things you see as duties?

Lord, help me to know what you want me to do, and to find joy in it. Help me to change my attitude to anything I do with a joyless sense of duty, and to find delight in doing Your will. Teach me to bring love to all I do. Show me how to enjoy living more. You created us for joy and to live fully and abundantly, and our joy shines the light of Your glory into the world. Show me how to live more fully in You. Help me to play with joy, and help me to do my duties with joy, seeing both as "living". Thank You!

CHAPTER SEVEN:
POLLYANNA AND PUNISHMENTS

At half-past one o'clock Timothy drove Miss Polly and her niece to the four or five principal dry goods stores, which were about half a mile from the homestead.

Fitting Pollyanna with a new wardrobe proved to be more or less of an exciting experience for all concerned. Miss Polly came out of it with the feeling of limp relaxation that one might have at finding oneself at last on solid earth after a perilous walk across the very thin crust of a volcano. The various clerks who had waited upon the pair came out of it with very red faces, and enough amusing stories of Pollyanna to keep their friends in gales of laughter the rest of the week. Pollyanna herself came out of it with radiant smiles and a heart content; for, as she expressed it to one of the clerks: "When you haven't had anybody but missionary barrels and Ladies' Aiders to dress you, it IS perfectly lovely to just walk right in and buy clothes that are brand-new, and that don't have to be tucked up or let down because they don't fit!"

The shopping expedition consumed the entire afternoon; then came supper and a delightful talk with Old Tom in the garden, and another with Nancy on the back porch, after the dishes were done, and while Aunt Polly paid a visit to a neighbor.

Old Tom told Pollyanna wonderful things of her mother, that made her very happy indeed; and Nancy told her all about the little farm six miles away at "The Corners," where lived her own dear mother, and her equally dear brother and sisters. She promised, too, that sometime, if Miss Polly were willing, Pollyanna should be taken to see them.

"And THEY'VE got lovely names, too. You'll like THEIR names," sighed Nancy. "They're 'Algernon,' and 'Florabelle' and 'Estelle.' I — I just hate 'Nancy'!"

"Oh, Nancy, what a dreadful thing to say! Why?"

"Because it isn't pretty like the others. You see, I was the first baby, and mother hadn't begun ter read so many stories with the pretty names in 'em, then."

"But I love 'Nancy,' just because it's you," declared Pollyanna.

"Humph! Well, I guess you could love 'Clarissa Mabelle' just as well," retorted Nancy, "and it would be a heap happier for me. I think THAT name's just grand!"

Pollyanna laughed.

"Well, anyhow," she chuckled, "you can be glad it isn't 'Hephzibah.'"

"Hephzibah!"

"Yes. Mrs. White's name is that. Her husband calls her 'Hep,' and she doesn't like it. She says when he calls out 'Hep — Hep!' she feels just as if the next minute he was going to yell 'Hurrah!' And she doesn't like to be hurrahed at."

Nancy's gloomy face relaxed into a broad smile.

"Well, if you don't beat the Dutch! Say, do you know? — I sha'n't never hear 'Nancy' now that I don't think o' that 'Hep — Hep!' and giggle. My, I guess I AM glad — " She stopped short and turned amazed eyes on the little girl. "Say, Miss Pollyanna, do you mean — was you playin' that 'ere game THEN — about my bein' glad I wa'n't named Hephzibah'?"

Pollyanna frowned; then she laughed.

"Why, Nancy, that's so! I WAS playing the game — but that's one of the times I just did it without thinking, I reckon. You see, you DO, lots of times; you get so used to it — looking for something to be glad about, you know. And most generally there is something about everything that you can be glad about, if you keep hunting long enough to find it."

"Well, m-maybe," granted Nancy, with open doubt.

At half-past eight Pollyanna went up to bed. The screens had not yet come, and the close little room was like an oven. With longing eyes Pollyanna looked at the two fast-closed windows — but she did not raise them. She undressed, folded her clothes neatly, said her prayers, blew out her candle and climbed into bed.

Just how long she lay in sleepless misery, tossing from side to side of the hot little cot, she did not know; but it seemed to her that it must have been hours before she finally slipped out of bed, felt her way across the room and opened her door.

Out in the main attic all was velvet blackness save where the moon flung a path of silver half-way across the floor from the east dormer window. With a resolute ignoring of that fearsome darkness to the right and to the left, Pollyanna drew a quick breath and pattered straight into that silvery path, and on to the window.

She had hoped, vaguely, that this window might have a screen, but it did not. Outside, however, there was a wide world of fairy-like beauty, and there was, too, she knew, fresh, sweet air that would feel so good to hot cheeks and hands!

As she stepped nearer and peered longingly out, she saw something else: she saw, only a little way below the window, the wide, flat tin roof of Miss Polly's sun parlor built over the porte-cochere. The sight filled her with longing. If only, now, she were out there!

Fearfully she looked behind her. Back there, somewhere, were her hot little room and her still hotter bed; but between her and them lay a horrid desert of blackness across which one must feel one's way with outstretched, shrinking arms; while before her, out on the sun-parlor roof, were the moonlight and the cool, sweet night air.

If only her bed were out there! And folks did sleep out of doors. Joel Hartley at home, who was so sick with the consumption, HAD to sleep out of doors.

Suddenly Pollyanna remembered that she had seen near this attic window a row of long white bags hanging from nails. Nancy had said that they contained the winter clothing, put away for the summer. A little fearfully now, Pollyanna felt her way to these bags, selected a nice fat soft one (it contained Miss Polly's sealskin coat) for a bed; and a thinner one to be doubled up for a pillow, and still another (which was so thin it seemed almost empty) for a covering. Thus equipped, Pollyanna in high glee pattered to the moonlit window again, raised the sash, stuffed her burden through to the roof below, then let herself down after it, closing the window carefully behind her — Pollyanna had not forgotten those flies with the marvellous feet that carried things.

How deliciously cool it was! Pollyanna quite danced up and down with delight, drawing in long, full breaths of the refreshing air. The tin roof under her feet crackled with little resounding snaps that Pollyanna rather liked. She walked, indeed, two or three times back and forth from end to end — it gave her such a pleasant sensation of airy space after her hot little room; and the roof was so broad and flat that she had no fear of falling off. Finally, with a sigh of content, she curled herself up on the sealskin-coat mattress, arranged one bag for a pillow and the other for a covering, and settled herself to sleep.

"I'm so glad now that the screens didn't come," she murmured, blinking up at the stars; "else I couldn't have had this!"

Down-stairs in Miss Polly's room next the sun parlor, Miss Polly herself was hurrying into dressing gown and slippers, her face white and frightened. A minute before she had been telephoning in a shaking voice to Timothy:

"Come up quick! — you and your father. Bring lanterns. Somebody is on the roof of the sun parlor. He must have climbed up the rose-trellis or somewhere, and of course he can get right into the house through the east window in the attic. I have locked the attic door down here — but hurry, quick!"

Some time later, Pollyanna, just dropping off to sleep, was startled by a lantern flash, and a trio of amazed ejaculations. She opened her eyes to find Timothy at the top of a ladder near her, Old Tom just getting through the window, and her aunt peering out at her from behind him.

"Pollyanna, what does this mean?" cried Aunt Polly then.

Pollyanna blinked sleepy eyes and sat up.

"Why, Mr. Tom — Aunt Polly!" she stammered. "Don't look so scared! It isn't that I've got the consumption, you know, like Joel Hartley. It's only that I was so hot — in there. But I shut the window, Aunt Polly, so the flies couldn't carry those germ-things in."

Timothy disappeared suddenly down the ladder. Old Tom, with almost equal precipitation, handed his lantern to Miss Polly, and followed his son.

Miss Polly bit her lip hard — until the men were gone; then she said sternly:

"Pollyanna, hand those things to me at once and come in here. Of all the extraordinary children!" she ejaculated a little later, as, with Pollyanna by her side, and the lantern in her hand, she turned back into the attic.

To Pollyanna the air was all the more stifling after that cool breath of the out of doors; but she did not complain. She only drew a long quivering sigh.

At the top of the stairs Miss Polly jerked out crisply:

"For the rest of the night, Pollyanna, you are to sleep in my bed with me. The screens will be here to-morrow, but until then I consider it my duty to keep you where I know where you are."

Pollyanna drew in her breath.

"With you? — in your bed?" she cried rapturously. "Oh, Aunt Polly, Aunt Polly, how perfectly lovely of you! And when I've so wanted to sleep with some one sometime — some one that belonged to me, you know; not a Ladies' Aider. I've HAD them. My! I reckon I am glad now those screens didn't come! Wouldn't you be?"

There was no reply. Miss Polly was stalking on ahead. Miss Polly, to tell the truth, was feeling curiously helpless. For the third time since Pollyanna's arrival, Miss Polly was punishing Pollyanna — and for the third time she was being confronted with the amazing fact that her punishment was being taken as a special reward of merit. No wonder Miss Polly was feeling curiously helpless.

CHAPTER 7
DEVOTIONAL & JOURNAL

"...most generally there is something about everything that you can be glad about, if you keep hunting long enough to find it."

Miss Polly is frustrated when Pollyanna doesn't respond to her punishments with the fear she expected, but gladness instead!

When things don't go how you hoped in your life, do you see that as God punishing you?

How does that feel?

How do you think God wants you to respond to the Biblical command to "fear" Him?

There's something wonderful in the trusting way Pollyanna responds to Miss Polly, with complete trust that Miss Polly is acting from love, with her best good at heart. I'm much more likely to respond to what I see as punishment with resentment and rebellion! I believe Pollyanna's way is how God wants us to respond to Him, with obedience, trust, and love. Unlike Miss Polly, God loves us perfectly and wants only the best for us, even when it doesn't feel that way.

> *Such love has no fear, because perfect love expels all fear.*
> *If we are afraid, it is for fear of punishment,*
> *and this shows that we have not fully experienced his perfect love.*
> 1 John 4:18 NLT

In the original Biblical Greek and Hebrew, there are different ways the words usually translated as "fear" in English can be interpreted. One meaning has a positive sense - we're commanded to have reverence for God, to respect and worship him. But as we grow in experiencing God's perfect love for us, we know and trust Him, and we can have faith that He always does what is best for us. We don't feel the cringing terror and torment of fear this verse is referring to. It's the difference between the good sort of fear that makes us fall to our knees in amazed wonder, and the bad sort of fear that makes us run and hide. God wants us to obey Him out of love, not fear.

It took me a long time to realize that when bad things happen in my life, it isn't God punishing me. Once we believe in Jesus, God doesn't punish us, because Jesus took the penalty for us. There is no more punishment. But there *is* discipline, and there are still consequences when we make wrong choices. God's discipline is training, to show us the way we should go, to make us into the people He created us to be. So when there is pain in my life, I'm learning to look and see if I've made wrong choices, if God is giving me a wake-up call to get my attention and remind me what He wants. Looking back, I can see that many of the times things went wrong and I got angry with God, it was my wrong choices that were the problem. God gives us free will, and when we make mistakes, those mistakes have consequences.

But I'm also learning this doesn't mean that every time I suffer, it's a consequence of my mistakes. We live in a fallen world, a world that is not the way God intended, and bad things happen. When they do, we have two choices – Trust God, focus on Him, and keep hold of hope; or give up, get angry, feel despair. Joy is always our choice!

Do you feel God *does* always intend what is best for you?

How can you feel glad again if you're angry with God over things that have happened differently to the way you hoped, that perhaps you felt were undeserved punishments?

Lord, it's painful and confusing sometimes when I can't understand Your reasons for things that happen in my life. Help me to trust You, even when things aren't turning out the way I hoped. Please help me to look at how I am living and the choices I've made, not to blame or beat myself up, but to confess any mistakes I've made to You, confident that You will forgive me and help me to do things differently from now on. Help me to trust that You will always do what is best for me. Things that don't happen how I wanted may not be punishments, but You working out a higher purpose in my life in ways I can't yet see. Help me to trust in Your love, Your grace, and Your mercy. Help me to surrender to Your will for me. Thank You!

CHAPTER EIGHT:
POLLYANNA PAYS A VISIT

It was not long before life at the Harrington homestead settled into something like order — though not exactly the order that Miss Polly had at first prescribed. Pollyanna sewed, practised, read aloud, and studied cooking in the kitchen, it is true; but she did not give to any of these things quite so much time as had first been planned. She had more time, also, to "just live," as she expressed it, for almost all of every afternoon from two until six o'clock was hers to do with as she liked — provided she did not "like" to do certain things already prohibited by Aunt Polly.

It is a question, perhaps, whether all this leisure time was given to the child as a relief to Pollyanna from work — or as a relief to Aunt Polly from Pollyanna. Certainly, as those first July days passed, Miss Polly found occasion many times to ejaculate "What an extraordinary child!" and certainly the reading and sewing lessons found her at their conclusion each day somewhat dazed and wholly exhausted.

Nancy, in the kitchen, fared better. She was not dazed nor exhausted. Wednesdays and Saturdays came to be, indeed, red-letter days to her.

There were no children in the immediate neighborhood of the Harrington homestead for Pollyanna to play with. The house itself was on the outskirts of the village, and though there were other houses not far away, they did not chance to contain any boys or girls near Pollyanna's age. This, however, did not seem to disturb Pollyanna in the least.

"Oh, no, I don't mind it at all," she explained to Nancy. "I'm happy just to walk around and see the streets and the houses and watch the people. I just love people. Don't you, Nancy?"

"Well, I can't say I do — all of 'em," retorted Nancy, tersely.

Almost every pleasant afternoon found Pollyanna begging for "an errand to run," so that she might be off for a walk in one direction or another; and it was on these walks that frequently she met the Man. To herself Pollyanna always called him "the Man," no matter if she met a dozen other men the same day.

The Man often wore a long black coat and a high silk hat — two things that the "just men" never wore. His face was clean shaven and rather pale, and his hair, showing below his hat, was somewhat gray. He walked erect, and rather rapidly, and he was always alone, which made Pollyanna vaguely sorry for him. Perhaps it was because of this that she one day spoke to him.

"How do you do, sir? Isn't this a nice day?" she called cheerily, as she approached him.

The man threw a hurried glance about him, then stopped uncertainly.

"Did you speak — to me?" he asked in a sharp voice.

"Yes, sir," beamed Pollyanna. "I say, it's a nice day, isn't it?"

"Eh? Oh! Humph!" he grunted; and strode on again.

Pollyanna laughed. He was such a funny man, she thought.

The next day she saw him again.

"'Tisn't quite so nice as yesterday, but it's pretty nice," she called out cheerfully.

"Eh? Oh! Humph!" grunted the man as before; and once again Pollyanna laughed happily.

When for the third time Pollyanna accosted him in much the same manner, the man stopped abruptly.

"See here, child, who are you, and why are you speaking to me every day?"

"I'm Pollyanna Whittier, and I thought you looked lonesome. I'm so glad you stopped. Now we're introduced — only I don't know your name yet."

"Well, of all the — " The man did not finish his sentence, but strode on faster than ever.

Pollyanna looked after him with a disappointed droop to her usually smiling lips.

"Maybe he didn't understand — but that was only half an introduction. I don't know HIS name, yet," she murmured, as she proceeded on her way.

Pollyanna was carrying calf's-foot jelly to Mrs. Snow to-day. Miss Polly Harrington always sent something to Mrs. Snow once a week. She said she thought that it was her duty, inasmuch as Mrs. Snow was poor, sick, and a member of her church — it was the duty of all the church members to look out for her, of course. Miss Polly did her duty by Mrs. Snow usually on Thursday afternoons — not personally, but through Nancy.

To-day Pollyanna had begged the privilege, and Nancy had promptly given it to her in accordance with Miss Polly's orders.

"And it's glad that I am ter get rid of it," Nancy had declared in private afterwards to Pollyanna; "though it's a shame ter be tuckin' the job off on ter you, poor lamb, so it is, it is!"

"But I'd love to do it, Nancy."

"Well, you won't — after you've done it once," predicted Nancy, sourly.

"Why not?"

"Because nobody does. If folks wa'n't sorry for her there wouldn't a soul go near her from mornin' till night, she's that cantankerous. All is, I pity her daughter what HAS ter take care of her."

"But, why, Nancy?"

Nancy shrugged her shoulders.

"Well, in plain words, it's just that nothin' what ever has happened, has happened right in Mis' Snow's eyes. Even the days of the week ain't run ter her mind. If it's Monday she's bound ter say she wished 'twas Sunday; and if you take her jelly you're pretty sure ter hear she wanted chicken — but if you DID bring her chicken, she'd be jest hankerin' for lamb broth!"

"Why, what a funny woman," laughed Pollyanna. "I think I shall like to go to see her. She must be so surprising and — and different. I love DIFFERENT folks."

"Humph! Well, Mis' Snow's 'different,' all right — I hope, for the sake of the rest of us!" Nancy had finished grimly.

Pollyanna was thinking of these remarks to-day as she turned in at the gate of the shabby little cottage. Her eyes were quite sparkling, indeed, at the prospect of meeting this "different" Mrs. Snow.

A pale-faced, tired-looking young girl answered her knock at the door.

"How do you do?" began Pollyanna politely. "I'm from Miss Polly Harrington, and I'd like to see Mrs. Snow, please."

"Well, if you would, you're the first one that ever 'liked' to see her," muttered the girl under her breath; but Pollyanna did not hear this. The girl had turned and was leading the way through the hall to a door at the end of it.

In the sick-room, after the girl had ushered her in and closed the door, Pollyanna blinked a little before she could accustom her eyes to the gloom. Then she saw, dimly outlined, a woman half-sitting up in the bed across the room. Pollyanna advanced at once.

"How do you do, Mrs. Snow? Aunt Polly says she hopes you are comfortable to-day, and she's sent you some calf's-foot jelly."

"Dear me! Jelly?" murmured a fretful voice. "Of course I'm very much obliged, but I was hoping 'twould be lamb broth to-day."

Pollyanna frowned a little.

"Why, I thought it was CHICKEN you wanted when folks brought you jelly," she said.

"What?" The sick woman turned sharply.

"Why, nothing, much," apologized Pollyanna, hurriedly; "and of course it doesn't really make any difference. It's only that Nancy said it was chicken you wanted when we brought jelly, and lamb broth when we brought chicken — but maybe 'twas the other way, and Nancy forgot."

The sick woman pulled herself up till she sat erect in the bed — a most unusual thing for her to do, though Pollyanna did not know this.

"Well, Miss Impertinence, who are you?" she demanded.

Pollyanna laughed gleefully.

"Oh, THAT isn't my name, Mrs. Snow — and I'm so glad 'tisn't, too! That would be worse than 'Hephzibah,' wouldn't it? I'm Pollyanna Whittier, Miss Polly Harrington's niece, and I've come to live with her. That's why I'm here with the jelly this morning."

All through the first part of this sentence, the sick woman had sat interestedly erect; but at the reference to the jelly she fell back on her pillow listlessly.

"Very well; thank you. Your aunt is very kind, of course, but my appetite isn't very good this morning, and I was wanting lamb — " She stopped suddenly, then went on with an abrupt change of subject. "I never slept a wink last night — not a wink!"

"O dear, I wish *I* didn't," sighed Pollyanna, placing the jelly on the little stand and seating herself comfortably in the nearest chair. "You lose such a lot of time just sleeping! Don't you think so?"

"Lose time — sleeping!" exclaimed the sick woman.

"Yes, when you might be just living, you know. It seems such a pity we can't live nights, too."

Once again the woman pulled herself erect in her bed.

"Well, if you ain't the amazing young one!" she cried. "Here! do you go to that window and pull up the curtain," she directed. "I should like to know what you look like!"

Pollyanna rose to her feet, but she laughed a little ruefully.

"O dear! then you'll see my freckles, won't you?" she sighed, as she went to the window; " — and just when I was being so glad it was dark and you couldn't see 'em. There! Now you can — oh!" she broke off excitedly, as she turned back to the bed; "I'm so glad you wanted to see me, because now I can see you! They didn't tell me you were so pretty!"

"Me! — pretty!" scoffed the woman, bitterly.

"Why, yes. Didn't you know it?" cried Pollyanna.

"Well, no, I didn't," retorted Mrs. Snow, dryly. Mrs. Snow had lived forty years, and for fifteen of those years she had been too busy wishing things were different to find much time to enjoy things as they were.

"Oh, but your eyes are so big and dark, and your hair's all dark, too, and curly," cooed Pollyanna. "I love black curls. (That's one of the things I'm going to have when I get to Heaven.) And you've got two little red spots in your cheeks. Why, Mrs. Snow, you ARE pretty! I should think you'd know it when you looked at yourself in the glass."

"The glass!" snapped the sick woman, falling back on her pillow. "Yes, well, I hain't done much prinkin' before the mirror these days — and you wouldn't, if you was flat on your back as I am!"

"Why, no, of course not," agreed Pollyanna, sympathetically. "But wait — just let me show you," she exclaimed, skipping over to the bureau and picking up a small hand-glass.

On the way back to the bed she stopped, eyeing the sick woman with a critical gaze.

"I reckon maybe, if you don't mind, I'd like to fix your hair just a little before I let you see it," she proposed. "May I fix your hair, please?"

"Why, I — suppose so, if you want to," permitted Mrs. Snow, grudgingly; "but 'twon't stay, you know."

"Oh, thank you. I love to fix people's hair," exulted Pollyanna, carefully laying down the hand-glass and reaching for a comb. "I sha'n't do much to-day, of course — I'm in such a hurry for you to see how pretty you are; but some day I'm going to take it all down and have a perfectly lovely time with it," she cried, touching with soft fingers the waving hair above the sick woman's forehead.

For five minutes Pollyanna worked swiftly, deftly, combing a refractory curl into fluffiness, perking up a drooping ruffle at the neck, or shaking a pillow into plumpness so that the head might have a better pose. Meanwhile the sick woman, frowning prodigiously, and openly scoffing at the whole procedure, was, in spite of herself, beginning to tingle with a feeling perilously near to excitement.

"There!" panted Pollyanna, hastily plucking a pink from a vase near by and tucking it into the dark hair where it would give the best effect. "Now I reckon we're ready to be looked at!" And she held out the mirror in triumph.

"Humph!" grunted the sick woman, eyeing her reflection severely. "I like red pinks better than pink ones; but then, it'll fade, anyhow, before night, so what's the difference!"

"But I should think you'd be glad they did fade," laughed Pollyanna, "'cause then you can have the fun of getting some more. I just love your hair fluffed out like that," she finished with a satisfied gaze. "Don't you?"

"Hm-m; maybe. Still — 'twon't last, with me tossing back and forth on the pillow as I do."

"Of course not — and I'm glad, too," nodded Pollyanna, cheerfully, "because then I can fix it again. Anyhow, I should think you'd be glad it's black — black shows up so much nicer on a pillow than yellow hair like mine does."

"Maybe; but I never did set much store by black hair — shows gray too soon," retorted Mrs. Snow. She spoke fretfully, but she still held the mirror before her face.

"Oh, I love black hair! I should be so glad if I only had it," sighed Pollyanna.

Mrs. Snow dropped the mirror and turned irritably.

"Well, you wouldn't! — not if you were me. You wouldn't be glad for black hair nor anything else — if you had to lie here all day as I do!"

Pollyanna bent her brows in a thoughtful frown.

"Why, 'twould be kind of hard — to do it then, wouldn't it?" she mused aloud.

"Do what?"

"Be glad about things."

"Be glad about things — when you're sick in bed all your days? Well, I should say it would," retorted Mrs. Snow. "If you don't think so, just tell me something to be glad about; that's all!"

To Mrs. Snow's unbounded amazement, Pollyanna sprang to her feet and clapped her hands.

"Oh, goody! That'll be a hard one — won't it? I've got to go, now, but I'll think and think all the way home; and maybe the next time I come I can tell it to you. Good-by. I've had a lovely time! Good-by," she called again, as she tripped through the doorway.

"Well, I never! Now, what does she mean by that?" ejaculated Mrs. Snow, staring after her visitor. By and by she turned her head and picked up the mirror, eyeing her reflection critically.

"That little thing HAS got a knack with hair and no mistake," she muttered under her breath. "I declare, I didn't know it could look so pretty. But then, what's the use?" she sighed, dropping the little glass into the bedclothes, and rolling her head on the pillow fretfully.

A little later, when Milly, Mrs. Snow's daughter, came in, the mirror still lay among the bedclothes — though it had been carefully hidden from sight.

"Why, mother — the curtain is up!" cried Milly, dividing her amazed stare between the window and the pink in her mother's hair.

"Well, what if it is?" snapped the sick woman. "I needn't stay in the dark all my life, if I am sick, need I?"

"Why, n-no, of course not," rejoined Milly, in hasty conciliation, as she reached for the medicine bottle. "It's only — well, you know very well that I've tried to get you to have a lighter room for ages and you wouldn't."

There was no reply to this. Mrs. Snow was picking at the lace on her nightgown. At last she spoke fretfully.

"I should think SOMEBODY might give me a new nightdress — instead of lamb broth, for a change!"

"Why — mother!"

No wonder Milly quite gasped aloud with bewilderment. In the drawer behind her at that moment lay two new nightdresses that Milly for months had been vainly urging her mother to wear.

CHAPTER 8
DEVOTIONAL & JOURNAL

"Mrs. Snow had lived forty years, and for fifteen of those years she had been too busy wishing things were different to find much time to enjoy things as they were."

Mrs. Snow is a poor widow, confined to bed by ill health, so clearly there are plenty of things in her life that she must wish different!

What parts of your life do you wish were different? Especially, which parts are so far from how you'd like them to be that they get in the way of you enjoying life? Make a list, using scrap paper if needed so you can destroy it afterwards.

Accepting "things as they are" can be hard, especially when those things are far from what we hoped for. Health, finances, work, relationships, and so much more can become sources of unhappiness when we compare what we have with what we hoped for.

I've struggled with this, over so many things and for so many years. When at last I reached sixteen weeks pregnant after four previous miscarriages, and then my waters suddenly broke, I prayed so frantically for God to work a miracle and let my baby survive. When His answer seemed to be "No," the pain felt brutal, impossible to bear. In anger and grief, I turned my back on Him for many years.

Only later did I realize He was still with me, all that time. No matter how much anger and accusation I hurled at Him, He didn't turn His back on me. He was still there, loving me, ready to hold me and support me.

It wasn't part of His plan for me to have the child I desired, not in that way, but it took me a long time to get the message I couldn't change His plan by disobeying His guidance. I wanted a baby, so badly! And God didn't seem to be doing anything to make it happen.

So I rushed into a relationship with a non-believer, rather than waiting on Him. I rushed into pregnancy after pregnancy, rather than waiting on His will. And I blamed Him when it all went wrong.

Only now am I learning to rest in Him and trust Him. To trust He wasn't punishing me for making wrong choices. To know that somehow, He has brought good out of my mistakes. I can't pretend to know His purposes, but I do know that each of those pregnancies gave a soul a chance to be embodied, even if only for a short time. At last, I can feel a peace about what was so painful at the time when I was fighting Him.

The Bible describes the way God shapes our lives as being like a potter shaping clay. All the clay needs to do is surrender to the potter's hands. If it fights back, or demands to be made a jug not a bowl, the potter will work even harder to push it into shape! Yet I know so many times in my life, I've fought back, argued with God about the shape He planned for my life. His way of making us fully His and remade in His image may be different from the way we expect. But He knows, and we need to let Him do his work. Fighting God's work in our lives brings only grief, obedience to Christ gives us joy.

I'm discovering what Jesus meant when He said:

> *"So don't be anxious about tomorrow. God will take care of your tomorrow too.*
> *Live one day at a time."*
> Matthew 6:34 TLB

God wants us to surrender all our wants and needs to Him, and to trust Him with them. Even when God's answers aren't the ones we desperately hope for, we can trust He is still with us, still working in our lives, and still taking care of us. He may not give us everything we want, but He never leaves us.

No matter what, He is with us.

Pray over the list you made, and take it to God, handing over each thing to Him.

Is God prompting you to make any changes to any of these things? Can you trust He will give you the courage and strength to make those changes? If not, ask Him to give you that courage.

Is God prompting you to accept that some of these things cannot be changed? Can you trust that He will give you grace to accept them? If not, ask Him to give you that acceptance.

Is God asking you to wait and allow His will to unfold on any of these things? Can you trust that He will give you patience to surrender and wait on His will? If not, ask Him to give you that patience.

What would it feel like to live one day at a time, finding joy in the moment?

THE SERENITY PRAYER (attributed to Reinhold Niebuhr)
God, give me grace to accept with serenity the things that cannot be changed,
Courage to change the things which should be changed,
and the Wisdom to distinguish the one from the other.
Living one day at a time,
Enjoying one moment at a time,
Accepting hardship as a pathway to peace,
Taking, as Jesus did,
This sinful world as it is,
Not as I would have it,
Trusting that You will make all things right,
If I surrender to Your will,
So that I may be reasonably happy in this life,
And supremely happy with You forever in the next.
Amen.

CHAPTER NINE:
WHICH TELLS OF THE MAN

It rained the next time Pollyanna saw the Man. She greeted him, however, with a bright smile.

"It isn't so nice to-day, is it?" she called blithesomely. "I'm glad it doesn't rain always, anyhow!"

The man did not even grunt this time, nor turn his head. Pollyanna decided that of course he did not hear her. The next time, therefore (which happened to be the following day), she spoke up louder. She thought it particularly necessary to do this, anyway, for the Man was striding along, his hands behind his back, and his eyes on the ground — which seemed, to Pollyanna, preposterous in the face of the glorious sunshine and the freshly-washed morning air: Pollyanna, as a special treat, was on a morning errand to-day.

"How do you do?" she chirped. "I'm so glad it isn't yesterday, aren't you?"

The man stopped abruptly. There was an angry scowl on his face.

"See here, little girl, we might just as well settle this thing right now, once for all," he began testily. "I've got something besides the weather to think of. I don't know whether the sun shines or not."

Pollyanna beamed joyously.

"No, sir; I thought you didn't. That's why I told you."

"Yes; well — Eh? What?" he broke off sharply, in sudden understanding of her words.

"I say, that's why I told you — so you would notice it, you know — that the sun shines, and all that. I knew you'd be glad it did if you only stopped to think of it — and you didn't look a bit as if you WERE thinking of it!"

"Well, of all the — " ejaculated the man, with an oddly impotent gesture. He started forward again, but after the second step he turned back, still frowning.

"See here, why don't you find some one your own age to talk to?"

"I'd like to, sir, but there aren't any 'round here, Nancy says. Still, I don't mind so very much. I like old folks just as well, maybe better, sometimes — being used to the Ladies' Aid, so."

"Humph! The Ladies' Aid, indeed! Is that what you took me for?" The man's lips were threatening to smile, but the scowl above them was still trying to hold them grimly stern.

Pollyanna laughed gleefully.

"Oh, no, sir. You don't look a mite like a Ladies' Aider — not but that you're just as good, of course — maybe better," she added in hurried politeness. "You see, I'm sure you're much nicer than you look!"

The man made a queer noise in his throat.

"Well, of all the — " he ejaculated again, as he turned and strode on as before.

The next time Pollyanna met the Man, his eyes were gazing straight into hers, with a quizzical directness that made his face look really pleasant, Pollyanna thought.

"Good afternoon," he greeted her a little stiffly. "Perhaps I'd better say right away that I KNOW the sun is shining to-day."

"But you don't have to tell me," nodded Pollyanna, brightly. "I KNEW you knew it just as soon as I saw you."

"Oh, you did, did you?"

"Yes, sir; I saw it in your eyes, you know, and in your smile."

"Humph!" grunted the man, as he passed on.

The Man always spoke to Pollyanna after this, and frequently he spoke first, though usually he said little but "good afternoon." Even that, however, was a great surprise to Nancy, who chanced to be with Pollyanna one day when the greeting was given.

"Sakes alive, Miss Pollyanna," she gasped, "did that man SPEAK TO YOU?"

"Why, yes, he always does — now," smiled Pollyanna.

"'He always does'! Goodness! Do you know who — he — is?" demanded Nancy.

Pollyanna frowned and shook her head.

"I reckon he forgot to tell me one day. You see, I did my part of the introducing, but he didn't."

Nancy's eyes widened.

"But he never speaks ter anybody, child — he hain't for years, I guess, except when he just has to, for business, and all that. He's John Pendleton. He lives all by himself in the big house on Pendleton Hill. He won't even have any one 'round ter cook for him — comes down ter the hotel for his meals three times a day. I know Sally Miner, who waits on him, and she says he hardly opens his head enough ter tell what he wants ter eat. She has ter guess it more'n half the time — only it'll be somethin' CHEAP! She knows that without no tellin'."

Pollyanna nodded sympathetically.

"I know. You have to look for cheap things when you're poor. Father and I took meals out a lot. We had beans and fish balls most generally. We used to say how glad we were we liked beans — that is, we said it specially when we were looking at the roast turkey place, you know, that was sixty cents. Does Mr. Pendleton like beans?"

"Like 'em! What if he does — or don't? Why, Miss Pollyanna, he ain't poor. He's got loads of money, John Pendleton has — from his father. There ain't nobody in town as rich as he is. He could eat dollar bills, if he wanted to — and not know it."

Pollyanna giggled.

"As if anybody COULD eat dollar bills and not know it, Nancy, when they come to try to chew 'em!"

"Ho! I mean he's rich enough ter do it," shrugged Nancy. "He ain't spendin' his money, that's all. He's a-savin' of it."

"Oh, for the heathen," surmised Pollyanna. "How perfectly splendid! That's denying yourself and taking up your cross. I know; father told me."

Nancy's lips parted abruptly, as if there were angry words all ready to come; but her eyes, resting on Pollyanna's jubilantly trustful face, saw something that prevented the words being spoken.

"Humph!" she vouchsafed. Then, showing her old-time interest, she went on: "But, say, it is queer, his speakin' to you, honestly, Miss Pollyanna. He don't speak ter no one; and he lives all alone in a great big lovely house all full of jest grand things, they say. Some says he's crazy, and some jest cross; and some says he's got a skeleton in his closet."

"Oh, Nancy!" shuddered Pollyanna. "How can he keep such a dreadful thing? I should think he'd throw it away!"

Nancy chuckled. That Pollyanna had taken the skeleton literally instead of figuratively, she knew very well; but, perversely, she refrained from correcting the mistake.

"And EVERYBODY says he's mysterious," she went on. "Some years he jest travels, week in and week out, and it's always in heathen countries — Egypt and Asia and the Desert of Sarah, you know."

"Oh, a missionary," nodded Pollyanna.

Nancy laughed oddly.

"Well, I didn't say that, Miss Pollyanna. When he comes back he writes books — queer, odd books, they say, about some gimcrack he's found in them heathen countries. But he don't never seem ter want ter spend no money here — leastways, not for jest livin'."

"Of course not — if he's saving it for the heathen," declared Pollyanna. "But he is a funny man, and he's different, too, just like Mrs. Snow, only he's a different different."

"Well, I guess he is — rather," chuckled Nancy.

"I'm gladder'n ever now, anyhow, that he speaks to me," sighed Pollyanna contentedly.

CHAPTER 9
DEVOTIONAL & JOURNAL

The man stopped abruptly. There was an angry scowl on his face.

"See here, little girl, we might just as well settle this thing right now, once for all," he began testily. "I've got something besides the weather to think of. I don't know whether the sun shines or not."

Pollyanna beamed joyously.

"No, sir; I thought you didn't. That's why I told you."

"Yes; well — Eh? What?" he broke off sharply, in sudden understanding of her words.

"I say, that's why I told you — so you would notice it, you know — that the sun shines, and all that. I knew you'd be glad it did if you only stopped to think of it — and you didn't look a bit as if you WERE thinking of it!"

Are you able to see the sun shining in your life? What clouds are getting in the way?

The thing I love most about Pollyanna is that despite having so much she could be miserable about — poor, orphaned, living with a dutiful but unloving aunt who gives her a bare attic room — she bubbles over with joy. She notices that the sun is shining! John Pendleton, on the other hand, allows a twenty year old lost love to blind him to friendship, wealth, and God's love.

I know that there is nothing better for people than to be happy and to do good while they live.
Ecclesiastes 3:12 NIV

God wants us to be happy. But life can feel so full of worries and concerns that, like John Pendleton, we don't notice the sun shining, either.

I know far too often, I focus on all that is wrong in my life. Whether that's my marriage, my health, my finances, relationships with others, my schedule – I spend so much time looking at the clouds, until I get so I can't see the sunshine anymore. Or old bitterness and resentment clouds my sight.

But there is still so much that is good! By changing my focus to God, His love for me, all He longs to bless me with, I can see the good that already exists, even in the most difficult situation.

Our mouths were filled with laughter, our tongues with songs of joy.
Then it was said among the nations, "The Lord has done great things for them."
Psalm 126:2

Can you surrender whatever trials you might be dealing with to God? If that's difficult, please post to the Facebook group & we'll pray for you – https://www.facebook.com/groups/LessonsfromPollyanna

List twenty ways the sun shines in your life today.:

Lord, you know the troubles I'm dealing with right now. You know the hurts my heart bears, the worries that sometimes seem to fill my mind. Please help me to release all those to You, trust You with them, and then see that the sun is shining. You designed me to see the sunshine and dance in it, like Pollyanna does. Help me to do that today. Help me to feel Your true joy and peace, Your loving support carrying me through the day. Thank You!

CHAPTER TEN:
A SURPRISE FOR MRS. SNOW

The next time Pollyanna went to see Mrs. Snow, she found that lady, as at first, in a darkened room.

"It's the little girl from Miss Polly's, mother," announced Milly, in a tired manner; then Pollyanna found herself alone with the invalid.

"Oh, it's you, is it?" asked a fretful voice from the bed. "I remember you. ANYbody'd remember you, I guess, if they saw you once. I wish you had come yesterday. I WANTED you yesterday."

"Did you? Well, I'm glad 'tisn't any farther away from yesterday than to-day is, then," laughed Pollyanna, advancing cheerily into the room, and setting her basket carefully down on a chair. "My! but aren't you dark here, though? I can't see you a bit," she cried, unhesitatingly crossing to the window and pulling up the shade. "I want to see if you've fixed your hair like I did — oh, you haven't! But, never mind; I'm glad you haven't, after all, 'cause maybe you'll let me do it — later. But now I want you to see what I've brought you."

The woman stirred restlessly.

"Just as if how it looks would make any difference in how it tastes," she scoffed — but she turned her eyes toward the basket. "Well, what is it?"

"Guess! What do you want?" Pollyanna had skipped back to the basket. Her face was alight. The sick woman frowned.

"Why, I don't WANT anything, as I know of," she sighed. "After all, they all taste alike!"
Pollyanna chuckled.

"This won't. Guess! If you DID want something, what would it be?"

The woman hesitated. She did not realize it herself, but she had so long been accustomed to wanting what she did not have, that to state off-hand what she DID want seemed impossible — until she knew what she had.

Obviously, however, she must say something. This extraordinary child was waiting.

"Well, of course, there's lamb broth — "

"I've got it!" crowed Pollyanna.

"But that's what I DIDN'T want," sighed the sick woman, sure now of what her stomach craved. "It was chicken I wanted."

"Oh, I've got that, too," chuckled Pollyanna.

The woman turned in amazement.

"Both of them?" she demanded.

"Yes — and calf's-foot jelly," triumphed Pollyanna. "I was just bound you should have what you wanted for once; so Nancy and I fixed it. Oh, of course, there's only a little of each — but there's some of all of 'em! I'm so glad you did want chicken," she went on contentedly, as she lifted the three little bowls from her basket. "You see, I got to thinking on the way here — what if you should say tripe, or onions, or something like that, that I didn't have! Wouldn't it have been a shame — when I'd tried so hard?" she laughed merrily.

There was no reply. The sick woman seemed to be trying — mentally to find something she had lost.

"There! I'm to leave them all," announced Pollyanna, as she arranged the three bowls in a row on the table. "Like enough it'll be lamb broth you want to-morrow. How do you do to-day?" she finished in polite inquiry.

"Very poorly, thank you," murmured Mrs. Snow, falling back into her usual listless attitude. "I lost my nap this morning. Nellie Higgins next door has begun music lessons, and her practising drives me nearly wild. She was at it all the morning — every minute! I'm sure, I don't know what I shall do!"

Polly nodded sympathetically.

"I know. It IS awful! Mrs. White had it once — one of my Ladies' Aiders, you know. She had rheumatic fever, too, at the same time, so she couldn't thrash 'round. She said 'twould have been easier if she could have. Can you?"

"Can I — what?"

"Thrash 'round — move, you know, so as to change your position when the music gets too hard to stand."

Mrs. Snow stared a little.

"Why, of course I can move — anywhere — in bed," she rejoined a little irritably.

"Well, you can be glad of that, then, anyhow, can't you?" nodded Pollyanna. "Mrs. White couldn't. You can't thrash when you have rheumatic fever — though you want to something awful, Mrs. White says. She told me afterwards she reckoned she'd have gone raving crazy if it hadn't been for Mr. White's sister's ears — being deaf, so."

"Sister's — EARS! What do you mean?"

Pollyanna laughed.

"Well, I reckon I didn't tell it all, and I forgot you didn't know Mrs. White. You see, Miss White was deaf — awfully deaf; and she came to visit 'em and to help take care of Mrs. White and the house. Well, they had such an awful time making her understand ANYTHING, that after that, every time the piano commenced to play across the street, Mrs. White felt so glad she COULD hear it, that she didn't mind so much that she DID hear it, 'cause she couldn't help thinking how awful 'twould be if she was deaf and couldn't hear anything, like her husband's sister. You see, she was playing the game, too. I'd told her about it."

"The — game?"

Pollyanna clapped her hands.

"There! I 'most forgot; but I've thought it up, Mrs. Snow — what you can be glad about."

"GLAD about! What do you mean?"

"Why, I told you I would. Don't you remember? You asked me to tell you something to be glad about — glad, you know, even though you did have to lie here abed all day."

"Oh!" scoffed the woman. "THAT? Yes, I remember that; but I didn't suppose you were in earnest any more than I was."

"Oh, yes, I was," nodded Pollyanna, triumphantly; "and I found it, too. But 'TWAS hard. It's all the more fun, though, always, when 'tis hard. And I will own up, honest to true, that I couldn't think of anything for a while. Then I got it."

"Did you, really? Well, what is it?" Mrs. Snow's voice was sarcastically polite.

Pollyanna drew a long breath.

"I thought — how glad you could be — that other folks weren't like you — all sick in bed like this, you know," she announced impressively.

Mrs. Snow stared. Her eyes were angry.

"Well, really!" she ejaculated then, in not quite an agreeable tone of voice.

"And now I'll tell you the game," proposed Pollyanna, blithely confident. "It'll be just lovely for you to play — it'll be so hard. And there's so much more fun when it is hard! You see, it's like this." And she began to tell of the missionary barrel, the crutches, and the doll that did not come.

The story was just finished when Milly appeared at the door.

"Your aunt is wanting you, Miss Pollyanna," she said with dreary listlessness. "She telephoned down to the Harlows' across the way. She says you're to hurry — that you've got some practising to make up before dark."

Pollyanna rose reluctantly.

"All right," she sighed. "I'll hurry." Suddenly she laughed. "I suppose I ought to be glad I've got legs to hurry with, hadn't I, Mrs. Snow?"

There was no answer. Mrs. Snow's eyes were closed. But Milly, whose eyes were wide open with surprise, saw that there were tears on the wasted cheeks.

"Good-by," flung Pollyanna over her shoulder, as she reached the door. "I'm awfully sorry about the hair — I wanted to do it. But maybe I can next time!"

One by one the July days passed. To Pollyanna, they were happy days, indeed. She often told her aunt, joyously, how very happy they were.

Whereupon her aunt would usually reply, wearily:

"Very well, Pollyanna. I am gratified, of course, that they are happy; but I trust that they are profitable, as well — otherwise I should have failed signally in my duty."

Generally Pollyanna would answer this with a hug and a kiss — a proceeding that was still always most disconcerting to Miss Polly; but one day she spoke. It was during the sewing hour.

"Do you mean that it wouldn't be enough then, Aunt Polly, that they should be just happy days?" she asked wistfully.

"That is what I mean, Pollyanna."

"They must be pro-fi-ta-ble as well?"

"Certainly."

"What is being pro-fi-ta-ble?"

"Why, it — it's just being profitable — having profit, something to show for it, Pollyanna. What an extraordinary child you are!"

"Then just being glad isn't pro-fi-ta-ble?" questioned Pollyanna, a little anxiously.

"Certainly not."

"O dear! Then you wouldn't like it, of course. I'm afraid, now, you won't ever play the game, Aunt Polly."

"Game? What game?"

"Why, that father — " Pollyanna clapped her hand to her lips. "N-nothing," she stammered.

Miss Polly frowned. "That will do for this morning, Pollyanna," she said tersely. And the sewing lesson was over.

It was that afternoon that Pollyanna, coming down from her attic room, met her aunt on the stairway.

"Why, Aunt Polly, how perfectly lovely!" she cried. "You were coming up to see me! Come right in. I love company," she finished, scampering up the stairs and throwing her door wide open.

Now Miss Polly had not been intending to call on her niece. She had been planning to look for a certain white wool shawl in the cedar chest near the east window. But to her unbounded surprise now, she found herself, not in the main attic before the cedar chest, but in Pollyanna's little room sitting in one of the straight-backed chairs — so many, many times since Pollyanna came, Miss Polly had found herself like this, doing some utterly unexpected, surprising thing, quite unlike the thing she had set out to do!

"I love company," said Pollyanna, again, flitting about as if she were dispensing the hospitality of a palace; "specially since I've had this room, all mine, you know. Oh, of course, I had a room, always, but 'twas a hired room, and hired rooms aren't half as nice as owned ones, are they? And of course I do own this one, don't I?"

"Why, y-yes, Pollyanna," murmured Miss Polly, vaguely wondering why she did not get up at once and go to look for that shawl.

"And of course NOW I just love this room, even if it hasn't got the carpets and curtains and pictures that I'd been want — " With a painful blush Pollyanna stopped short. She was plunging into an entirely different sentence when her aunt interrupted her sharply.

"What's that, Pollyanna?"

"N-nothing, Aunt Polly, truly. I didn't mean to say it."

"Probably not," returned Miss Polly, coldly; "but you did say it, so suppose we have the rest of it."

"But it wasn't anything, only that I'd been kind of planning on pretty carpets and lace curtains and things, you know. But, of course — ”

"PLANNING on them!" interrupted Miss Polly, sharply.

Pollyanna blushed still more painfully.

"I ought not to have, of course, Aunt Polly," she apologized. "It was only because I'd always wanted them and hadn't had them, I suppose. Oh, we'd had two rugs in the barrels, but they were little, you know, and one had ink spots, and the other holes; and there never were only those two pictures; the one fath — I mean the good one we sold, and the bad one that broke. Of course if it hadn't been for all that I shouldn't have wanted them, so — pretty things, I mean; and I shouldn't have got to planning all through the hall that first day how pretty mine would be here, and — and — but, truly, Aunt Polly, it wasn't but just a minute — I mean, a few minutes — before I was being glad that the bureau DIDN'T have a looking-glass, because it didn't show my freckles; and there couldn't be a nicer picture than the one out my window there; and you've been so good to me, that — ”

Miss Polly rose suddenly to her feet. Her face was very red.

"That will do, Pollyanna," she said stiffly. "You have said quite enough, I'm sure." The next minute she had swept down the stairs — and not until she reached the first floor did it suddenly occur to her that she had gone up into the attic to find a white wool shawl in the cedar chest near the east window.

Less than twenty-four hours later, Miss Polly said to Nancy, crisply:

"Nancy, you may move Miss Pollyanna's things down-stairs this morning to the room directly beneath. I have decided to have my niece sleep there for the present."

"Yes, ma'am," said Nancy aloud.

"O glory!" said Nancy to herself.

To Pollyanna, a minute later, she cried joyously:

"And won't ye jest be listenin' ter this, Miss Pollyanna. You're ter sleep down-stairs in the room straight under this. You are — you are!"

Pollyanna actually grew white.

"You mean — why, Nancy, not really — really and truly?"

"I guess you'll think it's really and truly," prophesied Nancy, exultingly, nodding her head to Pollyanna over the armful of dresses she had taken from the closet. "I'm told ter take down yer things, and I'm goin' ter take 'em, too, 'fore she gets a chance ter change her mind."

Pollyanna did not stop to hear the end of this sentence. At the imminent risk of being dashed headlong, she was flying down-stairs, two steps at a time.

Bang went two doors and a chair before Pollyanna at last reached her goal — Aunt Polly.

"Oh, Aunt Polly, Aunt Polly, did you mean it, really? Why, that room's got EVERYTHING — the carpet and curtains and three pictures, besides the one outdoors, too, 'cause the windows look the same way. Oh, Aunt Polly!"

"Very well, Pollyanna. I am gratified that you like the change, of course; but if you think so much of all those things, I trust you will take proper care of them; that's all. Pollyanna, please pick up that chair; and you have banged two doors in the last half-minute." Miss Polly spoke sternly, all the more sternly because, for some inexplicable reason, she felt inclined to cry — and Miss Polly was not used to feeling inclined to cry.

Pollyanna picked up the chair.

"Yes'm; I know I banged 'em — those doors," she admitted cheerfully. "You see I'd just found out about the room, and I reckon you'd have banged doors if — " Pollyanna stopped short and eyed her aunt with new interest. "Aunt Polly, DID you ever bang doors?"

"I hope — not, Pollyanna!" Miss Polly's voice was properly shocked.

"Why, Aunt Polly, what a shame!" Pollyanna's face expressed only concerned sympathy.

"A shame!" repeated Aunt Polly, too dazed to say more.

"Why, yes. You see, if you'd felt like banging doors you'd have banged 'em, of course; and if you didn't, that must have meant that you weren't ever glad over anything — or you would have banged 'em. You couldn't have helped it. And I'm so sorry you weren't ever glad over anything!"

"PollyANna!" gasped the lady; but Pollyanna was gone, and only the distant bang of the attic-stairway door answered for her. Pollyanna had gone to help Nancy bring down "her things."

Miss Polly, in the sitting room, felt vaguely disturbed; — but then, of course she HAD been glad — over some things!

CHAPTER 10
DEVOTIONAL & JOURNAL

Cheerfully giving, cheerfully receiving! Mrs. Snow, the fretful unhappy invalid, can never feel happy with whatever she has, because she always wants something else; Pollyanna, on the other hand, knows exactly what she wants, but is determined to make the best of what she has. And Pollyanna loves to give; while Miss Polly, despite having plenty of time and money, gives the minimum duty requires.

God makes the link between receiving and giving very clear. We can't give unless we first receive, but giving allows us to receive even more.

Freely you have received, freely give.
Matthew 10:8

Each of you should give what you have decided in your heart to give, not reluctantly or under compulsion, for God loves a cheerful giver. And God is able to bless you abundantly, so that in all things at all times, having all that you need, you will abound in every good work.
2 Corinthians 9:7-8 NIV

Yet in our own lives, we often either expect to receive without giving; or we expect ourselves to give without allowing ourselves to receive. Either way, we can find ourselves losing the true joy that should come from giving and receiving.

I know I do this. My husband does so much for me, yet like Mrs. Snow, I too often don't notice or thank him as I should, because I wanted something different. I don't recognize how generous he is and how much he's giving me, because he's giving me things I didn't ask for or things that aren't so obviously gifts, wrapped in pretty paper with a bow. The bunch of gas station flowers when I wanted roses. But to him, they're all flowers. He doesn't make the same distinction between romantic and unromantic flowers I do!

And I do the same with God. I pray, asking for things to turn out the way I want, and I can fail to see the good in what He gives me unless it's exactly what I asked for.

Or we can give too much without receiving in return. Professional givers, getting a sense of value and worth from giving but never asking for help. Always ready to volunteer, always offering to help, and ultimately getting overloaded to the point where we resent giving.

When that happens, our first response might become to say no, like Miss Polly (which makes us feel guilty, or leads to living a joyless and small life). I got caught in that cycle so often when I worked as a nurse. I couldn't say no to anything, I wanted to excel at my job, I wanted to meet all my patients' needs. But then I got so exhausted trying, the only way out in the end was to leave that job and hope it would be different next time. (Hint – it never was! I needed to learn to say no and set limits, and how to allow my own well to be filled first.)

Whether your normal response is yes or no, whether what's been asked for is time, money, or other resources, pray before you give that reflex answer! Unless it's an emergency, it's okay to say, "I need a little time to think about it." Discerning God's will gets easier with practice. Leaning on God's strength and accepting all He gives us so we can do the things He asks us to do gets easier with practice. Saying no to the things we're asked to do that aren't necessary for us to do gets easier with practice, too.

God intends to fill our needs first by letting Him give to us. He is always there, waiting to give. Freely receive, freely give.

Are you able to receive easily and thankfully? Which areas in your life have you been offered more, but been reluctant to take it?

What areas of your life do you find it easy to give cheerfully? What is it about those things that makes you glad to give?

Where do you feel you're giving reluctantly? Pray over each item. Is this something you know God wants you to do, and you need to do, even if you don't want to or find it difficult? If so, how can you decide to give willingly, rather than reluctantly? What would it take to shift this item to your list of things you're glad to give?

Let God know how hard you're finding giving in this area. Trust that He will give you the strength, energy, and resources you need to do what He asks you to do. Be open to Him providing this in unexpected ways!

Do you get the sense for some things that you've felt pressured to give time or money, or take on certain tasks, but God isn't asking you to do them? No matter how good or important they are, these things can drain us, and get in the way of us doing what God is truly calling us to do. Do you really have to do it, or could someone else do it? How would it feel to say no to this?

Ask God to show you His will for this, and to provide the way to gracefully back out of giving in this area if that what He wants. Make extra sure that you're not confusing His will with what you want!

Pray and ask yourself these questions every time you're asked to give.

Lord, I want to do Your will and be a cheerful giver and receiver, but it's not always easy. Help me to bring everything to You, and to seek your guidance. Help me to discern clearly what You want me to do, and what I've allowed people to pressure me into doing. Help me to trust that You will always provide all I need to do Your will, including enabling me to say no to things that aren't right for me to take on. Remind me how necessary it is that I call on Your help and don't try to do it on my own. You promise blessings when I give for the right reasons. Please help me to always know the difference. Thank You!

August came. August brought several surprises and some changes — none of which, however, were really a surprise to Nancy. Nancy, since Pollyanna's arrival, had come to look for surprises and changes.

First there was the kitten.

Pollyanna found the kitten mewing pitifully some distance down the road. When systematic questioning of the neighbors failed to find any one who claimed it, Pollyanna brought it home at once, as a matter of course.

"And I was glad I didn't find any one who owned it, too," she told her aunt in happy confidence; "'cause I wanted to bring it home all the time. I love kitties. I knew you'd be glad to let it live here."

Miss Polly looked at the forlorn little gray bunch of neglected misery in Pollyanna's arms, and shivered: Miss Polly did not care for cats — not even pretty, healthy, clean ones.

"Ugh! Pollyanna! What a dirty little beast! And it's sick, I'm sure, and all mangy and fleay."

"I know it, poor little thing," crooned Pollyanna, tenderly, looking into the little creature's frightened eyes. "And it's all trembly, too, it's so scared. You see it doesn't know, yet, that we're going to keep it, of course."

"No — nor anybody else," retorted Miss Polly, with meaning emphasis.

"Oh, yes, they do," nodded Pollyanna, entirely misunderstanding her aunt's words. "I told everybody we should keep it, if I didn't find where it belonged. I knew you'd be glad to have it — poor little lonesome thing!"

Miss Polly opened her lips and tried to speak; but in vain. The curious helpless feeling that had been hers so often since Pollyanna's arrival, had her now fast in its grip.

"Of course I knew," hurried on Pollyanna, gratefully, "that you wouldn't let a dear little lonesome kitty go hunting for a home when you'd just taken ME in; and I said so to Mrs. Ford when she asked if you'd let me keep it. Why, I had the Ladies' Aid, you know, and kitty didn't have anybody. I knew you'd feel that way," she nodded happily, as she ran from the room.

"But, Pollyanna, Pollyanna," remonstrated Miss Polly. "I don't — " But Pollyanna was already halfway to the kitchen, calling:

"Nancy, Nancy, just see this dear little kitty that Aunt Polly is going to bring up along with me!"

And Aunt Polly, in the sitting room — who abhorred cats — fell back in her chair with a gasp of dismay, powerless to remonstrate.

The next day it was a dog, even dirtier and more forlorn, perhaps, than was the kitten; and again Miss Polly, to her dumfounded amazement, found herself figuring as a kind protector and an angel of mercy — a role that Pollyanna so unhesitatingly thrust upon her as a matter of course, that the woman — who abhorred dogs even more than she did cats, if possible — found herself as before, powerless to remonstrate.

When, in less than a week, however, Pollyanna brought home a small, ragged boy, and confidently claimed the same protection for him, Miss Polly did have something to say. It happened after this wise.

On a pleasant Thursday morning Pollyanna had been taking calf's-foot jelly again to Mrs. Snow. Mrs. Snow and Pollyanna were the best of friends now. Their friendship had started from the third visit Pollyanna had made, the one after she had told Mrs. Snow of the game. Mrs. Snow herself was playing the game now, with Pollyanna. To be sure, she was not playing it very well — she had been sorry for everything for so long, that it was not easy to be glad for anything now. But under Pollyanna's cheery instructions and merry laughter at her mistakes, she was learning fast. To-day, even, to Pollyanna's huge delight, she had said that she was glad Pollyanna brought calf's-foot jelly, because that was just what she had been wanting — she did not know that Milly, at the front door, had told Pollyanna that the minister's wife had already that day sent over a great bowlful of that same kind of jelly.

Pollyanna was thinking of this now when suddenly she saw the boy.

The boy was sitting in a disconsolate little heap by the roadside, whittling half-heartedly at a small stick.

"Hullo," smiled Pollyanna, engagingly.

The boy glanced up, but he looked away again, at once.

"Hullo yourself," he mumbled.

Pollyanna laughed.

"Now you don't look as if you'd be glad even for calf's-foot jelly," she chuckled, stopping before him.

The boy stirred restlessly, gave her a surprised look, and began to whittle again at his stick, with the dull, broken-bladed knife in his hand.

Pollyanna hesitated, then dropped herself comfortably down on the grass near him. In spite of Pollyanna's brave assertion that she was "used to Ladies' Aiders," and "didn't mind," she had sighed at times for some companion of her own age. Hence her determination to make the most of this one.

"My name's Pollyanna Whittier," she began pleasantly. "What's yours?"

Again the boy stirred restlessly. He even almost got to his feet. But he settled back.

"Jimmy Bean," he grunted with ungracious indifference.

"Good! Now we're introduced. I'm glad you did your part — some folks don't, you know. I live at Miss Polly Harrington's house. Where do you live?"

"Nowhere."

"Nowhere! Why, you can't do that — everybody lives somewhere," asserted Pollyanna.

LESSONS FROM POLLYANNA: JOURNAL

"Well, I don't — just now. I'm huntin' up a new place."

"Oh! Where is it?"

The boy regarded her with scornful eyes.

"Silly! As if I'd be a-huntin' for it — if I knew!"

Pollyanna tossed her head a little. This was not a nice boy, and she did not like to be called "silly." Still, he was somebody besides — old folks. "Where did you live — before?" she queried.

"Well, if you ain't the beat'em for askin' questions!" sighed the boy impatiently.

"I have to be," retorted Pollyanna calmly, "else I couldn't find out a thing about you. If you'd talk more I wouldn't talk so much."

The boy gave a short laugh. It was a sheepish laugh, and not quite a willing one; but his face looked a little pleasanter when he spoke this time.

"All right then — here goes! I'm Jimmy Bean, and I'm ten years old goin' on eleven. I come last year ter live at the Orphans' Home; but they've got so many kids there ain't much room for me, an' I wa'n't never wanted, anyhow, I don't believe. So I've quit. I'm goin' ter live somewheres else — but I hain't found the place, yet. I'd LIKE a home — jest a common one, ye know, with a mother in it, instead of a Matron. If ye has a home, ye has folks; an' I hain't had folks since — dad died. So I'm a-huntin' now. I've tried four houses, but — they didn't want me — though I said I expected ter work, 'course. There! Is that all you want ter know?" The boy's voice had broken a little over the last two sentences.

"Why, what a shame!" sympathized Pollyanna. "And didn't there anybody want you? O dear! I know just how you feel, because after — after my father died, too, there wasn't anybody but the Ladies' Aid for me, until Aunt Polly said she'd take — " Pollyanna stopped abruptly. The dawning of a wonderful idea began to show in her face.

"Oh, I know just the place for you," she cried. "Aunt Polly'll take you — I know she will! Didn't she take me? And didn't she take Fluffy and Buffy, when they didn't have any one to love them, or any place to go? — and they're only cats and dogs. Oh, come, I know Aunt Polly'll take you! You don't know how good and kind she is!"

Jimmy Bean's thin little face brightened.

"Honest Injun? Would she, now? I'd work, ye know, an' I'm real strong!" He bared a small, bony arm.

"Of course she would! Why, my Aunt Polly is the nicest lady in the world — now that my mama has gone to be a Heaven angel. And there's rooms — heaps of 'em," she continued, springing to her feet, and tugging at his arm. "It's an awful big house. Maybe, though," she added a little anxiously, as they hurried on, "maybe you'll have to sleep in the attic room. I did, at first. But there's screens there now, so 'twon't be so hot, and the flies can't get in, either, to bring in the germ-things on their feet. Did you know about that? It's perfectly lovely! Maybe she'll let you read the book if you're good — I mean, if you're bad. And you've got freckles, too," — with a critical glance — "so you'll be glad there isn't any looking-glass; and the outdoor picture is nicer than any wall-one could be, so you won't mind sleeping in that room at all, I'm sure," panted Pollyanna, finding suddenly that she needed the rest of her breath for purposes other than talking.

"Gorry!" exclaimed Jimmy Bean tersely and uncomprehendingly, but admiringly. Then he added: "I shouldn't think anybody who could talk like that, runnin', would need ter ask no questions ter fill up time with!"

Pollyanna laughed.

"Well, anyhow, you can be glad of that," she retorted; "for when I'm talking, YOU don't have to!"

When the house was reached, Pollyanna unhesitatingly piloted her companion straight into the presence of her amazed aunt.

"Oh, Aunt Polly," she triumphed, "just look a-here! I've got something ever so much nicer, even, than Fluffy and Buffy for you to bring up. It's a real live boy. He won't mind a bit sleeping in the attic, at first, you know, and he says he'll work; but I shall need him the most of the time to play with, I reckon."

Miss Polly grew white, then very red. She did not quite understand; but she thought she understood enough.

"Pollyanna, what does this mean? Who is this dirty little boy? Where did you find him?" she demanded sharply.

The "dirty little boy" fell back a step and looked toward the door.

Pollyanna laughed merrily.

"There, if I didn't forget to tell you his name! I'm as bad as the Man. And he is dirty, too, isn't he? — I mean, the boy is — just like Fluffy and Buffy were when you took them in. But I reckon he'll improve all right by washing, just as they did, and — Oh, I 'most forgot again," she broke off with a laugh. "This is Jimmy Bean, Aunt Polly."

"Well, what is he doing here?"

"Why, Aunt Polly, I just told you!" Pollyanna's eyes were wide with surprise. "He's for you. I brought him home — so he could live here, you know. He wants a home and folks. I told him how good you were to me, and to Fluffy and Buffy, and that I knew you would be to him, because of course he's even nicer than cats and dogs."

Miss Polly dropped back in her chair and raised a shaking hand to her throat. The old helplessness was threatening once more to overcome her.

With a visible struggle, however, Miss Polly pulled herself suddenly erect.

"That will do, Pollyanna. This is a little the most absurd thing you've done yet. As if tramp cats and mangy dogs weren't bad enough but you must needs bring home ragged little beggars from the street, who — "

There was a sudden stir from the boy. His eyes flashed and his chin came up. With two strides of his sturdy little legs he confronted Miss Polly fearlessly.

"I ain't a beggar, marm, an' I don't want nothin' o' you. I was cal'latin' ter work, of course, fur my board an' keep. I wouldn't have come ter your old house, anyhow, if this 'ere girl hadn't 'a' made me, a-tellin' me how you was so good an' kind that you'd be jest dyin' ter take me in. So, there!" And he wheeled about and stalked from the room with a dignity that would have been absurd had it not been so pitiful.

"Oh, Aunt Polly," choked Pollyanna. "Why, I thought you'd be GLAD to have him here! I'm sure, I should think you'd be glad — "

Miss Polly raised her hand with a peremptory gesture of silence. Miss Polly's nerves had snapped at last. The "good and kind" of the boy's words were still ringing in her ears, and the old helplessness was almost upon her, she knew. Yet she rallied her forces with the last atom of her will power.

"Pollyanna," she cried sharply, "WILL you stop using that everlasting word 'glad'! It's 'glad' — 'glad' — 'glad' from morning till night until I think I shall grow wild!"

From sheer amazement Pollyanna's jaw dropped.

"Why, Aunt Polly," she breathed, "I should think you'd be glad to have me gl — Oh!" she broke off, clapping her hand to her lips and hurrying blindly from the room.

Before the boy had reached the end of the driveway, Pollyanna overtook him.

"Boy! Boy! Jimmy Bean, I want you to know how — how sorry I am," she panted, catching him with a detaining hand.

"Sorry nothin'! I ain't blamin' you," retorted the boy, sullenly. "But I ain't no beggar!" he added, with sudden spirit.

"Of course you aren't! But you mustn't blame auntie," appealed Pollyanna. "Probably I didn't do the introducing right, anyhow; and I reckon I didn't tell her much who you were. She is good and kind, really — she's always been; but I probably didn't explain it right. I do wish I could find some place for you, though!"

The boy shrugged his shoulders and half turned away.

"Never mind. I guess I can find one myself. I ain't no beggar, you know."

Pollyanna was frowning thoughtfully. Of a sudden she turned, her face illumined.

"Say, I'll tell you what I WILL do! The Ladies' Aid meets this afternoon. I heard Aunt Polly say so. I'll lay your case before them. That's what father always did, when he wanted anything — educating the heathen and new carpets, you know."

The boy turned fiercely.

"Well, I ain't a heathen or a new carpet. Besides — what is a Ladies' Aid?"

Pollyanna stared in shocked disapproval.

Why, Jimmy Bean, wherever have you been brought up? — not to know what a Ladies' Aid is!"

"Oh, all right — if you ain't tellin'," grunted the boy, turning and beginning to walk away indifferently.

Pollyanna sprang to his side at once.

"It's — it's — why, it's just a lot of ladies that meet and sew and give suppers and raise money and — and talk; that's what a Ladies' Aid is. They're awfully kind — that is, most of mine was, back home. I haven't seen this one here, but they're always good, I reckon. I'm going to tell them about you this afternoon."

Again the boy turned fiercely.

"Not much you will! Maybe you think I'm goin' ter stand 'round an' hear a whole LOT o' women call me a beggar, instead of jest ONE! Not much!"

"Oh, but you wouldn't be there," argued Pollyanna, quickly. "I'd go alone, of course, and tell them."

"You would?"

"Yes; and I'd tell it better this time," hurried on Pollyanna, quick to see the signs of relenting in the boy's face. "And there'd be some of 'em, I know, that would be glad to give you a home."

"I'd work — don't forget ter say that," cautioned the boy.

"Of course not," promised Pollyanna, happily, sure now that her point was gained. "Then I'll let you know tomorrow."

"Where?"

"By the road — where I found you to-day; near Mrs. Snow's house."

"All right. I'll be there." The boy paused before he went on slowly: "Maybe I'd better go back, then, for ter-night, ter the Home. You see I hain't no other place ter stay; and — and I didn't leave till this mornin'. I slipped out. I didn't tell 'em I wasn't comin' back, else they'd pretend I couldn't come — though I'm thinkin' they won't do no worryin' when I don't show up sometime. They ain't like FOLKS, ye know. They don't CARE!"

"I know," nodded Pollyanna, with understanding eyes. "But I'm sure, when I see you to-morrow, I'll have just a common home and folks that do care all ready for you. Good-by!" she called brightly, as she turned back toward the house.

In the sitting-room window at that moment, Miss Polly, who had been watching the two children, followed with sombre eyes the boy until a bend of the road hid him from sight. Then she sighed, turned, and walked listlessly up-stairs — and Miss Polly did not usually move listlessly. In her ears still was the boy's scornful "you was so good and kind." In her heart was a curious sense of desolation — as of something lost.

CHAPTER 11
DEVOTIONAL & JOURNAL

"Miss Polly, who had been watching the two children, followed with sombre eyes the boy until a bend of the road hid him from sight. Then she sighed, turned, and walked listlessly up-stairs — and Miss Polly did not usually move listlessly. In her ears still was the boy's scornful "you was so good and kind." In her heart was a curious sense of desolation — as of something lost."

Miss Polly feels she's lost something, and she has — her peace of mind based on her usual sureness she is right!

Though we can be right with God and still feel unhappy over other things, we can't have true joy *without* being right with God. Feeling guilty or ashamed kills our happiness, as we simply can't feel guilty and genuinely happy at the same time.

> *How happy is the one whose wrongs are forgiven, whose sin is hidden from sight.*
> *How happy is the person whose sin the Eternal will not take into account.*
> *How happy are those who no longer lie, to themselves or others.*
> *When I refused to admit my wrongs, I was miserable...*
> Psalm 32:1-3 VOICE

> *If we confess our sins, he is faithful and just and will forgive us our sins*
> *and purify us from all unrighteousness*
> 1 John 1:9 NIV

Like so many of us, I felt a wonderful surge of joy and freedom when I first became a Christian. But I lost that over time. Part of the problem was feeling guilty. I didn't grow up feeling loved, and God's unconditional love was a very difficult concept to accept. It seemed too easy to simply ask His forgiveness, and believe I was forgiven! What I needed to learn was that God does what He says. Whether or not I *felt* forgiven, if I confessed my mistakes and asked His forgiveness, I *was* forgiven.

Of course, sometimes we do have reason to feel guilty. Unconfessed sins damage our closeness with God. Sin and God can't co-exist. To maintain our joy, we need to keep giving ourselves to God, rededicating our hearts and lives to Him.

Pastor Rick Warren talks about doing a spiritual inventory morning and evening, a few quiet minutes with God to admit any new or unconfessed sins to Him and ask His forgiveness, and in return receive His blessing and cleansing. Not to beat ourselves up or feel guilty, but to let God correct our course if we've drifted off the right path. To simply know we're right with God, so we can take hold of His promise of forgiveness with full confidence. This needn't take long to do, and as a spiritual practice I've found it adds so much to my joy.

Once we've confessed a sin and asked His forgiveness, we don't need to feel guilty over it. God's mercy has no end, and He *is* faithful and just. He does forgive as soon as we ask Him, just as he promises!

What do you need to release to God today, so that He can forgive you and clear your conscience?

Can you make time each day to do a spiritual inventory?

Can you trust that if you ask God's forgiveness and ask His help to do better, you *are* forgiven?

Let us come near to God with a sincere heart and a sure faith, because we have been made free from a guilty conscience, and our bodies have been washed with pure water.
Hebrews 10:22 NCV

Lord, Thank You that You died for us so that we could be forgiven and made right with You. Help me to admit my wrongs and ask Your forgiveness. Free me from shame and guilt, wash me clean, and bless me with the sure faith and joy that comes from knowing I am right with You. Help me to forgive myself too, and to keep my focus on You, knowing that You have forgiven me and You are working in my life. Thank You!

CHAPTER TWELVE:
BEFORE THE LADIES' AID

Dinner, which came at noon in the Harrington homestead, was a silent meal on the day of the Ladies' Aid meeting. Pollyanna, it is true, tried to talk; but she did not make a success of it, chiefly because four times she was obliged to break off a "glad" in the middle of it, much to her blushing discomfort. The fifth time it happened, Miss Polly moved her head wearily.

"There, there, child, say it, if you want to," she sighed. "I'm sure I'd rather you did than not if it's going to make all this fuss."

Pollyanna's puckered little face cleared.

"Oh, thank you. I'm afraid it would be pretty hard — not to say it. You see I've played it so long."

"You've — what?" demanded Aunt Polly.

"Played it — the game, you know, that father — " Pollyanna stopped with a painful blush at finding herself so soon again on forbidden ground.

Aunt Polly frowned and said nothing. The rest of the meal was a silent one.

Pollyanna was not sorry to hear Aunt Polly tell the minister's wife over the telephone, a little later, that she would not be at the Ladies' Aid meeting that afternoon, owing to a headache. When Aunt Polly went up-stairs to her room and closed the door, Pollyanna tried to be sorry for the headache; but she could not help feeling glad that her aunt was not to be present that afternoon when she laid the case of Jimmy Bean before the Ladies' Aid. She could not forget that Aunt Polly had called Jimmy Bean a little beggar; and she did not want Aunt Polly to call him that — before the Ladies' Aid.

Pollyanna knew that the Ladies' Aid met at two o'clock in the chapel next the church, not quite half a mile from home. She planned her going, therefore, so that she should get there a little before three.

"I want them all to be there," she said to herself; "else the very one that wasn't there might be the one who would be wanting to give Jimmy Bean a home; and, of course, two o'clock always means three, really — to Ladies' Aiders."

Quietly, but with confident courage, Pollyanna ascended the chapel steps, pushed open the door and entered the vestibule. A soft babel of feminine chatter and laughter came from the main room. Hesitating only a brief moment Pollyanna pushed open one of the inner doors.

The chatter dropped to a surprised hush. Pollyanna advanced a little timidly. Now that the time had come, she felt unwontedly shy. After all, these half-strange, half-familiar faces about her were not her own dear Ladies' Aid.

"How do you do, Ladies' Aiders?" she faltered politely. "I'm Pollyanna Whittier. I — I reckon some of you know me, maybe; anyway, I do YOU — only I don't know you all together this way."

The silence could almost be felt now. Some of the ladies did know this rather extraordinary niece of their fellow-member, and nearly all had heard of her; but not one of them could think of anything to say, just then.

"I — I've come to — to lay the case before you," stammered Pollyanna, after a moment, unconsciously falling into her father's familiar phraseology.

There was a slight rustle.

"Did — did your aunt send you, my dear?" asked Mrs. Ford, the minister's wife.

Pollyanna colored a little.

"Oh, no. I came all by myself. You see, I'm used to Ladies' Aiders. It was Ladies' Aiders that brought me up — with father."

Somebody tittered hysterically, and the minister's wife frowned.

"Yes, dear. What is it?"

"Well, it — it's Jimmy Bean," sighed Pollyanna. "He hasn't any home except the Orphan one, and they're full, and don't want him, anyhow, he thinks; so he wants another. He wants one of the common kind, that has a mother instead of a Matron in it — folks, you know, that'll care. He's ten years old going on eleven. I thought some of you might like him — to live with you, you know."

"Well, did you ever!" murmured a voice, breaking the dazed pause that followed Pollyanna's words.

With anxious eyes Pollyanna swept the circle of faces about her.

"Oh, I forgot to say; he will work," she supplemented eagerly.

Still there was silence; then, coldly, one or two women began to question her. After a time they all had the story and began to talk among themselves, animatedly, not quite pleasantly.

Pollyanna listened with growing anxiety. Some of what was said she could not understand. She did gather, after a time, however, that there was no woman there who had a home to give him, though every woman seemed to think that some of the others might take him, as there were several who had no little boys of their own already in their homes. But there was no one who agreed herself to take him. Then she heard the minister's wife suggest timidly that they, as a society, might perhaps assume his support and education instead of sending quite so much money this year to the little boys in far-away India.

A great many ladies talked then, and several of them talked all at once, and even more loudly and more unpleasantly than before. It seemed that their society was famous for its offering to Hindu missions, and several said they should die of mortification if it should be less this year.

Some of what was said at this time Pollyanna again thought she could not have understood, too, for it sounded almost as if they did not care at all what the money DID, so long as the sum opposite the name of their society in a certain "report" "headed the list" —

and of course that could not be what they meant at all! But it was all very confusing, and not quite pleasant, so that Pollyanna was glad, indeed, when at last she found herself outside in the hushed, sweet air — only she was very sorry, too: for she knew it was not going to be easy, or anything but sad, to tell Jimmy Bean to-morrow that the Ladies' Aid had decided that they would rather send all their money to bring up the little India boys than to save out enough to bring up one little boy in their own town, for which they would not get "a bit of credit in the report," according to the tall lady who wore spectacles.

"Not but that it's good, of course, to send money to the heathen, and I shouldn't want 'em not to send SOME there," sighed Pollyanna to herself, as she trudged sorrowfully along. "But they acted as if little boys HERE weren't any account — only little boys 'way off. I should THINK, though, they'd rather see Jimmy Bean grow — than just a report!"

CHAPTER 12
DEVOTIONAL & JOURNAL

"Some of what was said at this time Pollyanna again thought she could not have understood, too, for it sounded almost as if they did not care at all what the money DID, so long as the sum opposite the name of their society in a certain "report" "headed the list" — and of course that could not be what they meant at all!"

Good deeds, bad motives.

"Be careful! When you do something good, don't do it in front of others so that they will see you. If you do that, you will have no reward from your Father in heaven... Don't be like the hypocrites... They want everyone to praise them. The truth is, that's all the reward they will get... Your Father can see what is done in private, and he will reward you."
Matthew 6:1-4 ERV

Clearly, the Beldingsville Ladies' Aid hadn't read these verses, or if they had, they still cared more about looking good than doing good. I love the gentle satire here. The original audience for the book would have been church-going ladies, maybe even members of their local Ladies' Aid, as *Pollyanna* was first published as a serial in a Christian women's magazine. In her innocence, Pollyanna finds it hard to believe that The Ladies' Aid refuse to help her orphaned friend Jimmy, because giving funds to help him might mean they wouldn't come first on the list of donors to overseas missions.

Any time I post on Facebook that I've given to a charity, that I'm doing a Bible study, or I'm praying over some issue I need to be sure my motivation is helping others by letting them know about the charity or the Bible verses, or seeking to support others by letting them know they're prayed for. Not bigging myself up and saying "Look how good I am!" like the people Jesus talked about.

When we feel the need for the recognition and approval of others, instead of judging ourselves, it's worth digging deeper. I know at times I've done the right things not so people notice me, but so God does! If we don't feel we deserve His love or we've never experienced unconditional love, we can get into trying to *earn* His approval and love. But there's no sense of joy or peace there, because we always feel we need to do more, try harder. It never feels enough. Only resting in God's love and grace and trusting in His love for us is enough.

But God's mercy is so abundant, and his love for us is so great, that while we were spiritually dead in our disobedience he brought us to life with Christ. It is by God's grace that you have been saved.
Ephesians 2:4-6 ERV

God loves us, we can be sure of that no matter what. And He see our hearts. He wants love for Him and others to be our only motive.

Can you see anywhere in your life where you care more about being *seen* to do the right thing, about what other people think, than you do about actually doing the right thing for its own sake?

Is there anywhere you are doing the right thing because you hope God will love and approve of you more if you do it?

What do you think and feel God might want you to do differently?

How can you bring more love for God and others into the good things you do?

Lord, please help me to do the right things for the right reasons — love of you and other people. Help what I do to be done to serve others in Your name and to give You the glory, not for people to notice and praise me. Help me to know that You love me, no matter what I do, that I don't have to prove my love for You or earn Your love. Show me what You want me to do differently, or where I can do the same things but bring more genuine love to them. Thank You!

CHAPTER THIRTEEN:
IN PENDLETON WOODS

Pollyanna had not turned her steps toward home, when she left the chapel. She had turned them, instead, toward Pendleton Hill. It had been a hard day, for all it had been a "vacation one" (as she termed the infrequent days when there was no sewing or cooking lesson), and Pollyanna was sure that nothing would do her quite so much good as a walk through the green quiet of Pendleton Woods. Up Pendleton Hill, therefore, she climbed steadily, in spite of the warm sun on her back.

"I don't have to get home till half-past five, anyway," she was telling herself; "and it'll be so much nicer to go around by the way of the woods, even if I do have to climb to get there."

It was very beautiful in the Pendleton Woods, as Pollyanna knew by experience. But to-day it seemed even more delightful than ever, notwithstanding her disappointment over what she must tell Jimmy Bean to-morrow.

"I wish they were up here — all those ladies who talked so loud," sighed Pollyanna to herself, raising her eyes to the patches of vivid blue between the sunlit green of the tree-tops. "Anyhow, if they were up here, I just reckon they'd change and take Jimmy Bean for their little boy, all right," she finished, secure in her conviction, but unable to give a reason for it, even to herself.

Suddenly Pollyanna lifted her head and listened. A dog had barked some distance ahead. A moment later he came dashing toward her, still barking.

"Hullo, doggie — hullo!" Pollyanna snapped her fingers at the dog and looked expectantly down the path. She had seen the dog once before, she was sure. He had been then with the Man, Mr. John Pendleton. She was looking now, hoping to see him. For some minutes she watched eagerly, but he did not appear. Then she turned her attention toward the dog.

The dog, as even Pollyanna could see, was acting strangely. He was still barking — giving little short, sharp yelps, as if of alarm. He was running back and forth, too, in the path ahead. Soon they reached a side path, and down this the little dog fairly flew, only to come back at once, whining and barking.

"Ho! That isn't the way home," laughed Pollyanna, still keeping to the main path.

The little dog seemed frantic now. Back and forth, back and forth, between Pollyanna and the side path he vibrated, barking and whining pitifully. Every quiver of his little brown body, and every glance from his beseeching brown eyes were eloquent with appeal — so eloquent that at last Pollyanna understood, turned, and followed him.

Straight ahead, now, the little dog dashed madly; and it was not long before Pollyanna came upon the reason for it all: a man lying motionless at the foot of a steep, overhanging mass of rock a few yards from the side path.

A twig cracked sharply under Pollyanna's foot, and the man turned his head. With a cry of dismay Pollyanna ran to his side.

"Mr. Pendleton! Oh, are you hurt?"

"Hurt? Oh, no! I'm just taking a siesta in the sunshine," snapped the man irritably. "See here, how much do you know? What can you do? Have you got any sense?"

Pollyanna caught her breath with a little gasp, but — as was her habit — she answered the questions literally, one by one.

"Why, Mr. Pendleton, I — I don't know so very much, and I can't do a great many things; but most of the Ladies' Aiders, except Mrs. Rawson, said I had real good sense. I heard 'em say so one day — they didn't know I heard, though."

The man smiled grimly.

"There, there, child, I beg your pardon, I'm sure; it's only this confounded leg of mine. Now listen." He paused, and with some difficulty reached his hand into his trousers pocket and brought out a bunch of keys, singling out one between his thumb and forefinger. "Straight through the path there, about five minutes' walk, is my house. This key will admit you to the side door under the porte-cochere. Do you know what a porte-cochere is?"

"Oh, yes, sir. Auntie has one with a sun parlor over it. That's the roof I slept on — only I didn't sleep, you know. They found me."

"Eh? Oh! Well, when you get into the house, go straight through the vestibule and hall to the door at the end. On the big, flat-topped desk in the middle of the room you'll find a telephone. Do you know how to use a telephone?"

"Oh, yes, sir! Why, once when Aunt Polly — "

"Never mind Aunt Polly now," cut in the man scowlingly, as he tried to move himself a little.

"Hunt up Dr. Thomas Chilton's number on the card you'll find somewhere around there — it ought to be on the hook down at the side, but it probably won't be. You know a telephone card, I suppose, when you see one!"

"Oh, yes, sir! I just love Aunt Polly's. There's such a lot of queer names, and — "

"Tell Dr. Chilton that John Pendleton is at the foot of Little Eagle Ledge in Pendleton Woods with a broken leg, and to come at once with a stretcher and two men. He'll know what to do besides that. Tell him to come by the path from the house."

"A broken leg? Oh, Mr. Pendleton, how perfectly awful!" shuddered Pollyanna. "But I'm so glad I came! Can't *I* do — "

"Yes, you can — but evidently you won't! WILL you go and do what I ask and stop talking," moaned the man, faintly.

And, with a little sobbing cry, Pollyanna went.

Pollyanna did not stop now to look up at the patches of blue between the sunlit tops of the trees. She kept her eyes on the ground to make sure that no twig nor stone tripped her hurrying feet.

It was not long before she came in sight of the house. She had seen it before, though never so near as this. She was almost frightened now at the massiveness of the great pile of gray stone with its pillared verandas and its imposing entrance. Pausing only a moment, however, she sped across the big neglected lawn and around the house to the side door under the porte-cochere. Her fingers, stiff from their tight clutch upon the keys, were anything but skilful in their efforts to turn the bolt in the lock; but at last the heavy, carved door swung slowly back on its hinges.

Pollyanna caught her breath. In spite of her feeling of haste, she paused a moment and looked fearfully through the vestibule to the wide, sombre hall beyond, her thoughts in a whirl. This was John Pendleton's house; the house of mystery; the house into which no one but its master entered; the house which sheltered, somewhere — a skeleton. Yet she, Pollyanna, was expected to enter alone these fearsome rooms, and telephone the doctor that the master of the house lay now —

With a little cry Pollyanna, looking neither to the right nor the left, fairly ran through the hall to the door at the end and opened it.

The room was large, and sombre with dark woods and hangings like the hall; but through the west window the sun threw a long shaft of gold across the floor, gleamed dully on the tarnished brass andirons in the fireplace, and touched the nickel of the telephone on the great desk in the middle of the room. It was toward this desk that Pollyanna hurriedly tiptoed.

The telephone card was not on its hook; it was on the floor. But Pollyanna found it, and ran her shaking forefinger down through the C's to "Chilton." In due time she had Dr. Chilton himself at the other end of the wires, and was tremblingly delivering her message and answering the doctor's terse, pertinent questions. This done, she hung up the receiver and drew a long breath of relief.

Only a brief glance did Pollyanna give about her; then, with a confused vision in her eyes of crimson draperies, book-lined walls, a littered floor, an untidy desk, innumerable closed doors (any one of which might conceal a skeleton), and everywhere dust, dust, dust, she fled back through the hall to the great carved door, still half open as she had left it.

In what seemed, even to the injured man, an incredibly short time, Pollyanna was back in the woods at the man's side.

"Well, what is the trouble? Couldn't you get in?" he demanded.

Pollyanna opened wide her eyes.

"Why, of course I could! I'm HERE," she answered. "As if I'd be here if I hadn't got in! And the doctor will be right up just as soon as possible with the men and things. He said he knew just where you were, so I didn't stay to show him. I wanted to be with you."

"Did you?" smiled the man, grimly. "Well, I can't say I admire your taste. I should think you might find pleasanter companions."

"Do you mean — because you're so — cross?"

"Thanks for your frankness. Yes."

Pollyanna laughed softly.

"But you're only cross OUTSIDE — You aren't cross inside a bit!"

"Indeed! How do you know that?" asked the man, trying to change the position of his head without moving the rest of his body.

"Oh, lots of ways; there — like that — the way you act with the dog," she added, pointing to the long, slender hand that rested on the dog's sleek head near him. "It's funny how dogs and cats know the insides of folks better than other folks do, isn't it? Say, I'm going to hold your head," she finished abruptly.

The man winced several times and groaned once; softly while the change was being made; but in the end he found Pollyanna's lap a very welcome substitute for the rocky hollow in which his head had lain before.

"Well, that is — better," he murmured faintly.

He did not speak again for some time. Pollyanna, watching his face, wondered if he were asleep. She did not think he was. He looked as if his lips were tight shut to keep back moans of pain. Pollyanna herself almost cried aloud as she looked at his great, strong body lying there so helpless. One hand, with fingers tightly clenched, lay outflung, motionless. The other, limply open, lay on the dog's head. The dog, his wistful, eager eyes on his master's face, was motionless, too.

Minute by minute the time passed. The sun dropped lower in the west and the shadows grew deeper under the trees. Pollyanna sat so still she hardly seemed to breathe. A bird alighted fearlessly within reach of her hand, and a squirrel whisked his bushy tail on a tree-branch almost under her nose — yet with his bright little eyes all the while on the motionless dog.

At last the dog pricked up his ears and whined softly; then he gave a short, sharp bark. The next moment Pollyanna heard voices, and very soon their owners appeared three men carrying a stretcher and various other articles.

The tallest of the party — a smooth-shaven, kind-eyed man whom Pollyanna knew by sight as "Dr. Chilton" — advanced cheerily.

"Well, my little lady, playing nurse?"

"Oh, no, sir," smiled Pollyanna. "I've only held his head — I haven't given him a mite of medicine. But I'm glad I was here."

"So am I," nodded the doctor, as he turned his absorbed attention to the injured man.

CHAPTER 13
DEVOTIONAL & JOURNAL

Pollyanna laughed softly. "But you're only cross OUTSIDE. You arn't cross inside a bit!"

"Indeed! How do you know that?" asked the man, trying to change the position of his head without moving the rest of his body.

"Oh, lots of ways; there — like that — the way you act with the dog," she added, pointing to the long, slender hand that rested on the dog's sleek head near him. "It's funny how dogs and cats know the insides of folks better than other folks do, isn't it?"

To his surprise, Pollyanna sees grumpy and wounded John Pendleton as God sees each of us and asks us to see ourselves and each other — with love and compassion.

Dear friends, since God so loved us, we also ought to love one another.
1 John 4:11

For many of us, our biggest challenges as Christians is to learn to love like Jesus loves. No matter how life has broken and warped a person, God holds the image of them as He created them to be, and how someday, if they choose to turn to Him and give Him Lordship of their life, He will make them over to be.

But if we grew up seeing ourselves as unlovable, only having value for what we did, then it's hard to fully accept and believe in God's love, and it's equally hard to love others. Often, we're harder on ourselves than anyone else. Yet we're on that same journey of being made new by God, made over into the person He intended us to be.

If we really know He loves us and what that means, then we can live the abundant live full of joy and peace He promised us. If we learn to love ourselves and other people with His love, not just our lives will be transformed, the world around us can be changed!

You are the people of God; he loved you and chose you for his own.
So then, you must clothe yourselves with compassion, kindness, humility, gentleness, and patience.
Colossians 3:12 GNT

One way I notice how I'm failing to love myself and others is when I get irritated with people. It's a sure sign!

The way to fix it isn't to wish the other person was different or try to get them to change, but to focus on God. If I surrender the situation to Him, and claim His promises of love, I allow His love and joy to flood into the situation, and my heart.

I can't love like Jesus does on my own, only God loves like that. But He can love though me. And he does!

Is God asking you to respond to yourself with more compassion, kindness, gentleness and patience? In what areas of your life?

How can you show that changed attitude toward yourself? What will you do differently?

Are there any difficult people in your life who God is calling you to respond to with a more compassionate heart?

Pray for them, asking God's best for them, and asking God to change your attitude toward them. Besides prayer, how can you show that change?

Lord, show me how to love the way You love me. Help me to see every person in my life, including myself, as You do. Flawed, broken, damaged by our choices in this fallen world, but still created to reflect Your image, still worthy of love and compassion. I can't yet love perfectly, but You can. Please love through me. Help me to treat myself and others with love, kindness, understanding, gentleness and patience, seeing the reality of who You intend them to be, the best of who they are, who they could be if they were whole and complete in You. When I feel unloving, help me to surrender the situation to You and pray for them instead. Thank You!

CHAPTER FOURTEEN:
JUST A MATTER OF JELLY

Pollyanna was a little late for supper on the night of the accident to John Pendleton; but, as it happened, she escaped without reproof.

Nancy met her at the door.

"Well, if I ain't glad ter be settin' my two eyes on you," she sighed in obvious relief. "It's half-past six!"

"I know it," admitted Pollyanna anxiously; "but I'm not to blame — truly I'm not. And I don't think even Aunt Polly will say I am, either."

"She won't have the chance," retorted Nancy, with huge satisfaction. "She's gone."

"Gone!" gasped Pollyanna. "You don't mean that I've driven her away?" Through Pollyanna's mind at the moment trooped remorseful memories of the morning with its unwanted boy, cat, and dog, and its unwelcome "glad" and forbidden "father" that would spring to her forgetful little tongue. "Oh, I DIDN'T drive her away?"

"Not much you did," scoffed Nancy. "Her cousin died suddenly down to Boston, and she had ter go. She had one o' them yeller telegram letters after you went away this afternoon, and she won't be back for three days. Now I guess we're glad all right. We'll be keepin' house tergether, jest you and me, all that time. We will, we will!"

Pollyanna looked shocked.

"Glad! Oh, Nancy, when it's a funeral?"

"Oh, but 'twa'n't the funeral I was glad for, Miss Pollyanna. It was — " Nancy stopped abruptly. A shrewd twinkle came into her eyes. "Why, Miss Pollyanna, as if it wa'n't yerself that was teachin' me ter play the game," she reproached her gravely.

Pollyanna puckered her forehead into a troubled frown.

"I can't help it, Nancy," she argued with a shake of her head. "It must be that there are some things that 'tisn't right to play the game on — and I'm sure funerals is one of them. There's nothing in a funeral to be glad about."

Nancy chuckled.

"We can be glad 'tain't our'n," she observed demurely. But Pollyanna did not hear. She had begun to tell of the accident; and in a moment Nancy, open-mouthed, was listening.

At the appointed place the next afternoon, Pollyanna met Jimmy Bean according to agreement. As was to be expected, of course, Jimmy showed keen disappointment that the Ladies' Aid preferred a little India boy to himself.

"Well, maybe 'tis natural," he sighed. "Of course things you don't know about are always nicer'n things you do, same as the pertater on 'tother side of the plate is always the biggest.

But I wish I looked that way ter somebody 'way off. Wouldn't it be jest great, now, if only somebody over in India wanted ME?"

Pollyanna clapped her hands.

"Why, of course! That's the very thing, Jimmy! I'll write to my Ladies' Aiders about you. They aren't over in India; they're only out West — but that's awful far away, just the same. I reckon you'd think so if you'd come all the way here as I did!"

Jimmy's face brightened.

"Do you think they would — truly — take me?" he asked.

"Of course they would! Don't they take little boys in India to bring up? Well, they can just play you are the little India boy this time. I reckon you're far enough away to make a report, all right. You wait. I'll write 'em. I'll write Mrs. White. No, I'll write Mrs. Jones. Mrs. White has got the most money, but Mrs. Jones gives the most — which is kind of funny, isn't it? — when you think of it. But I reckon some of the Aiders will take you."

"All right — but don't furgit ter say I'll work fur my board an' keep," put in Jimmy. "I ain't no beggar, an' biz'ness is biz'ness, even with Ladies' Aiders, I'm thinkin'." He hesitated, then added: "An' I s'pose I better stay where I be fur a spell yet — till you hear."

"Of course," nodded Pollyanna emphatically. "Then I'll know just where to find you. And they'll take you — I'm sure you're far enough away for that. Didn't Aunt Polly take — Say!" she broke off, suddenly, "DO you suppose I was Aunt Polly's little girl from India?"

"Well, if you ain't the queerest kid," grinned Jimmy, as he turned away.

It was about a week after the accident in Pendleton Woods that Pollyanna said to her aunt one morning:

"Aunt Polly, please would you mind very much if I took Mrs. Snow's calf's-foot jelly this week to some one else? I'm sure Mrs. Snow wouldn't — this once."

"Dear me, Pollyanna, what ARE you up to now?" sighed her aunt. "You ARE the most extraordinary child!"

Pollyanna frowned a little anxiously.

"Aunt Polly, please, what is extraordinary? If you're EXtraordinary you can't be ORdinary, can you?"

"You certainly can not."

"Oh, that's all right, then. I'm glad I'm EXtraordinary," sighed Pollyanna, her face clearing. "You see, Mrs. White used to say Mrs. Rawson was a very ordinary woman — and she disliked Mrs. Rawson something awful. They were always fight — I mean, father had — that is, I mean, WE had more trouble keeping peace between them than we did between any of the rest of the Aiders," corrected Pollyanna, a little breathless from her efforts to steer between the Scylla of her father's past commands in regard to speaking of church quarrels, and the Charybdis of her aunt's present commands in regard to speaking of her father.

"Yes, yes; well, never mind," interposed Aunt Polly, a trifle impatiently. "You do run on so, Pollyanna, and no matter what we're talking about you always bring up at those Ladies' Aiders!"

"Yes'm," smiled Pollyanna, cheerfully, "I reckon I do, maybe. But you see they used to bring me up, and — "

"That will do, Pollyanna," interrupted a cold voice. "Now what is it about this jelly?"

"Nothing, Aunt Polly, truly, that you would mind, I'm sure. You let me take jelly to HER, so I thought you would to HIM — this once. You see, broken legs aren't like — like lifelong invalids, so his won't last forever as Mrs. Snow's does, and she can have all the rest of the things after just once or twice."

"'Him'? 'He'? 'Broken leg'? What are you talking about, Pollyanna?"

Pollyanna stared; then her face relaxed.

"Oh, I forgot. I reckon you didn't know. You see, it happened while you were gone. It was the very day you went that I found him in the woods, you know; and I had to unlock his house and telephone for the men and the doctor, and hold his head, and everything. And of course then I came away and haven't seen him since. But when Nancy made the jelly for Mrs. Snow this week I thought how nice it would be if I could take it to him instead of her, just this once. Aunt Polly, may I?"

"Yes, yes, I suppose so," acquiesced Miss Polly, a little wearily. "Who did you say he was?"

"The Man. I mean, Mr. John Pendleton."

Miss Polly almost sprang from her chair.

"JOHN PENDLETON!"

"Yes. Nancy told me his name. Maybe you know him."

Miss Polly did not answer this. Instead she asked:

"Do YOU know him?"

Pollyanna nodded.

"Oh, yes. He always speaks and smiles — now. He's only cross OUTSIDE, you know. I'll go and get the jelly. Nancy had it 'most fixed when I came in," finished Pollyanna, already halfway across the room.

"Pollyanna, wait! Miss Polly's voice was suddenly very stern. I've changed my mind. I would prefer that Mrs. Snow had that jelly to-day — as usual. That is all. You may go now."

Pollyanna's face fell.

"Oh, but Aunt Polly, HERS will last. She can always be sick and have things, you know; but his is just a broken leg, and legs don't last — I mean, broken ones. He's had it a whole week now."

"Yes, I remember. I heard Mr. John Pendleton had met with an accident," said Miss Polly, a little stiffly; "but — I do not care to be sending jelly to John Pendleton, Pollyanna."

"I know, he is cross — outside," admitted Pollyanna, sadly, "so I suppose you don't like him. But I wouldn't say 'twas you sent it. I'd say 'twas me. I like him. I'd be glad to send him jelly."

Miss Polly began to shake her head again. Then, suddenly, she stopped, and asked in a curiously quiet voice:

"Does he know who you — are, Pollyanna?"

The little girl sighed.

"I reckon not. I told him my name, once, but he never calls me it — never."

"Does he know where you — live?"

"Oh, no. I never told him that."

"Then he doesn't know you're my — niece?"

"I don't think so."

For a moment there was silence. Miss Polly was looking at Pollyanna with eyes that did not seem to see her at all. The little girl, shifting impatiently from one small foot to the other, sighed audibly. Then Miss Polly roused herself with a start.

"Very well, Pollyanna," she said at last, still in that queer voice, so unlike her own; "you may you may take the jelly to Mr. Pendleton as your own gift. But understand: I do not send it. Be very sure that he does not think I do!"

"Yes'm — no'm — thank you, Aunt Polly," exulted Pollyanna, as she flew through the door.

CHAPTER 14
DEVOTIONAL & JOURNAL

"Aunt Polly, please, what is extraordinary? If you're EXtraordinary you can't be ORdinary, can you?"

"You certainly can not."

"Oh, that's all right, then. I'm glad I'm EXtraordinary,"

Miss Polly doesn't mean "extraordinary" as the compliment Pollyanna takes it as!

It's part of being human to place a lot of value on conforming. Whether conforming to what is fashionable or "normal" in society, conforming to the expectations of our friends or our family, or being like the others in our church, we want to fit in.

Different, yes, our unique selves, but not *too* different!

As a teen and in my twenties, I wanted so desperately to belong, to be normal and ordinary (I wasn't!). Pollyanna though is willing to be truly different, even extraordinary, rather than live an ordinary life.

> *But you are a chosen generation, a royal priesthood, a holy nation,*
> *His own special people, that you may proclaim the praises of Him*
> *who called you out of darkness into His marvelous light*
> 1 Peter 2:9 NKJV

God has called us to be special, His own people, different from those who don't know Him. He wants us to stand in His light, singing His praises!

> *...let yourselves be pulled into a way of life shaped by God's life,*
> *a life energetic and blazing with holiness.*
> 1 Peter 1:16 MSG

I love the sound of that – a life energetic and blazing with God's holiness!

God doesn't call us to be odd or weird. He calls us to be unique. To be authentically who He created us to be, not cookie-cuttered into what society expects of us. I don't want to be ordinary any more.

Do not allow this world to mold you in its own image.
Instead, be transformed from the inside out by renewing your mind.
As a result, you will be able to discern what God wills
and whatever God finds good, pleasing, and complete.
Romans 12:2 VOICE

Do you feel God is calling you to fit in, or to stand out? How do you feel about that?

Are there any areas in your life where you're aware you've been conforming to the world in ways that don't feel right for you?

What might God be asking you to do instead?

Lord, show me how You want me to be extraordinary for You. Show me how You want me to do Your will, to be different, to live the life "blazing with holiness" that You intend for me. Please transform me and make me new, all You created me to be. All I need to do is focus on You not the world, trust You, and allow You to work in me. You will do the rest. Thank You!

CHAPTER FIFTEEN:
DR. CHILTON

The great gray pile of masonry looked very different to Pollyanna when she made her second visit to the house of Mr. John Pendleton. Windows were open, an elderly woman was hanging out clothes in the back yard, and the doctor's gig stood under the porte-cochere.

As before Pollyanna went to the side door. This time she rang the bell — her fingers were not stiff to-day from a tight clutch on a bunch of keys.

A familiar-looking small dog bounded up the steps to greet her, but there was a slight delay before the woman who had been hanging out the clothes opened the door.

"If you please, I've brought some calf's-foot jelly for Mr. Pendleton," smiled Pollyanna.

"Thank you," said the woman, reaching for the bowl in the little girl's hand. "Who shall I say sent it? And it's calf's-foot jelly?"

The doctor, coming into the hall at that moment, heard the woman's words and saw the disappointed look on Pollyanna's face. He stepped quickly forward.

"Ah! Some calf's-foot jelly?" he asked genially. "That will be fine! Maybe you'd like to see our patient, eh?"

"Oh, yes, sir," beamed Pollyanna; and the woman, in obedience to a nod from the doctor, led the way down the hall at once, though plainly with vast surprise on her face.

Behind the doctor, a young man (a trained nurse from the nearest city) gave a disturbed exclamation.

"But, Doctor, didn't Mr. Pendleton give orders not to admit — any one?"

"Oh, yes," nodded the doctor, imperturbably. "But I'm giving orders now. I'll take the risk." Then he added whimsically: "You don't know, of course; but that little girl is better than a six-quart bottle of tonic any day. If anything or anybody can take the grouch out of Pendleton this afternoon, she can. That's why I sent her in."

"Who is she?"

For one brief moment the doctor hesitated.

"She's the niece of one of our best known residents. Her name is Pollyanna Whittier. I — I don't happen to enjoy a very extensive personal acquaintance with the little lady as yet; but lots of my patients do — I'm thankful to say!"

The nurse smiled.

"Indeed! And what are the special ingredients of this wonder-working — tonic of hers?"

The doctor shook his head.

"I don't know. As near as I can find out it is an overwhelming, unquenchable gladness for everything that has happened or is going to happen. At any rate, her quaint speeches are constantly being repeated to me, and, as near as I can make out, 'just being glad' is the tenor of most of them. All is," he added, with another whimsical smile, as he stepped out on to the porch, "I wish I could prescribe her — and buy her — as I would a box of pills; — though if there gets to be many of her in the world, you and I might as well go to ribbon-selling and ditch-digging for all the money we'd get out of nursing and doctoring," he laughed, picking up the reins and stepping into the gig.

Pollyanna, meanwhile, in accordance with the doctor's orders, was being escorted to John Pendleton's rooms.

Her way led through the great library at the end of the hall, and, rapid as was her progress through it, Pollyanna saw at once that great changes had taken place. The book-lined walls and the crimson curtains were the same; but there was no litter on the floor, no untidiness on the desk, and not so much as a grain of dust in sight. The telephone card hung in its proper place, and the brass andirons had been polished. One of the mysterious doors was open, and it was toward this that the maid led the way. A moment later Pollyanna found herself in a sumptuously furnished bedroom while the maid was saying in a frightened voice:

"If you please, sir, here — here's a little girl with some jelly. The doctor said I was to — to bring her in."

The next moment Pollyanna found herself alone with a very cross-looking man lying flat on his back in bed.

"See here, didn't I say — " began an angry voice. "Oh, it's you!" it broke off not very graciously, as Pollyanna advanced toward the bed.

"Yes, sir," smiled Pollyanna. "Oh, I'm so glad they let me in! You see, at first the lady 'most took my jelly, and I was so afraid I wasn't going to see you at all. Then the doctor came, and he said I might. Wasn't he lovely to let me see you?"

In spite of himself the man's lips twitched into a smile; but all he said was "Humph!"

"And I've brought you some jelly," resumed Pollyanna; " — calf's-foot. I hope you like it?" There was a rising inflection in her voice.

"Never ate it." The fleeting smile had gone, and the scowl had come back to the man's face.

For a brief instant Pollyanna's countenance showed disappointment; but it cleared as she set the bowl of jelly down.

"Didn't you? Well, if you didn't, then you can't know you DON'T like it, anyhow, can you? So I reckon I'm glad you haven't, after all. Now, if you knew — "

"Yes, yes; well, there's one thing I know all right, and that is that I'm flat on my back right here this minute, and that I'm liable to stay here — till doomsday, I guess."

Pollyanna looked shocked.

"Oh, no! It couldn't be till doomsday, you know, when the angel Gabriel blows his trumpet, unless it should come quicker than we think it will — oh, of course, I know the Bible says it may come quicker than we think, but I don't think it will — that is, of course I believe the Bible; but I mean I don't think it will come as much quicker as it would if it should come now, and — "

John Pendleton laughed suddenly — and aloud. The nurse, coming in at that moment, heard the laugh, and beat a hurried — but a very silent — retreat. He had the air of a frightened cook who, seeing the danger of a breath of cold air striking a half-done cake, hastily shuts the oven door.

"Aren't you getting a little mixed?" asked John Pendleton of Pollyanna.

The little girl laughed.

"Maybe. But what I mean is, that legs don't last — broken ones, you know — like lifelong invalids, same as Mrs. Snow has got. So yours won't last till doomsday at all. I should think you could be glad of that."

"Oh, I am," retorted the man grimly.

"And you didn't break but one. You can be glad 'twasn't two." Pollyanna was warming to her task.

"Of course! So fortunate," sniffed the man, with uplifted eyebrows; "looking at it from that standpoint, I suppose I might be glad I wasn't a centipede and didn't break fifty!"

Pollyanna chuckled.

"Oh, that's the best yet," she crowed. "I know what a centipede is; they've got lots of legs. And you can be glad — "

"Oh, of course," interrupted the man, sharply, all the old bitterness coming back to his voice; "I can be glad, too, for all the rest, I suppose — the nurse, and the doctor, and that confounded woman in the kitchen!"

"Why, yes, sir — only think how bad 'twould be if you DIDN'T have them!"

"Well, I — eh?" he demanded sharply.

"Why, I say, only think how bad it would be if you didn't have 'em — and you lying here like this!"

"As if that wasn't the very thing that was at the bottom of the whole matter," retorted the man, testily, "because I *am* lying here like this! And yet you expect me to say I'm glad because of a fool woman who disarranges the whole house and calls it 'regulating,' and a man who aids and abets her in it, and calls it 'nursing,' to say nothing of the doctor who eggs 'em both on — and the whole bunch of them, meanwhile, expecting me to pay them for it, and pay them well, too!"

Pollyanna frowned sympathetically.

"Yes, I know. THAT part is too bad — about the money — when you've been saving it, too, all this time."

"When — eh?"

"Saving it — buying beans and fish balls, you know. Say, DO you like beans? — or do you like turkey better, only on account of the sixty cents?"

"Look a-here, child, what are you talking about?"

Pollyanna smiled radiantly.

"About your money, you know — denying yourself, and saving it for the heathen. You see, I found out about it. Why, Mr. Pendleton, that's one of the ways I knew you weren't cross inside. Nancy told me."

The man's jaw dropped.

"Nancy told you I was saving money for the — Well, may I inquire who Nancy is?"

"Our Nancy. She works for Aunt Polly."

"Aunt Polly! Well, who is Aunt Polly?"

"She's Miss Polly Harrington. I live with her."

The man made a sudden movement.

"Miss — Polly — Harrington!" he breathed. "You live with — HER!"

"Yes; I'm her niece. She's taken me to bring up — on account of my mother, you know," faltered Pollyanna, in a low voice. "She was her sister. And after father — went to be with her and the rest of us in Heaven, there wasn't any one left for me down here but the Ladies' Aid; so she took me."

The man did not answer. His face, as he lay back on the pillow now, was very white — so white that Pollyanna was frightened. She rose uncertainly to her feet.

"I reckon maybe I'd better go now," she proposed. "I — I hope you'll like — the jelly."

The man turned his head suddenly, and opened his eyes. There was a curious longing in their dark depths which even Pollyanna saw, and at which she marvelled.

"And so you are — Miss Polly Harrington's niece," he said gently.

"Yes, sir."

Still the man's dark eyes lingered on her face, until Pollyanna, feeling vaguely restless, murmured:

"I — I suppose you know — her."

John Pendleton's lips curved in an odd smile.

"Oh, yes; I know her." He hesitated, then went on, still with that curious smile. "But — you don't mean — you can't mean that it was Miss Polly Harrington who sent that jelly — to me?" he said slowly.

Pollyanna looked distressed.

"N-no, sir: she didn't. She said I must be very sure not to let you think she did send it. But I — "

"I thought as much," vouchsafed the man, shortly, turning away his head.

And Pollyanna, still more distressed, tiptoed from the room.

Under the porte-cochère she found the doctor waiting in his gig. The nurse stood on the steps.

"Well, Miss Pollyanna, may I have the pleasure of seeing you home?" asked the doctor smilingly. "I started to drive on a few minutes ago; then it occurred to me that I'd wait for you."

"Thank you, sir. I'm glad you did. I just love to ride," beamed Pollyanna, as he reached out his hand to help her in.

"Do you?" smiled the doctor, nodding his head in farewell to the young man on the steps. "Well, as near as I can judge, there are a good many things you 'love' to do — eh?" he added, as they drove briskly away.

Pollyanna laughed.

"Why, I don't know. I reckon perhaps there are," she admitted. "I like to do 'most everything that's LIVING. Of course I don't like the other things very well — sewing, and reading out loud, and all that. But THEY aren't LIVING."

"No? What are they, then?"

"Aunt Polly says they're 'learning to live,'" sighed Pollyanna, with a rueful smile.

The doctor smiled now — a little queerly.

"Does she? Well, I should think she might say — just that."

"Yes," responded Pollyanna. "But I don't see it that way at all. I don't think you have to LEARN how to live. I didn't, anyhow."

The doctor drew a long sigh.

"After all, I'm afraid some of us — do have to, little girl," he said.

Then, for a time he was silent. Pollyanna, stealing a glance at his face, felt vaguely sorry for him. He looked so sad. She wished, uneasily, that she could "do something." It was this, perhaps, that caused her to say in a timid voice:

"Dr. Chilton, I should think being a doctor would, be the very gladdest kind of a business there was."

The doctor turned in surprise.

"'Gladdest'! — when I see so much suffering always, everywhere I go?" he cried.

She nodded.

"I know; but you're HELPING it — don't you see? — and of course you're glad to help it! And so that makes you the gladdest of any of us, all the time."

The doctor's eyes filled with sudden hot tears. The doctor's life was a singularly lonely one. He had no wife and no home save his two-room office in a boarding house. His profession was very dear to him. Looking now into Pollyanna's shining eyes, he felt as if a loving hand had been suddenly laid on his head in blessing. He knew, too, that never again would a long day's work or a long night's weariness be quite without that new-found exaltation that had come to him through Pollyanna's eyes.

"God bless you, little girl," he said unsteadily. Then, with the bright smile his patients knew and loved so well, he added: "And I'm thinking, after all, that it was the doctor, quite as much as his patients, that needed a draft of that tonic!" All of which puzzled Pollyanna very much — until a chipmunk, running across the road, drove the whole matter from her mind.

The doctor left Pollyanna at her own door, smiled at Nancy, who was sweeping off the front porch, then drove rapidly away.

"I've had a perfectly beautiful ride with the doctor," announced Pollyanna, bounding up the steps. "He's lovely, Nancy!"

"Is he?"

"Yes. And I told him I should think his business would be the very gladdest one there was."

"What! — goin' ter see sick folks — an' folks what ain't sick but thinks they is, which is worse?" Nancy's face showed open skepticism.

Pollyanna laughed gleefully.

"Yes. That's 'most what he said, too; but there is a way to be glad, even then. Guess!"

Nancy frowned in meditation. Nancy was getting so she could play this game of "being glad" quite successfully, she thought. She rather enjoyed studying out Pollyanna's "posers," too, as she called some of the little girl's questions.

"Oh, I know," she chuckled. "It's just the opposite from what you told Mis' Snow."

"Opposite?" repeated Pollyanna, obviously puzzled.

"Yes. You told her she could be glad because other folks wasn't like her — all sick, you know."

"Yes," nodded Pollyanna.

"Well, the doctor can be glad because he isn't like other folks — the sick ones, I mean, what he doctors," finished Nancy in triumph.

It was Pollyanna's turn to frown.

"Why, y-yes," she admitted. "Of course that IS one way, but it isn't the way I said; and — someway, I don't seem to quite like the sound of it. It isn't exactly as if he said he was glad they WERE sick, but — You do play the game so funny, sometimes Nancy," she sighed, as she went into the house.

Pollyanna found her aunt in the sitting room.

"Who was that man — the one who drove into the yard, Pollyanna?" questioned the lady a little sharply.

"Why, Aunt Polly, that was Dr. Chilton! Don't you know him?"

"Dr. Chilton! What was he doing — here?"

"He drove me home. Oh, and I gave the jelly to Mr. Pendleton, and — "

Miss Polly lifted her head quickly.

"Pollyanna, he did not think I sent it?"

"Oh, no, Aunt Polly. I told him you didn't."

Miss Polly grew a sudden vivid pink.

"You TOLD him I didn't!"

Pollyanna opened wide her eyes at the remonstrative dismay in her aunt's voice.

"Why, Aunt Polly, you SAID to!"

Aunt Polly sighed.

"I SAID, Pollyanna, that I did not send it, and for you to be very sure that he did not think I DID! — which is a very different matter from TELLING him outright that I did not send it." And she turned vexedly away.

"Dear me! Well, I don't see where the difference is," sighed Pollyanna, as she went to hang her hat on the one particular hook in the house upon which Aunt Polly had said that it must be hung.

CHAPTER 15
DEVOTIONAL & JOURNAL

"Yes," responded Pollyanna. "But I don't see it that way at all. I don't think you have to LEARN how to live. I didn't, anyhow."

The doctor drew a long sigh.

"After all, I'm afraid some of us — do have to, little girl," he said.

Pollyanna knows how to live a full and joyous life, but most of us, like Dr. Chilton, need to learn how. Usually, because we need to unlearn some old joyless lessons many of us learned growing up first. Things like feeling we have to work hard to be good enough to earn God's love, like holding onto old disappointments and hurts, like feeling guilt over past mistakes and failures. We need to let go of whatever burdens we currently carry.

"Come to me, all you who are weary and burdened, and I will give you rest. Take my yoke upon you and learn from me, for I am gentle and humble in heart, and you will find rest for your souls. For my yoke is easy and my burden is light."
Matthew 11:28-30

Jesus used the metaphor of a well-fitted and well-balanced yoke, a harness linking two oxen side by side to haul the same load. The stronger ox always takes the heaviest part of the load. The same Greek word used for "yoke" is used when marriage is mentioned in the New Testament, so the way a couple work together in a good marriage is another way to look at it.

Or in this lovely paraphrase:

"Are you tired? Worn out? Burned out on religion? Come to me. Get away with me and you'll recover your life. I'll show you how to take a real rest. Walk with me and work with me—watch how I do it. Learn the unforced rhythms of grace. I won't lay anything heavy or ill-fitting on you. Keep company with me and you'll learn to live freely and lightly."
Matthew 11:28-30 MSG

Yet I've had so much trouble with this! I lay my burdens at the Lord's feet, then snatch them straight back again! For some crazy reason I believe it's my job to carry them. It's like I've been walking along the road, carrying a heavy parcel. Yet when a friend stops in their car to offer me a ride to my destination, instead of putting the suitcase in the trunk as they suggest, I still insist on lifting it up in my tired aching arms.

To experience the fullness of God's grace, we need to trust Jesus not just with our salvation, the ride to get us where we're going, but with our everyday burdens too. He made us, and he knows every cell of our bodies and every hair on our heads. And He has experienced everything we experience, knows every burden we carry too.

He wants us to live freely, lightly, and with joy.

What makes you feel tired, worn out, and burdened? Are there any areas of your life you're holding burdens back from Jesus, still carrying the load?

What is He asking you to let go of? What burdens can you hand over to Him now?

Are you pulling away from Jesus in any part of your life, trying to lead the way instead of letting Him lead you?

What do you feel He might be asking you to do differently?

Lord, thank You that You free me from my burdens of guilt, past hurts, not feeling good enough, and so much else. Help me to feel how light Your yoke is and how joyfully and freely I can live when I follow You, If in any areas I'm experiencing my walk with You as heavy, please help me to see why. Am I not allowing You to carry the weight, and still trying to carry more of the burden than I need to? Am I holding onto unconfessed sin and guilt? Instead of walking beside You, am I pulling in an opposite direction trying to go my own way? Or am I impatient with Your timing and so dragging back or trying to race ahead of You? Help me to trust You. Help me to let it all go and be willing to truly be yoked to You. Help me to learn to live more fully and joyfully, resting in You the way You want me to. Thank You!

CHAPTER SIXTEEN:
A RED ROSE AND A LACE SHAWL

It was on a rainy day about a week after Pollyanna's visit to Mr. John Pendleton, that Miss Polly was driven by Timothy to an early afternoon committee meeting of the Ladies' Aid Society. When she returned at three o'clock, her cheeks were a bright, pretty pink, and her hair, blown by the damp wind, had fluffed into kinks and curls wherever the loosened pins had given leave.

Pollyanna had never before seen her aunt look like this.

"Oh — oh — oh! Why, Aunt Polly, you've got 'em, too," she cried rapturously, dancing round and round her aunt, as that lady entered the sitting room.

"Got what, you impossible child?"

Pollyanna was still revolving round and round her aunt.

"And I never knew you had 'em! Can folks have 'em when you don't know they've got 'em? DO you suppose I could? — 'fore I get to Heaven, I mean," she cried, pulling out with eager fingers the straight locks above her ears. "But then, they wouldn't be black, if they did come. You can't hide the black part."

"Pollyanna, what does all this mean?" demanded Aunt Polly, hurriedly removing her hat, and trying to smooth back her disordered hair.

"No, no — please, Aunt Polly!" Pollyanna's jubilant voice turned to one of distressed appeal. "Don't smooth 'em out! It's those that I'm talking about — those darling little black curls. Oh, Aunt Polly, they're so pretty!"

"Nonsense! What do you mean, Pollyanna, by going to the Ladies' Aid the other day in that absurd fashion about that beggar boy?"

"But it isn't nonsense," urged Pollyanna, answering only the first of her aunt's remarks. "You don't know how pretty you look with your hair like that! Oh, Aunt Polly, please, mayn't I do your hair like I did Mrs. Snow's, and put in a flower? I'd so love to see you that way! Why, you'd be ever so much prettier than she was!"

"Pollyanna!" (Miss Polly spoke very sharply — all the more sharply because Pollyanna's words had given her an odd throb of joy: when before had anybody cared how she, or her hair looked? When before had anybody "loved" to see her "pretty"?) "Pollyanna, you did not answer my question. Why did you go to the Ladies' Aid in that absurd fashion?"

"Yes'm, I know; but, please, I didn't know it was absurd until I went and found out they'd rather see their report grow than Jimmy. So then I wrote to MY Ladies' Aiders — 'cause Jimmy is far away from them, you know; and I thought maybe he could be their little India boy same as — Aunt Polly, WAS I your little India girl? And, Aunt Polly, you WILL let me do your hair, won't you?"

Aunt Polly put her hand to her throat — the old, helpless feeling was upon her, she knew.

"But, Pollyanna, when the ladies told me this afternoon how you came to them, I was so ashamed! I — "

Pollyanna began to dance up and down lightly on her toes.

"You didn't! — You didn't say I COULDN'T do your hair," she crowed triumphantly; "and so I'm sure it means just the other way 'round, sort of — like it did the other day about Mr. Pendleton's jelly that you didn't send, but didn't want me to say you didn't send, you know. Now wait just where you are. I'll get a comb."

"But Pollyanna, Pollyanna," remonstrated Aunt Polly, following the little girl from the room and panting up-stairs after her.

"Oh, did you come up here?" Pollyanna greeted her at the door of Miss Polly's own room. "That'll be nicer yet! I've got the comb. Now sit down, please, right here. Oh, I'm so glad you let me do it!"

"But, Pollyanna, I — I — "

Miss Polly did not finish her sentence. To her helpless amazement she found herself in the low chair before the dressing table, with her hair already tumbling about her ears under ten eager, but very gentle fingers.

"Oh, my! what pretty hair you've got," prattled Pollyanna; "and there's so much more of it than Mrs. Snow has, too! But, of course, you need more, anyhow, because you're well and can go to places where folks can see it. My! I reckon folks'll be glad when they do see it — and surprised, too, 'cause you've hid it so long. Why, Aunt Polly, I'll make you so pretty everybody'll just love to look at you!"

"Pollyanna!" gasped a stifled but shocked voice from a veil of hair. "I — I'm sure I don't know why I'm letting you do this silly thing."

"Why, Aunt Polly, I should think you'd be glad to have folks like to look at you! Don't you like to look at pretty things? I'm ever so much happier when I look at pretty folks, 'cause when I look at the other kind I'm so sorry for them."

"But — but — "

"And I just love to do folks' hair," purred Pollyanna, contentedly. "I did quite a lot of the Ladies' Aiders' — but there wasn't any of them so nice as yours. Mrs. White's was pretty nice, though, and she looked just lovely one day when I dressed her up in — Oh, Aunt Polly, I've just happened to think of something! But it's a secret, and I sha'n't tell. Now your hair is almost done, and pretty quick I'm going to leave you just a minute; and you must promise — promise — PROMISE not to stir nor peek, even, till I come back. Now remember!" she finished, as she ran from the room.

Aloud Miss Polly said nothing. To herself she said that of course she should at once undo the absurd work of her niece's fingers, and put her hair up properly again. As for "peeking" just as if she cared how —

At that moment — unaccountably — Miss Polly caught a glimpse of herself in the mirror of the dressing table. And what she saw sent such a flush of rosy color to her cheeks that — she only flushed the more at the sight.

She saw a face — not young, it is true — but just now alight with excitement and surprise. The cheeks were a pretty pink. The eyes sparkled. The hair, dark, and still damp from the outdoor air, lay in loose waves about the forehead and curved back over the ears in wonderfully becoming lines, with softening little curls here and there.

So amazed and so absorbed was Miss Polly with what she saw in the glass that she quite forgot her determination to do over her hair, until she heard Pollyanna enter the room again. Before she could move, then, she felt a folded something slipped across her eyes and tied in the back.

"Pollyanna, Pollyanna! What are you doing?" she cried.

Pollyanna chuckled.

"That's just what I don't want you to know, Aunt Polly, and I was afraid you WOULD peek, so I tied on the handkerchief. Now sit still. It won't take but just a minute, then I'll let you see."

"But, Pollyanna," began Miss Polly, struggling blindly to her feet, "you must take this off! You — child, child! what ARE you doing?" she gasped, as she felt a soft something slipped about her shoulders.

Pollyanna only chuckled the more gleefully. With trembling fingers she was draping about her aunt's shoulders the fleecy folds of a beautiful lace shawl, yellowed from long years of packing away, and fragrant with lavender. Pollyanna had found the shawl the week before when Nancy had been regulating the attic; and it had occurred to her to-day that there was no reason why her aunt, as well as Mrs. White of her Western home, should not be "dressed up."

Her task completed, Pollyanna surveyed her work with eyes that approved, but that saw yet one touch wanting. Promptly, therefore, she pulled her aunt toward the sun parlor where she could see a belated red rose blooming on the trellis within reach of her hand.

"Pollyanna, what are you doing? Where are you taking me to?" recoiled Aunt Polly, vainly trying to hold herself back. "Pollyanna, I shall not — "

"It's just to the sun parlor — only a minute! I'll have you ready now quicker'n no time," panted Pollyanna, reaching for the rose and thrusting it into the soft hair above Miss Polly's left ear. "There!" she exulted, untying the knot of the handkerchief and flinging the bit of linen far from her. "Oh, Aunt Polly, now I reckon you'll be glad I dressed you up!"

For one dazed moment Miss Polly looked at her bedecked self, and at her surroundings; then she gave a low cry and fled to her room. Pollyanna, following the direction of her aunt's last dismayed gaze, saw, through the open windows of the sun parlor, the horse and gig turning into the driveway. She recognized at once the man who held the reins. Delightedly she leaned forward.

"Dr. Chilton, Dr. Chilton! Did you want to see me? I'm up here."

"Yes," smiled the doctor, a little gravely. "Will you come down, please?"

In the bedroom Pollyanna found a flushed-faced, angry-eyed woman plucking at the pins that held a lace shawl in place.

"Pollyanna, how could you?" moaned the woman. "To think of your rigging me up like this, and then letting me — BE SEEN!"

Pollyanna stopped in dismay.

"But you looked lovely — perfectly lovely, Aunt Polly; and — "

"'Lovely'!" scorned the woman, flinging the shawl to one side and attacking her hair with shaking fingers.

"Oh, Aunt Polly, please, please let the hair stay!"

"Stay? Like this? As if I would!" And Miss Polly pulled the locks so tightly back that the last curl lay stretched dead at the ends of her fingers.

"O dear! And you did look so pretty," almost sobbed Pollyanna, as she stumbled through the door.

Down-stairs Pollyanna found the doctor waiting in his gig.

"I've prescribed you for a patient, and he's sent me to get the prescription filled," announced the doctor. "Will you go?"

"You mean — an errand — to the drug store?" asked Pollyanna, a little uncertainly. "I used to go some — for the Ladies' Aiders."

The doctor shook his head with a smile.

"Not exactly. It's Mr. John Pendleton. He would like to see you to-day, if you'll be so good as to come. It's stopped raining, so I drove down after you. Will you come? I'll call for you and bring you back before six o'clock."

"I'd love to!" exclaimed Pollyanna. "Let me ask Aunt Polly."

In a few moments she returned, hat in hand, but with rather a sober face.

"Didn't — your aunt want you to go?" asked the doctor, a little diffidently, as they drove away.

"Y-yes," sighed Pollyanna. "She — she wanted me to go TOO much, I'm afraid."

"Wanted you to go TOO MUCH!"

Pollyanna sighed again.

"Yes. I reckon she meant she didn't want me there. You see, she said: 'Yes, yes, run along, run along — do! I wish you'd gone before.'"

The doctor smiled — but with his lips only. His eyes were very grave. For some time he said nothing; then, a little hesitatingly, he asked:

"Wasn't it — your aunt I saw with you a few minutes ago — in the window of the sun parlor?"

Pollyanna drew a long breath.

"Yes; that's what's the whole trouble, I suppose. You see I'd dressed her up in a perfectly lovely lace shawl I found up-stairs, and I'd fixed her hair and put on a rose, and she looked so pretty. Didn't YOU think she looked just lovely?"

For a moment the doctor did not answer. When he did speak his voice was so low Pollyanna could but just hear the words.

"Yes, Pollyanna, I — I thought she did look — just lovely."

"Did you? I'm so glad! I'll tell her," nodded the little girl, contentedly.

To her surprise the doctor gave a sudden exclamation.

"Never! Pollyanna, I — I'm afraid I shall have to ask you not to tell her — that."

"Why, Dr. Chilton! Why not? I should think you'd be glad — "

"But she might not be," cut in the doctor.

Pollyanna considered this for a moment.

"That's so — maybe she wouldn't," she sighed. "I remember now; 'twas 'cause she saw you that she ran. And she — she spoke afterwards about her being seen in that rig."

"I thought as much," declared the doctor, under his breath.

"Still, I don't see why," maintained Pollyanna, " — when she looked so pretty!"

The doctor said nothing. He did not speak again, indeed, until they were almost to the great stone house in which John Pendleton lay with a broken leg.

CHAPTER 16
DEVOTIONAL & JOURNAL

"But you looked lovely — perfectly lovely, Aunt Polly; and — "

"'Lovely'!" scorned the woman, flinging the shawl to one side and attacking her hair with shaking fingers.

"Oh, Aunt Polly, please, please let the hair stay!"

"Stay? Like this? As if I would!" And Miss Polly pulled the locks so tightly back that the last curl lay stretched dead at the ends of her fingers.

"O dear! And you did look so pretty," almost sobbed Pollyanna, as she stumbled through the door.

Aunt Polly resists allowing her beauty to show, so much that being seen looking pretty after Pollyanna does her hair in a softer style, is a cause for anger and shame. She chooses to make herself look plain and deny her God-given beauty, not because of any spiritual belief about avoiding adornment, but because of bitterness and hurt.

There's so much focus on external beauty in our society! How we feel about ourselves as women is too often measured by how we feel about how we look. There seems to be two ways to deal with this – opting in or opting out of the beauty contest. I know women who rarely wear make-up and who don't style their hair more than dragging a comb through it. I also know women who won't leave the house without a full make-up, and who get up hours before they need to because they need the time to style their hair. Yet probably just as many women in each group consider themselves plain, and certainly just as many are beautiful!

I always put myself in the first group – the opt-outs. I realized early I didn't measure up to the idea of beauty. I wasn't tall and slender, but on the plump side. I didn't have long straight blonde hair, but reddish hair with an annoying kink. I freckle, and never tan. My eyelashes are short, my brows unruly. So I didn't try to play the beauty game. No make-up, no hair styling, no need to worry about managing my weight, because I'd never be good enough. For the longest time, my sense of worth as a woman was in the pits, and I was painfully shy because of it.

Yet right when I was feeling worst about myself, beating myself up for being overweight, believing I was ugly not just on the outside but on the inside, I met one of the most beautiful women I've ever known. She wore only the lightest make-up, and let her curly hair run wild. Her features weren't especially lovely. She was heavier than I was. Yet she had an amazing beauty, a joy in life and a vitality that radiated out of her. Meeting her was such a God-given blessing, because He showed me I needed to think again about beauty and stop defining myself by worldly standards.

Your beauty should not come from outward adornment, such as elaborate hairstyles and the wearing of gold jewelry or fine clothes. Rather, it should be that of your inner self, the unfading beauty of a gentle and quiet spirit, which is of great worth in God's sight.
1 Peter 3:3-4 NIV

Many versions translate that as "Your beauty should not come *only* from outward adornment." It's not adornment that's the problem! I love this quote from Laura Lawson Visconti: "Peter isn't saying women ought to stray from wearing jewelry and fixing their hair, but that it shouldn't define them. He's saying a woman's beauty is an inner light, one that only grows brighter and stronger with age.... Let's stop trying to define beauty and allow it to organically unfold as we pursue other, more exciting things. Let's stop yearning. Women, let's focus on our internal beauty yes, but then let's allow our external beauty to blossom as well! Our beauty is not something to be afraid of — it's a God-given gift, each of ours completely unique and completely exquisite."

Taking some care over our appearance and ensuring we look the best we can isn't wrong, but it shouldn't be a major concern. Most importantly, we need to avoid making the mistake of defining ourselves by our looks, and defining beauty as whatever the current fashion says it should be. Physical beauty shouldn't become an idol.

That sort of beauty is transient. God wants us to focus on what lasts. When we have a true definition of beauty, we can all be truly beautiful.

He has made everything beautiful in its time.
Ecclesiastes 13:11

Do you feel it's wrong to want to look beautiful?

How do you feel about your physical appearance?

Do concerns about your physical beauty or time spent on clothes, hair and beauty routines steal your joy?

What does having "a gentle and quiet spirit" mean to you?

How can you redefine your concept of beauty?

Lord, help me to know that You created me to have my own unique beauty, inside and out. Help me to accept and embrace the beauty You gave me. Help me to focus on You, and to develop the lasting beauty and inner quietness of a woman at peace with You and herself, radiating the joy and delight of walking with You. Help me to blossom in every way You intend me to, inside and out. Thank You!

CHAPTER SEVENTEEN:
"JUST LIKE A BOOK"

John Pendleton greeted Pollyanna to-day with a smile.

"Well, Miss Pollyanna, I'm thinking you must be a very forgiving little person, else you wouldn't have come to see me again to-day."

"Why, Mr. Pendleton, I was real glad to come, and I'm sure I don't see why I shouldn't be, either."

"Oh, well, you know, I was pretty cross with you, I'm afraid, both the other day when you so kindly brought me the jelly, and that time when you found me with the broken leg at first. By the way, too, I don't think I've ever thanked you for that. Now I'm sure that even you would admit that you were very forgiving to come and see me, after such ungrateful treatment as that!"

Pollyanna stirred uneasily.

"But I was glad to find you — that is, I don't mean I was glad your leg was broken, of course," she corrected hurriedly.

John Pendleton smiled.

"I understand. Your tongue does get away with you once in a while, doesn't it, Miss Pollyanna? I do thank you, however; and I consider you a very brave little girl to do what you did that day. I thank you for the jelly, too," he added in a lighter voice.

"Did you like it?" asked Pollyanna with interest.

"Very much. I suppose — there isn't any more to-day that — that Aunt Polly DIDN'T send, is there?" he asked with an odd smile.

His visitor looked distressed.

"N-no, sir." She hesitated, then went on with heightened color. "Please, Mr. Pendleton, I didn't mean to be rude the other day when I said Aunt Polly did NOT send the jelly."

There was no answer. John Pendleton was not smiling now. He was looking straight ahead of him with eyes that seemed to be gazing through and beyond the object before them. After a time he drew a long sigh and turned to Pollyanna. When he spoke his voice carried the old nervous fretfulness.

"Well, well, this will never do at all! I didn't send for you to see me moping this time. Listen! Out in the library — the big room where the telephone is, you know — you will find a carved box on the lower shelf of the big case with glass doors in the corner not far from the fireplace. That is, it'll be there if that confounded woman hasn't 'regulated' it to somewhere else! You may bring it to me. It is heavy, but not too heavy for you to carry, I think."

"Oh, I'm awfully strong," declared Pollyanna, cheerfully, as she sprang to her feet. In a minute she had returned with the box.

It was a wonderful half-hour that Pollyanna spent then. The box was full of treasures — curios that John Pendleton had picked up in years of travel — and concerning each there was some entertaining story, whether it were a set of exquisitely carved chessmen from China, or a little jade idol from India.

It was after she had heard the story about the idol that Pollyanna murmured wistfully:

"Well, I suppose it WOULD be better to take a little boy in India to bring up — one that didn't know any more than to think that God was in that doll-thing — than it would be to take Jimmy Bean, a little boy who knows God is up in the sky. Still, I can't help wishing they had wanted Jimmy Bean, too, besides the India boys."

John Pendleton did not seem to hear. Again his, eyes were staring straight before him, looking at nothing. But soon he had roused himself, and had picked up another curio to talk about.

The visit, certainly, was a delightful one, but before it was over, Pollyanna was realizing that they were talking about something besides the wonderful things in the beautiful carved box. They were talking of herself, of Nancy, of Aunt Polly, and of her daily life. They were talking, too, even of the life and home long ago in the far Western town.

Not until it was nearly time for her to go, did the man say, in a voice Pollyanna had never before heard from stern John Pendleton:

"Little girl, I want you to come to see me often. Will you? I'm lonesome, and I need you. There's another reason — and I'm going to tell you that, too. I thought, at first, after I found out who you were, the other day, that I didn't want you to come any more. You reminded me of — of something I have tried for long years to forget. So I said to myself that I never wanted to see you again; and every day, when the doctor asked if I wouldn't let him bring you to me, I said no.

"But after a time I found I was wanting to see you so much that — that the fact that I WASN'T seeing you was making me remember all the more vividly the thing I was so wanting to forget. So now I want you to come. Will you — little girl?"

"Why, yes, Mr. Pendleton," breathed Pollyanna, her eyes luminous with sympathy for the sad-faced man lying back on the pillow before her. "I'd love to come!"

"Thank you," said John Pendleton, gently.

After supper that evening, Pollyanna, sitting on the back porch, told Nancy all about Mr. John Pendleton's wonderful carved box, and the still more wonderful things it contained.

"And ter think," sighed Nancy, "that he SHOWED ye all them things, and told ye about 'em like that — him that's so cross he never talks ter no one — no one!"

"Oh, but he isn't cross, Nancy, only outside," demurred Pollyanna, with quick loyalty. "I don't see why everybody thinks he's so bad, either. They wouldn't, if they knew him. But even Aunt Polly doesn't like him very well. She wouldn't send the jelly to him, you know, and she was so afraid he'd think she *did* send it!"

"Probably she didn't call him no duty," shrugged Nancy. "But what beats me is how he happened ter take ter you so, Miss Pollyanna — meanin' no offence ter you, of course — but he ain't the sort o' man what gen'rally takes ter kids; he ain't, he ain't."

Pollyanna smiled happily.

"But he did, Nancy," she nodded, "only I reckon even he didn't want to — ALL the time. Why, only to-day he owned up that one time he just felt he never wanted to see me again, because I reminded him of something he wanted to forget. But afterwards — "

"What's that?" interrupted Nancy, excitedly. "He said you reminded him of something he wanted to forget?"

"Yes. But afterwards — "

"What was it?" Nancy was eagerly insistent.

"He didn't tell me. He just said it was something."

"THE MYSTERY!" breathed Nancy, in an awestruck voice. "That's why he took to you in the first place. Oh, Miss Pollyanna! Why, that's just like a book — I've read lots of 'em; 'Lady Maud's Secret,' and 'The Lost Heir,' and 'Hidden for Years' — all of 'em had mysteries and things just like this. My stars and stockings! Just think of havin' a book lived right under yer nose like this an' me not knowin' it all this time! Now tell me everythin' — everythin' he said, Miss Pollyanna, there's a dear! No wonder he took ter you; no wonder — no wonder!"

"But he didn't," cried Pollyanna, "not till *I* talked to HIM, first. And he didn't even know who I was till I took the calf's-foot jelly, and had to make him understand that Aunt Polly didn't send it, and — "

Nancy sprang to her feet and clasped her hands together suddenly.

"Oh, Miss Pollyanna, I know, I know — I KNOW I know!" she exulted rapturously. The next minute she was down at Pollyanna's side again. "Tell me — now think, and answer straight and true," she urged excitedly. "It was after he found out you was Miss Polly's niece that he said he didn't ever want ter see ye again, wa'n't it?"

"Oh, yes. I told him that the last time I saw him, and he told me this to-day."

"I thought as much," triumphed Nancy. "And Miss Polly wouldn't send the jelly herself, would she?"

"No."

"And you told him she didn't send it?"

"Why, yes; I — "

"And he began ter act queer and cry out sudden after he found out you was her niece. He did that, didn't he?"

"Why, y-yes; he did act a little queer — over that jelly," admitted Pollyanna, with a thoughtful frown.

Nancy drew a long sigh.

"Then I've got it, sure! Now listen. MR. JOHN PENDLETON WAS MISS POLLY HARRINGTON'S LOVER!" she announced impressively, but with a furtive glance over her shoulder.

"Why, Nancy, he couldn't be! She doesn't like him," objected Pollyanna.

Nancy gave her a scornful glance.

"Of course she don't! THAT'S the quarrel!"

Pollyanna still looked incredulous, and with another long breath Nancy happily settled herself to tell the story.

"It's like this. Just before you come, Mr. Tom told me Miss Polly had had a lover once. I didn't believe it. I couldn't — her and a lover! But Mr. Tom said she had, and that he was livin' now right in this town. And NOW I know, of course. It's John Pendleton. Hain't he got a mystery in his life? Don't he shut himself up in that grand house alone, and never speak ter no one? Didn't he act queer when he found out you was Miss Polly's niece? And now hain't he owned up that you remind him of somethin' he wants ter forget? Just as if ANYBODY couldn't see 'twas Miss Polly! — an' her sayin' she wouldn't send him no jelly, too. Why, Miss Pollyanna, it's as plain as the nose on yer face; it is, it is!"

"Oh-h!" breathed Pollyanna, in wide-eyed amazement. "But, Nancy, I should think if they loved each other they'd make up some time. Both of 'em all alone, so, all these years. I should think they'd be glad to make up!"

Nancy sniffed disdainfully.

"I guess maybe you don't know much about lovers, Miss Pollyanna. You ain't big enough yet, anyhow. But if there IS a set o' folks in the world that wouldn't have no use for that 'ere 'glad game' o' your'n, it'd be a pair o' quarrellin' lovers; and that's what they be. Ain't he cross as sticks, most gen'rally? — and ain't she — "

Nancy stopped abruptly, remembering just in time to whom, and about whom, she was speaking. Suddenly, however, she chuckled.

"I ain't sayin', though, Miss Pollyanna, but what it would be a pretty slick piece of business if you could GET 'em ter playin' it — so they WOULD be glad ter make up. But, my land! wouldn't folks stare some — Miss Polly and him! I guess, though, there ain't much chance, much chance!"

Pollyanna said nothing; but when she went into the house a little later, her face was very thoughtful.

CHAPTER 17
DEVOTIONAL & JOURNAL

"Well, I suppose it WOULD be better to take a little boy in India to bring up — one that didn't know any more than to think that God was in that doll-thing — than it would be to take Jimmy Bean, a little boy who knows God is up in the sky."

When John Pendleton shows Pollyanna a box of curios collected on his travels, one of the items is a carved Indian idol. Pollyanna's response, coming from her child-like understanding of God taught to her in Sunday School, is interesting. Were you taught the same about God, that He "is up in the sky"?

What is your personal concept of God and where He can be found?

Does God feel near to you, or a long way away?

I'd rather know and trust God was right here with me than believe He lives away up in the sky! Feeling Him near me makes life so much better and easier.

But my spiritual life feels like it's been a roller-coaster ride! I've had ecstatically joyful moments of feeling God's presence as so real and true, and long deserts of despair where He has felt so far away from me, I've even doubted His existence.

"You can be sure that I will be with you always. I will continue with you until the end of time."
Matthew 28:20

Jesus, who is also called *Immanuel, God with us* (Matthew 1:23) promises that He will never leave us. I'm still learning that even when we don't feel his nearness, we can trust it is true – He keeps His promises! And trusting in His presence is essential for our joy.

Rejoice in the Lord always. I will say it again: Rejoice!
Philippians 4:4 NIV

Rejoicing can seem hard to do when life is full of challenges! But it is possible. We can change our mindset and rejoice "in the Lord", by focusing on his presence with us instead of our worries. That's how we return to the source of all joy. And since we can trust He is always with us, we can rejoice always, too.

Do not be anxious about anything, but in every situation, by prayer and petition, with thanksgiving, present your requests to God. And the peace of God, which transcends all understanding, will guard your hearts and your minds in Christ Jesus.
Philippians 4:6-7 NIV

It's not easy for an "I'll do it" person like me to let go of anxiety, but I'm finding life is so much better when I stop stressing and worrying about things, and hand it over to God. Like anything, the more we practice it, the better we get. As I surrender more and more to God, trusting He is there and He will take care of it, trusting Him becomes easier. The more I trust Him, the more peace and joy I feel. It's a wonderful uplifting circle.

But first, we need to trust in His promises *without* feeling it, trust in His presence, trust in His love, trust in His care for us, believing the feelings will follow.

When have you felt God's presence with you? How did it feel? Can you trust He is there with you even when you *don't* feel it?

Have you experienced praying about something and feeling less anxious about it, better able to cope with it, even though nothing has changed yet?

What worries can you take to God in prayer today?

Lord, thank You that You are with me, all the time and in all circumstances. Help me to stay focused on You as my source of joy and to trust that You will never leave me. Help me to feel Your joy in all things today as I walk with You. Help me to surrender all of my concerns to You in prayer and trust that You will take care of them for me. Thank You!

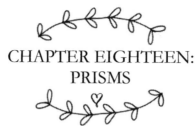

CHAPTER EIGHTEEN:
PRISMS

As the warm August days passed, Pollyanna went very frequently to the great house on Pendleton Hill. She did not feel, however, that her visits were really a success. Not but that the man seemed to want her there — he sent for her, indeed, frequently; but that when she was there, he seemed scarcely any the happier for her presence — at least, so Pollyanna thought.

He talked to her, it was true, and he showed her many strange and beautiful things — books, pictures, and curios. But he still fretted audibly over his own helplessness, and he chafed visibly under the rules and "regulatings" of the unwelcome members of his household. He did, indeed, seem to like to hear Pollyanna talk, however, and Pollyanna talked, Pollyanna liked to talk — but she was never sure that she would not look up and find him lying back on his pillow with that white, hurt look that always pained her; and she was never sure which — if any — of her words had brought it there. As for telling him the "glad game," and trying to get him to play it — Pollyanna had never seen the time yet when she thought he would care to hear about it. She had twice tried to tell him; but neither time had she got beyond the beginning of what her father had said — John Pendleton had on each occasion turned the conversation abruptly to another subject.

Pollyanna never doubted now that John Pendleton was her Aunt Polly's one-time lover; and with all the strength of her loving, loyal heart, she wished she could in some way bring happiness into their — to her mind — miserably lonely lives.

Just how she was to do this, however, she could not see. She talked to Mr. Pendleton about her aunt; and he listened, sometimes politely, sometimes irritably, frequently with a quizzical smile on his usually stern lips. She talked to her aunt about Mr. Pendleton — or rather, she tried to talk to her about him. As a general thing, however, Miss Polly would not listen — long. She always found something else to talk about. She frequently did that, however, when Pollyanna was talking of others — of Dr. Chilton, for instance. Pollyanna laid this, though, to the fact that it had been Dr. Chilton who had seen her in the sun parlor with the rose in her hair and the lace shawl draped about her shoulders.

Aunt Polly, indeed, seemed particularly bitter against Dr. Chilton, as Pollyanna found out one day when a hard cold shut her up in the house.

"If you are not better by night I shall send for the doctor," Aunt Polly said.

"Shall you? Then I'm going to be worse," gurgled Pollyanna. "I'd love to have Dr. Chilton come to see me!"

She wondered, then, at the look that came to her aunt's face.

"It will not be Dr. Chilton, Pollyanna," Miss Polly said sternly. "Dr. Chilton is not our family physician. I shall send for Dr. Warren — if you are worse."

Pollyanna did not grow worse, however, and Dr. Warren was not summoned.

"And I'm so glad, too," Pollyanna said to her aunt that evening. "Of course I like Dr. Warren, and all that; but I like Dr. Chilton better, and I'm afraid he'd feel hurt if I didn't have him. You see, he wasn't really to blame, after all, that he happened to see you when I'd dressed you up so pretty that day, Aunt Polly," she finished wistfully.

"That will do, Pollyanna. I really do not wish to discuss Dr. Chilton — or his feelings," reproved Miss Polly, decisively.

Pollyanna looked at her for a moment with mournfully interested eyes; then she sighed:

"I just love to see you when your cheeks are pink like that, Aunt Polly; but I would so like to fix your hair. If — Why, Aunt Polly!" But her aunt was already out of sight down the hall.

It was toward the end of August that Pollyanna, making an early morning call on John Pendleton, found the flaming band of blue and gold and green edged with red and violet lying across his pillow. She stopped short in awed delight.

"Why, Mr. Pendleton, it's a baby rainbow — a real rainbow come in to pay you a visit!" she exclaimed, clapping her hands together softly. "Oh — oh — oh, how pretty it is! But how DID it get in?" she cried.

The man laughed a little grimly: John Pendleton was particularly out of sorts with the world this morning.

"Well, I suppose it 'got in' through the bevelled edge of that glass thermometer in the window," he said wearily. "The sun shouldn't strike it at all but it does in the morning."

"Oh, but it's so pretty, Mr. Pendleton! And does just the sun do that? My! if it was mine I'd have it hang in the sun all day long!"

"Lots of good you'd get out of the thermometer, then," laughed the man. "How do you suppose you could tell how hot it was, or how cold it was, if the thermometer hung in the sun all day?"

"I shouldn't care," breathed Pollyanna, her fascinated eyes on the brilliant band of colors across the pillow. "Just as if anybody'd care when they were living all the time in a rainbow!"

The man laughed. He was watching Pollyanna's rapt face a little curiously. Suddenly a new thought came to him. He touched the bell at his side.

"Nora," he said, when the elderly maid appeared at the door, "bring me one of the big brass candle-sticks from the mantel in the front drawing-room."

"Yes, sir," murmured the woman, looking slightly dazed. In a minute she had returned. A musical tinkling entered the room with her as she advanced wonderingly toward the bed. It came from the prism pendants encircling the old-fashioned candelabrum in her hand.

"Thank you. You may set it here on the stand," directed the man. "Now get a string and fasten it to the sash-curtain fixtures of that window there. Take down the sash-curtain, and let the string reach straight across the window from side to side. That will be all. Thank you," he said, when she had carried out his directions.

As she left the room he turned smiling eyes toward the wondering Pollyanna.

"Bring me the candlestick now, please, Pollyanna."

With both hands she brought it; and in a moment he was slipping off the pendants, one by one, until they lay, a round dozen of them, side by side, on the bed.

"Now, my dear, suppose you take them and hook them to that little string Nora fixed across the window. If you really WANT to live in a rainbow — I don't see but we'll have to have a rainbow for you to live in!"

Pollyanna had not hung up three of the pendants in the sunlit window before she saw a little of what was going to happen. She was so excited then she could scarcely control her shaking fingers enough to hang up the rest. But at last her task was finished, and she stepped back with a low cry of delight.

It had become a fairyland — that sumptuous, but dreary bedroom. Everywhere were bits of dancing red and green, violet and orange, gold and blue. The wall, the floor, and the furniture, even to the bed itself, were aflame with shimmering bits of color.

"Oh, oh, oh, how lovely!" breathed Pollyanna; then she laughed suddenly. "I just reckon the sun himself is trying to play the game now, don't you?" she cried, forgetting for the moment that Mr. Pendleton could not know what she was talking about. "Oh, how I wish I had a lot of those things! How I would like to give them to Aunt Polly and Mrs. Snow and — lots of folks. I reckon THEN they'd be glad all right! Why, I think even Aunt Polly'd get so glad she couldn't help banging doors if she lived in a rainbow like that. Don't you?"

Mr. Pendleton laughed.

"Well, from my remembrance of your aunt, Miss Pollyanna, I must say I think it would take something more than a few prisms in the sunlight to — to make her bang many doors — for gladness. But come, now, really, what do you mean?"

Pollyanna stared slightly; then she drew a long breath.

"Oh, I forgot. You don't know about the game. I remember now."

"Suppose you tell me, then."

And this time Pollyanna told him. She told him the whole thing from the very first — from the crutches that should have been a doll. As she talked, she did not look at his face. Her rapt eyes were still on the dancing flecks of color from the prism pendants swaying in the sunlit window.

"And that's all," she sighed, when she had finished. "And now you know why I said the sun was trying to play it — that game."

For a moment there was silence. Then a low voice from the bed said unsteadily:

"Perhaps; but I'm thinking that the very finest prism of them all is yourself, Pollyanna."

"Oh, but I don't show beautiful red and green and purple when the sun shines through me, Mr. Pendleton!"

"Don't you?" smiled the man. And Pollyanna, looking into his face, wondered why there were tears in his eyes.

"No," she said. Then, after a minute she added mournfully: "I'm afraid, Mr. Pendleton, the sun doesn't make anything but freckles out of me. Aunt Polly says it DOES make them!"

The man laughed a little; and again Pollyanna looked at him: the laugh had sounded almost like a sob.

CHAPTER 18
DEVOTIONAL & JOURNAL

"I shouldn't care," breathed Pollyanna, her fascinated eyes on the brilliant band of colors across the pillow. "Just as if anybody'd care when they were living all the time in a rainbow!"...

..."Perhaps; but I'm thinking that the very finest prism of them all is yourself, Pollyanna."

"Oh, but I don't show beautiful red and green and purple when the sun shines through me, Mr. Pendleton!"

"Don't you?"

John Pendleton hasn't noticed the "baby rainbow" that gives Pollyanna so much delight. Are there any sources of joy you're ignoring in your life?

Could you give thanks for them right now?

A rainbow happens when light shines into glass, crystal, or water droplets, and the different colors that make up the light separate, which we see as a rainbow. It only forms when the light hits something clear enough to shine through, at just the right angle.

Letting myself shine is something I've always been uncomfortable with. I'm more of a hiding myself away under that bushel basket type of girl, except now I'm a bit too big to fit! (Could I have a plus-size basket, please?)

I was always embarrassed at the idea of being seen. I thought only special people shone, not ordinary average people like me. What I realize now is that it's not me that's seen, it's God's light shining through me once I let him clear away the sin that blocks the light. Just like Pollyanna doesn't notice the angled cut glass the sunlight shines through, only the rainbow it makes. We don't need to be special to shine, it's the light shining through that's the special part. All the glass needs to do is be in the light, and let the light do the work.

You are to live clean, innocent lives as children of God in a dark world
full of people who are crooked and stubborn.
Shine out among them like beacon lights.
Philippians 2:15 TLB

When we surrender ourselves fully to God, He washes us clean and clear, so He can shine through us and light up the dark places of the world. The people in the dark don't see us, but they do see God's light, through us.

God intends for us all to make rainbows, as Pollyanna does. All we need to do is be still in the light of His love, and let Him shine through us. The rainbows will happen!

How does the idea of being a shining light for Jesus feel?

How could you allow His light to shine through you more brightly?

Lord, Thank You for the rainbows You shine into my life, the ones I see and the ones I don't see as well. Help me to notice them more. Please help me also to shine, reflecting Your light of love into the world. Help me to live a life of such joy and gratitude that those around me see Your light more truly as it shines through me. Thank you!

CHAPTER NINETEEN:
WHICH IS SOMEWHAT SURPRISING

Pollyanna entered school in September. Preliminary examinations showed that she was well advanced for a girl of her years, and she was soon a happy member of a class of girls and boys her own age.

School, in some ways, was a surprise to Pollyanna; and Pollyanna, certainly, in many ways, was very much of a surprise to school. They were soon on the best of terms, however, and to her aunt Pollyanna confessed that going to school WAS living, after all — though she had had her doubts before.

In spite of her delight in her new work, Pollyanna did not forget her old friends. True, she could not give them quite so much time now, of course; but she gave them what time she could. Perhaps John Pendleton, of them all, however, was the most dissatisfied.

One Saturday afternoon he spoke to her about it.

"See here, Pollyanna, how would you like to come and live with me?" he asked, a little impatiently. "I don't see anything of you, nowadays."

Pollyanna laughed — Mr. Pendleton was such a funny man!

"I thought you didn't like to have folks 'round," she said.

He made a wry face.

"Oh, but that was before you taught me to play that wonderful game of yours. Now I'm glad to be waited on, hand and foot! Never mind, I'll be on my own two feet yet, one of these days; then I'll see who steps around," he finished, picking up one of the crutches at his side and shaking it playfully at the little girl. They were sitting in the great library to-day.

"Oh, but you aren't really glad at all for things; you just SAY you are," pouted Pollyanna, her eyes on the dog, dozing before the fire. "You know you don't play the game right EVER, Mr. Pendleton — you know you don't!"

The man's face grew suddenly very grave.

"That's why I want you, little girl — to help me play it. Will you come?"

Pollyanna turned in surprise.

"Mr. Pendleton, you don't really mean — that?"

"But I do. I want you. Will you come?"

Pollyanna looked distressed.

"Why, Mr. Pendleton, I can't — you know I can't. Why, I'm — Aunt Polly's!"

A quick something crossed the man's face that Pollyanna could not quite understand. His head came up almost fiercely.

"You're no more hers than — Perhaps she would let you come to me," he finished more gently. "Would you come — if she did?"

Pollyanna frowned in deep thought.

"But Aunt Polly has been so — good to me," she began slowly; "and she took me when I didn't have anybody left but the Ladies' Aid, and — "

Again that spasm of something crossed the man's face; but this time, when he spoke, his voice was low and very sad.

"Pollyanna, long years ago I loved somebody very much. I hoped to bring her, some day, to this house. I pictured how happy we'd be together in our home all the long years to come."

"Yes," pitied Pollyanna, her eyes shining with sympathy.

"But — well, I didn't bring her here. Never mind why. I just didn't that's all. And ever since then this great gray pile of stone has been a house — never a home. It takes a woman's hand and heart, or a child's presence, to make a home, Pollyanna; and I have not had either. Now will you come, my dear?"

Pollyanna sprang to her feet. Her face was fairly illumined.

"Mr. Pendleton, you — you mean that you wish you — you had had that woman's hand and heart all this time?"

"Why, y-yes, Pollyanna."

"Oh, I'm so glad! Then it's all right," sighed the little girl. "Now you can take us both, and everything will be lovely."

"Take — you — both?" repeated the man, dazedly.

A faint doubt crossed Pollyanna's countenance.

"Well, of course, Aunt Polly isn't won over, yet; but I'm sure she will be if you tell it to her just as you did to me, and then we'd both come, of course."

A look of actual terror leaped to the man's eyes.

"Aunt Polly come — HERE!"

Pollyanna's eyes widened a little.

"Would you rather go THERE?" she asked. "Of course the house isn't quite so pretty, but it's nearer — "

"Pollyanna, what ARE you talking about?" asked the man, very gently now.

"Why, about where we're going to live, of course," rejoined Pollyanna, in obvious surprise. "I THOUGHT you meant here, at first. You said it was here that you had wanted Aunt Polly's hand and heart all these years to make a home, and — "

An inarticulate cry came from the man's throat. He raised his hand and began to speak; but the next moment he dropped his hand nervelessly at his side.

"The doctor, sir," said the maid in the doorway.

Pollyanna rose at once.

John Pendleton turned to her feverishly.

"Pollyanna, for Heaven's sake, say nothing of what I asked you — yet," he begged, in a low voice.

Pollyanna dimpled into a sunny smile.

"Of course not! Just as if I didn't know you'd rather tell her yourself!" she called back merrily over her shoulder.

John Pendleton fell limply back in his chair.

"Why, what's up?" demanded the doctor, a minute later, his fingers on his patient's galloping pulse.

A whimsical smile trembled on John Pendleton's lips.

"Overdose of your tonic, I guess," he laughed, as he noted the doctor's eyes following Pollyanna's little figure down the driveway.

CHAPTER 19
DEVOTIONAL & JOURNAL

"Oh, but you aren't really glad at all for things; you just SAY you are," pouted Pollyanna, her eyes on the dog, dozing before the fire. "You know you don't play the game right EVER, Mr. Pendleton — you know you don't!"

Pollyanna recognizes that Mr. Pendleton only pretends to play the Glad Game because he's too caught up in disappointment from the past to truly feel glad. Our own wants and regrets can do the same to us. Dwelling on the past destroys our present happiness.

Are there any areas in your life where you know you're saying you're glad for things only because you feel you should be glad, when in your heart you're not?

Does pretending to feel happy make you feel better or worse?

When we've been badly hurt, the memory of the pain we suffered can stop us feeling joy now. When we're like this, it can seem as if all we can think about is how we've been hurt, and what is wrong in our life. We may pretend to put on a happy face, but it doesn't help as much as we'd like. Behind the mask, nothing has changed.

The thought of my pain... is bitter poison. I think of it constantly, and my spirit is depressed.
Lamentations 3:19, 20 GNT

I've done this when things have happened that have hurt and badly disappointed me. Broken relationships, dreams that didn't work out, plans that failed. We need to mourn them. It can feel like we have the right to be bitter, the right to stay heartbroken. But the more we dwell on what was wrong, the more it poisons our present joy and our relationships, and the worse we feel. It's too easy to slide into this cycle of despair, even get stuck in it for many years. The past isn't past when it's ruining our lives in the present!

The only way out is to focus on God instead of the pain. Trying to be glad can feel better temporarily, but it doesn't heal our bitterness and it doesn't give us hope things can be better.

Only God gives hope. And hope and joy go hand in hand.

Yet hope returns when I remember this one thing:
The Lord's unfailing love and mercy still continue, fresh as the morning, as sure as the sunrise.
The Lord is all I have, and so in him I put my hope.
Lamentations 3:21-24 GNT

May the God who gives hope fill you with great joy. May you have perfect peace as you trust in him.
May the power of the Holy Spirit fill you with hope.
Romans 15:13

Trust God. Let the past be past. Surrender anything that gets in the way of your joy to Him. Open your heart to hope.

What past disappointments, hurts, or losses get in the way of your present joy?

Can you let go of those things now and hand them over to God, so you can step more fully into your inheritance of joy?

Lord, please help me to let go of anything from the past that is stopping me from living fully in Your joy. Whether that's anger, sadness, hurt, bitterness, or other disappointments, I'm willing now to open my heart and mind to You and let them go. Fill the spaces left behind with Your joy instead please Lord, so that I can learn to live each moment of my life with gladness in You, and look to an even better future — eternal life with You in glory, perfected and joyful. Thank You!

CHAPTER TWENTY:
WHICH IS MORE SURPRISING

Sunday mornings Pollyanna usually attended church and Sunday school. Sunday afternoons she frequently went for a walk with Nancy. She had planned one for the day after her Saturday afternoon visit to Mr. John Pendleton; but on the way home from Sunday school Dr. Chilton overtook her in his gig, and brought his horse to a stop.

"Suppose you let me drive you home, Pollyanna," he suggested. "I want to speak to you a minute. I was just driving out to your place to tell you," he went on, as Pollyanna settled herself at his side. "Mr. Pendleton sent a special request for you to go to see him this afternoon, SURE. He says it's very important."

Pollyanna nodded happily.

"Yes, it is, I know. I'll go."

The doctor eyed her with some surprise.

"I'm not sure I shall let you, after all," he declared, his eyes twinkling. "You seemed more upsetting than soothing yesterday, young lady."

Pollyanna laughed.

"Oh, it wasn't me, truly — not really, you know; not so much as it was Aunt Polly."

The doctor turned with a quick start.

"Your — aunt!" he ejaculated.

Pollyanna gave a happy little bounce in her seat.

"Yes. And it's so exciting and lovely, just like a story, you know. I — I'm going to tell you," she burst out, with sudden decision. "He said not to mention it; but he wouldn't mind your knowing, of course. He meant not to mention it to HER."

"HER?"

"Yes; Aunt Polly. And, of course he WOULD want to tell her himself instead of having me do it — lovers, so!"

"Lovers!" As the doctor said the word, the horse started violently, as if the hand that held the reins had given them a sharp jerk.

"Yes," nodded Pollyanna, happily. "That's the story-part, you see. I didn't know it till Nancy told me. She said Aunt Polly had a lover years ago, and they quarrelled. She didn't know who it was at first. But we've found out now. It's Mr. Pendleton, you know."

The doctor relaxed suddenly. The hand holding the reins fell limply to his lap.

"Oh! No; I — didn't know," he said quietly.

Pollyanna hurried on — they were nearing the Harrington homestead. "Yes; and I'm so glad now. It's come out lovely. Mr. Pendleton asked me to come and live with him, but of course I wouldn't leave Aunt Polly like that — after she'd been so good to me. Then he told me all about the woman's hand and heart that he used to want, and I found out that he wanted it now; and I was so glad! For of course if he wants to make up the quarrel, everything will be all right now, and Aunt Polly and I will both go to live there, or else he'll come to live with us. Of course Aunt Polly doesn't know yet, and we haven't got everything settled; so I suppose that is why he wanted to see me this afternoon, sure."

The doctor sat suddenly erect. There was an odd smile on his lips.

"Yes; I can well imagine that Mr. John Pendleton does — want to see you, Pollyanna," he nodded, as he pulled his horse to a stop before the door.

"There's Aunt Polly now in the window," cried Pollyanna; then, a second later: "Why, no, she isn't — but I thought I saw her!"

"No; she isn't there — now," said the doctor, His lips had suddenly lost their smile.

Pollyanna found a very nervous John Pendleton waiting for her that afternoon.

"Pollyanna," he began at once. "I've been trying all night to puzzle out what you meant by all that, yesterday — about my wanting your Aunt Polly's hand and heart here all those years. What did you mean?"

"Why, because you were lovers, you know once; and I was so glad you still felt that way now."

"Lovers! — your Aunt Polly and I?"

At the obvious surprise in the man's voice, Pollyanna opened wide her eyes.

"Why, Mr. Pendleton, Nancy said you were!"

The man gave a short little laugh.

"Indeed! Well, I'm afraid I shall have to say that Nancy — didn't know."

"Then you — weren't lovers?" Pollyanna's voice was tragic with dismay.

"Never!"

"And it ISN'T all coming out like a book?"

There was no answer. The man's eyes were moodily fixed out the window.

"O dear! And it was all going so splendidly," almost sobbed Pollyanna.

"I'd have been so glad to come — with Aunt Polly."

"And you won't — now?" The man asked the question without turning his head.

"Of course not! I'm Aunt Polly's."

The man turned now, almost fiercely.

"Before you were hers, Pollyanna, you were — your mother's. And — it was your mother's hand and heart that I wanted long years ago."

"My mother's!"

"Yes. I had not meant to tell you, but perhaps it's better, after all, that I do — now." John Pendleton's face had grown very white. He was speaking with evident difficulty.

Pollyanna, her eyes wide and frightened, and her lips parted, was gazing at him fixedly.

"I loved your mother; but she — didn't love me. And after a time she went away with — your father. I did not know until then how much I did — care. The whole world suddenly seemed to turn black under my fingers, and — But, never mind. For long years I have been a cross, crabbed, unlovable, unloved old man — though I'm not nearly sixty, yet, Pollyanna. Then, one day, like one of the prisms that you love so well, little girl, you danced into my life, and flecked my dreary old world with dashes of the purple and gold and scarlet of your own bright cheeriness. I found out, after a time, who you were, and — and I thought then I never wanted to see you again. I didn't want to be reminded of — your mother. But — you know how that came out. I just had to have you come. And now I want you always. Pollyanna, won't you come NOW?"

"But, Mr. Pendleton, I — There's Aunt Polly!" Pollyanna's eyes were blurred with tears.

The man made an impatient gesture.

"What about me? How do you suppose I'm going to be 'glad' about anything — without you? Why, Pollyanna, it's only since you came that I've been even half glad to live! But if I had you for my own little girl, I'd be glad for — anything; and I'd try to make you glad, too, my dear. You shouldn't have a wish ungratified. All my money, to the last cent, should go to make you happy."

Pollyanna looked shocked.

"Why, Mr. Pendleton, as if I'd let you spend it on me — all that money you've saved for the heathen!"

A dull red came to the man's face. He started to speak, but Pollyanna was still talking.

"Besides, anybody with such a lot of money as you have doesn't need me to make you glad about things. You're making other folks so glad giving them things that you just can't help being glad yourself! Why, look at those prisms you gave Mrs. Snow and me, and the gold piece you gave Nancy on her birthday, and — "

"Yes, yes — never mind about all that," interrupted the man. His face was very, very red now — and no wonder, perhaps: it was not for "giving things" that John Pendleton had been best known in the past. "That's all nonsense. 'Twasn't much, anyhow — but what there was, was because of you. YOU gave those things; not I! Yes, you did," he repeated, in answer to the shocked denial in her face. "And that only goes to prove all the more how I need you, little girl," he added, his voice softening into tender pleading once more. "If ever, ever I am to play the 'glad game,' Pollyanna, you'll have to come and play it with me."

The little girl's forehead puckered into a wistful frown.

"Aunt Polly has been so good to me," she began; but the man interrupted her sharply. The old irritability had come back to his face. Impatience which would brook no opposition had been a part of John Pendleton's nature too long to yield very easily now to restraint.

"Of course she's been good to you! But she doesn't want you, I'll warrant, half so much as I do," he contested.

"Why, Mr. Pendleton, she's glad, I know, to have — "

"Glad!" interrupted the man, thoroughly losing his patience now. "I'll wager Miss Polly doesn't know how to be glad — for anything! Oh, she does her duty, I know. She's a very DUTIFUL woman. I've had experience with her 'duty,' before. I'll acknowledge we haven't been the best of friends for the last fifteen or twenty years. But I know her. Every one knows her — and she isn't the 'glad' kind, Pollyanna. She doesn't know how to be. As for your coming to me — you just ask her and see if she won't let you come. And, oh, little girl, little girl, I want you so!" he finished brokenly.

Pollyanna rose to her feet with a long sigh.

"All right. I'll ask her," she said wistfully. "Of course I don't mean that I wouldn't like to live here with you, Mr. Pendleton, but — " She did not complete her sentence. There was a moment's silence, then she added: "Well, anyhow, I'm glad I didn't tell her yesterday; — 'cause then I supposed SHE was wanted, too."

John Pendleton smiled grimly.

"Well, yes, Pollyanna; I guess it is just as well you didn't mention it — yesterday."

"I didn't — only to the doctor; and of course he doesn't count."

"The doctor!" cried John Pendleton, turning quickly. "Not — Dr. — Chilton?"

"Yes; when he came to tell me you wanted to see me to-day, you know."

"Well, of all the — " muttered the man, falling back in his chair. Then he sat up with sudden interest. "And what did Dr. Chilton say?" he asked.

Pollyanna frowned thoughtfully.

"Why, I don't remember. Not much, I reckon. Oh, he did say he could well imagine you did want to see me."

"Oh, did he, indeed!" answered John Pendleton. And Pollyanna wondered why he gave that sudden queer little laugh.

CHAPTER 20
DEVOTIONAL & JOURNAL

"What about me? How do you suppose I'm going to be 'glad' about anything — without you? Why, Pollyanna, it's only since you came that I've been even half glad to live! But if I had you for my own little girl, I'd be glad for — anything; and I'd try to make you glad, too, my dear."

Emotional blackmail or what? Thankfully, Pollyanna doesn't fall for it! But we almost all at times believe someone or something will give us happiness. Have you ever felt this?

Did it work how you hoped?

I've done this too many times. Not the emotional blackmail part, trying to make someone else feel responsible for my happiness, but thinking having someone or something would solve my problems and I'd be happy. All through my life, there's been something I've hoped would give me happiness.

I'll be happy when I have a boyfriend. I'll be happy when I leave home. I'll be happy when someone loves me. I'll be happy when I get married. I'll be happy when I have a baby. I'll be happy when I have a new job. I'll be happy when I move house. I'll be happy when I have a bestselling book. I'll be happy when I'm well.

Even: I'll be happy when I learn to play the piano. Not sure where that came from, but I really did go through a stage where that was my focus!

Well, I didn't have a baby, and I never did learn to play the piano. I'm still a little stuck on wanting to be well again. But being well didn't make me happy before, so chances are, if I'm healed, it won't work like magic to make me happy then, either. The same with moving house.

People of the world who don't know God pursue these things,
but you have a Father caring for you, a Father who knows all your needs.
Luke 12:30 VOICE

What you should want most is God's kingdom and doing what he wants you to do.
Then he will give you all these other things you need.
Matthew 6:33 ERV

What I'm doing by thinking these things will make me happy is putting them ahead of God, which is the same as making idols of them. Bad idea.

"Teacher, which command in God's Law is the most important?"
Jesus said, "Love the Lord your God with all your passion and prayer and intelligence.'
This is the most important, the first on any list. But there is a second to set alongside it:
'Love others as well as you love yourself.'"
Matthew 22:36-39 MSG

Jesus tells us what our priorities should be: 1. Love God 2. Love people. We're to love God above all else, with all our heart, mind, and spirit. Then we're to love others (including ourselves). Then after that, we can want all that other stuff.

The funny thing about all those things I thought would make me happy is that they didn't, and they couldn't. Loving God really is the only thing that can make us happy. I don't have most of the things on my happy list, yet I can truly say I have more joy now than I've ever had. When I focus on God, that's when I'm happy.

How do you show that you love God?

Is there anything, either relationships with others or things you want, that you put ahead of God?

What ways do you feel it's important for people to show their love for others? Do you treat other people in your life like that? Do you treat yourself like that?

Lord, please help me to give thanks for my possessions and my relationships, but to put You first. Nothing but You will truly make me happy. Help me to love You more than anything else, and to feel and show my love for You. Help me to love others and myself the way You love us, with a true accepting, forgiving, unconditional love. Help me know that You are the only real source of lasting joy, and to find my joy in You. Thank You!

CHAPTER TWENTY-ONE:
A QUESTION ANSWERED

The sky was darkening fast with what appeared to be an approaching thunder shower when Pollyanna hurried down the hill from John Pendleton's house. Half-way home she met Nancy with an umbrella. By that time, however, the clouds had shifted their position and the shower was not so imminent.

"Guess it's goin' 'round ter the north," announced Nancy, eyeing the sky critically. "I thought 'twas, all the time, but Miss Polly wanted me ter come with this. She was WORRIED about ye!"

"Was she?" murmured Pollyanna abstractedly, eyeing the clouds in her turn.

Nancy sniffed a little.

"You don't seem ter notice what I said," she observed aggrievedly. "I said yer aunt was WORRIED about ye!"

"Oh," sighed Pollyanna, remembering suddenly the question she was so soon to ask her aunt. "I'm sorry. I didn't mean to scare her."

"Well, I'm glad," retorted Nancy, unexpectedly. "I am, I am."

Pollyanna stared.

"GLAD that Aunt Polly was scared about me! Why, Nancy, THAT isn't the way to play the game — to be glad for things like that!" she objected.

"There wa'n't no game in it," retorted Nancy. "Never thought of it. YOU don't seem ter sense what it means ter have Miss Polly WORRIED about ye, child!"

"Why, it means worried — and worried is horrid — to feel," maintained Pollyanna. "What else can it mean?"

Nancy tossed her head.

"Well, I'll tell ye what it means. It means she's at last gettin' down somewheres near human — like folks; an' that she ain't jest doin' her duty by ye all the time."

"Why, Nancy," demurred the scandalized Pollyanna, "Aunt Polly always does her duty. She — she's a very dutiful woman!" Unconsciously Pollyanna repeated John Pendleton's words of half an hour before.

Nancy chuckled.

"You're right she is — and she always was, I guess! But she's somethin' more, now, since you came."

Pollyanna's face changed. Her brows drew into a troubled frown.

"There, that's what I was going to ask you, Nancy," she sighed. "Do you think Aunt Polly likes to have me here? Would she mind — if… if I wasn't here any more?"

131

Nancy threw a quick look into the little girl's absorbed face. She had expected to be asked this question long before, and she had dreaded it. She had wondered how she should answer it — how she could answer it honestly without cruelly hurting the questioner. But now, NOW, in the face of the new suspicions that had become convictions by the afternoon's umbrella-sending — Nancy only welcomed the question with open arms. She was sure that, with a clean conscience to-day, she could set the love-hungry little girl's heart at rest.

"Likes ter have ye here? Would she miss ye if ye wa'n't here?" cried Nancy, indignantly. "As if that wa'n't jest what I was tellin' of ye! Didn't she send me posthaste with an umbrella 'cause she see a little cloud in the sky? Didn't she make me tote yer things all down-stairs, so you could have the pretty room you wanted? Why, Miss Pollyanna, when ye remember how at first she hated ter have — "

With a choking cough Nancy pulled herself up just in time.

"And it ain't jest things I can put my fingers on, neither," rushed on Nancy, breathlessly. "It's little ways she has, that shows how you've been softenin' her up an' mellerin' her down — the cat, and the dog, and the way she speaks ter me, and oh, lots o' things. Why, Miss Pollyanna, there ain't no tellin' how she'd miss ye — if ye wa'n't here," finished Nancy, speaking with an enthusiastic certainty that was meant to hide the perilous admission she had almost made before. Even then she was not quite prepared for the sudden joy that illumined Pollyanna's face.

"Oh, Nancy, I'm so glad — glad — glad! You don't know how glad I am that Aunt Polly — wants me!"

"As if I'd leave her now!" thought Pollyanna, as she climbed the stairs to her room a little later. "I always knew I wanted to live with Aunt Polly — but I reckon maybe I didn't know quite how much I wanted Aunt Polly — to want to live with ME!"

The task of telling John Pendleton of her decision would not be an easy one, Pollyanna knew, and she dreaded it. She was very fond of John Pendleton, and she was very sorry for him — because he seemed to be so sorry for himself. She was sorry, too, for the long, lonely life that had made him so unhappy; and she was grieved that it had been because of her mother that he had spent those dreary years. She pictured the great gray house as it would be after its master was well again, with its silent rooms, its littered floors, its disordered desk; and her heart ached for his loneliness. She wished that somewhere, some one might be found who — And it was at this point that she sprang to her feet with a little cry of joy at the thought that had come to her.

As soon as she could, after that, she hurried up the hill to John Pendleton's house; and in due time she found herself in the great dim library, with John Pendleton himself sitting near her, his long, thin hands lying idle on the arms of his chair, and his faithful little dog at his feet.

"Well, Pollyanna, is it to be the 'glad game' with me, all the rest of my life?" asked the man, gently.

"Oh, yes," cried Pollyanna. "I've thought of the very gladdest kind of a thing for you to do, and — "

"With — YOU?" asked John Pendleton, his mouth growing a little stern at the corners.

"N-no; but — "

"Pollyanna, you aren't going to say no!" interrupted a voice deep with emotion.

"I — I've got to, Mr. Pendleton; truly I have. Aunt Polly — "

"Did she REFUSE — to let you — come?"

"I — I didn't ask her," stammered the little girl, miserably.

"Pollyanna!"

Pollyanna turned away her eyes. She could not meet the hurt, grieved gaze of her friend.

"So you didn't even ask her!"

"I couldn't, sir — truly," faltered Pollyanna. "You see, I found out — without asking. Aunt Polly WANTS me with her, and — and I want to stay, too," she confessed bravely. "You don't know how good she's been to me; and — and I think, really, sometimes she's beginning to be glad about things — lots of things. And you know she never used to be. You said it yourself. Oh, Mr. Pendleton, I COULDN'T leave Aunt Polly — now!"

There was a long pause. Only the snapping of the wood fire in the grate broke the silence. At last, however, the man spoke.

"No, Pollyanna; I see. You couldn't leave her — now," he said. "I won't ask you — again." The last word was so low it was almost inaudible; but Pollyanna heard.

"Oh, but you don't know about the rest of it," she reminded him eagerly. "There's the very gladdest thing you CAN do — truly there is!"

"Not for me, Pollyanna."

"Yes, sir, for you. You SAID it. You said only a — a woman's hand and heart or a child's presence could make a home. And I can get it for you — a child's presence; — not me, you know, but another one."

"As if I would have any but you!" resented an indignant voice.

"But you will — when you know; you're so kind and good! Why, think of the prisms and the gold pieces, and all that money you save for the heathen, and — "

"Pollyanna!" interrupted the man, savagely. "Once for all let us end that nonsense! I've tried to tell you half a dozen times before. There is no money for the heathen. I never sent a penny to them in my life. There!"

He lifted his chin and braced himself to meet what he expected — the grieved disappointment of Pollyanna's eyes. To his amazement, however, there was neither grief nor disappointment in Pollyanna's eyes. There was only surprised joy.

"Oh, oh!" she cried, clapping her hands. "I'm so glad! That is," she corrected, coloring distressfully, "I don't mean that I'm not sorry for the heathen, only just now I can't help being glad that you don't want the little India boys, because all the rest have wanted them. And so I'm glad you'd rather have Jimmy Bean. Now I know you'll take him!"

"Take — WHO?"

"Jimmy Bean. He's the 'child's presence,' you know; and he'll be so glad to be it. I had to tell him last week that even my Ladies' Aid out West wouldn't take him, and he was so disappointed. But now — when he hears of this — he'll be so glad!"

"Will he? Well, I won't," ejaculated the man, decisively. "Pollyanna, this is sheer nonsense!"

"You don't mean — you won't take him?"

"I certainly do mean just that."

"But he'd be a lovely child's presence," faltered Pollyanna. She was almost crying now. "And you COULDN'T be lonesome — with Jimmy 'round."

"I don't doubt it," rejoined the man; "but — I think I prefer the lonesomeness."

It was then that Pollyanna, for the first time in weeks, suddenly remembered something Nancy had once told her. She raised her chin aggrievedly.

"Maybe you think a nice live little boy wouldn't be better than that old dead skeleton you keep somewhere; but I think it would!"

"SKELETON?"

"Yes. Nancy said you had one in your closet, somewhere."

"Why, what — " Suddenly the man threw back his head and laughed. He laughed very heartily indeed — so heartily that Pollyanna began to cry from pure nervousness. When he saw that, John Pendleton sat erect very promptly. His face grew grave at once.

"Pollyanna, I suspect you are right — more right than you know," he said gently. "In fact, I KNOW that a 'nice live little boy' would be far better than — my skeleton in the closet; only — we aren't always willing to make the exchange. We are apt to still cling to — our skeletons, Pollyanna. However, suppose you tell me a little more about this nice little boy."

And Pollyanna told him.

Perhaps the laugh cleared the air; or perhaps the pathos of Jimmy Bean's story as told by Pollyanna's eager little lips touched a heart already strangely softened. At all events, when Pollyanna went home that night she carried with her an invitation for Jimmy Bean himself to call at the great house with Pollyanna the next Saturday afternoon.

"And I'm so glad, and I'm sure you'll like him," sighed Pollyanna, as she said good-by. "I do so want Jimmy Bean to have a home — and folks that care, you know."

CHAPTER 21
DEVOTIONAL & JOURNAL

"Maybe you think a nice live little boy wouldn't be better than that old dead skeleton you keep somewhere; but I think it would!"

"SKELETON?"

"Yes. Nancy said you had one in your closet, somewhere."...

"Pollyanna, I suspect you are right — more right than you know," he said gently. "In fact, I KNOW that a 'nice live little boy' would be far better than — my skeleton in the closet; only — we aren't always willing to make the exchange. We are apt to still cling to — our skeletons, Pollyanna. However, suppose you tell me a little more about this nice little boy."

I love how literal minded Pollyanna is, thinking John Pendleton really does have a skeleton hidden in a closet somewhere! But keeping his skeleton rather than adopting a boy is such a good image of how we can do the same — turn down the offer of something better, hold onto to an unsatisfying life, old dead dried out bones, rather than let God exchange it for a new aliveness.

I've been there in the desert, clinging to the dry bones I don't want to release. Lugging around remnants of the past I didn't want to let go of, dead dreams, lost hopes, regrets.

Thankfully, we have a God who can clothe dry bones in flesh again and bring them back to life:

> *I will breathe My Spirit into you, and you will be alive once again.*
> Ezekiel 37:14

And who can turn the worst desert of a messed-up past into a life that blossoms like a well-watered garden:

> *"Forget the former things; do not dwell on the past.*
> *See, I am doing a new thing! Now it springs up; do you not perceive it?*
> *I am making a way in the wilderness and streams in the wasteland."*
> Isaiah 43:18-19 NIV

Releasing our past hurts and regrets can be one of the hardest things to do, but is so necessary to live the joyful life God wants is to have. It's not betraying our past, but it's putting it where it belongs – behind us. It's trusting that He is in control, and He something far better planned for us than we hoped for. We'll see it if we keep our focus on Him not the past, trust in Him, and keep moving toward Him.

He's waiting for us to say yes to the life He wants to give us.

Yes!

Are there any "skeletons", old remainders of things from your past, you're still clinging to? This might be regret, blame, guilt, unforgiveness, secrets, relationships or habits we don't want to let go, anything that has happened to us that we don't feel good about and know is wrong for us.

How does holding onto that get in the way of your present joy?

What new things could God create in your life if you made room for them by handing the past to Him?

Is there anything you need to let go of now into God's loving hands, to make space for His plan to blossom into fullness?

Lord, I so want the joy of Your blossoming garden to replace the old dry desert of past hurts and regrets. I want to live abundantly, free and full-bodied rather than as a dusty lifeless skeleton. Please show me where I'm holding onto from my past, looking back rather than forward. Help me to release anything that gets in the way of my joy in You, even if letting go is painful. Help me to feel You peace and our comfort as I release to You anything that gets in the way of the life You intend for me. Thank You!

CHAPTER TWENTY-TWO:
SERMONS AND WOODBOXES

On the afternoon that Pollyanna told John Pendleton of Jimmy Bean, the Rev. Paul Ford climbed the hill and entered the Pendleton Woods, hoping that the hushed beauty of God's out-of-doors would still the tumult that His children of men had wrought.

The Rev. Paul Ford was sick at heart. Month by month, for a year past, conditions in the parish under him had been growing worse and worse; until it seemed that now, turn which way he would, he encountered only wrangling, backbiting, scandal, and jealousy. He had argued, pleaded, rebuked, and ignored by turns; and always and through all he had prayed — earnestly, hopefully. But to-day, miserably, he was forced to own that matters were no better, but rather worse.

Two of his deacons were at swords' points over a silly something that only endless brooding had made of any account. Three of his most energetic women workers had withdrawn from the Ladies' Aid Society because a tiny spark of gossip had been fanned by wagging tongues into a devouring flame of scandal. The choir had split over the amount of solo work given to a fanciedly preferred singer. Even the Christian Endeavor Society was in a ferment of unrest owing to open criticism of two of its officers. As to the Sunday school — it had been the resignation of its superintendent and two of its teachers that had been the last straw, and that had sent the harassed minister to the quiet woods for prayer and meditation.

Under the green arch of the trees the Rev. Paul Ford faced the thing squarely. To his mind, the crisis had come. Something must be done — and done at once. The entire work of the church was at a standstill. The Sunday services, the week-day prayer meeting, the missionary teas, even the suppers and socials were becoming less and less well attended. True, a few conscientious workers were still left. But they pulled at cross purposes, usually; and always they showed themselves to be acutely aware of the critical eyes all about them, and of the tongues that had nothing to do but to talk about what the eyes saw.

And because of all this, the Rev. Paul Ford understood very well that he (God's minister), the church, the town, and even Christianity itself was suffering; and must suffer still more unless —

Clearly something must be done, and done at once. But what?

Slowly the minister took from his pocket the notes he had made for his next Sunday's sermon. Frowningly he looked at them. His mouth settled into stern lines, as aloud, very impressively, he read the verses on which he had determined to speak:

"'But woe unto you, scribes and Pharisees, hypocrites! for ye shut up the kingdom of heaven against men: for ye neither go in yourselves, neither suffer ye them that are entering to go in.'

"'Woe unto you, scribes and Pharisees, hypocrites! for ye devour widows' houses, and for a pretence make long prayer: therefore ye shall receive the greater damnation.'

"'Woe unto you, scribes and Pharisees, hypocrites! for ye pay tithe of mint and anise and cummin, and have omitted the weightier matters of the law, judgment, mercy, and faith: these ought ye to have done, and not to leave the other undone.'"

It was a bitter denunciation. In the green aisles of the woods, the minister's deep voice rang out with scathing effect. Even the birds and squirrels seemed hushed into awed silence. It brought to the minister a vivid realization of how those words would sound the next Sunday when he should utter them before his people in the sacred hush of the church.

His people! — they WERE his people. Could he do it? Dare he do it? Dare he not do it? It was a fearful denunciation, even without the words that would follow — his own words. He had prayed and prayed. He had pleaded earnestly for help, for guidance. He longed — oh, how earnestly he longed! — to take now, in this crisis, the right step. But was this — the right step?

Slowly the minister folded the papers and thrust them back into his pocket. Then, with a sigh that was almost a moan, he flung himself down at the foot of a tree, and covered his face with his hands.

It was there that Pollyanna, on her way home from the Pendleton house, found him. With a little cry she ran forward.

"Oh, oh, Mr. Ford! You — YOU haven't broken YOUR leg or — or anything, have you?" she gasped.

The minister dropped his hands, and looked up quickly. He tried to smile.

"No, dear — no, indeed! I'm just — resting."

"Oh," sighed Pollyanna, falling back a little. "That's all right, then. You see, Mr. Pendleton HAD broken his leg when I found him — but he was lying down, though. And you are sitting up."

"Yes, I am sitting up; and I haven't broken anything — that doctors can mend."

The last words were very low, but Pollyanna heard them. A swift change crossed her face. Her eyes glowed with tender sympathy.

"I know what you mean — something plagues you. Father used to feel like that, lots of times. I reckon ministers do — most generally. You see there's such a lot depends on 'em, somehow."

The Rev. Paul Ford turned a little wonderingly.

"Was YOUR father a minister, Pollyanna?"

"Yes, sir. Didn't you know? I supposed everybody knew that. He married Aunt Polly's sister, and she was my mother."

"Oh, I understand. But, you see, I haven't been here many years, so I don't know all the family histories."

"Yes, sir — I mean, no, sir," smiled Pollyanna.

There was a long pause. The minister, still sitting at the foot of the tree, appeared to have forgotten Pollyanna's presence. He had pulled some papers from his pocket and unfolded them; but he was not looking at them. He was gazing, instead, at a leaf on the ground a little distance away — and it was not even a pretty leaf. It was brown and dead.

Pollyanna, looking at him, felt vaguely sorry for him.

"It — it's a nice day," she began hopefully.

For a moment there was no answer; then the minister looked up with a start.

"What? Oh! — yes, it is a very nice day."

"And 'tisn't cold at all, either, even if 'tis October," observed

Pollyanna, still more hopefully. "Mr. Pendleton had a fire, but he said he didn't need it. It was just to look at. I like to look at fires, don't you?"

There was no reply this time, though Pollyanna waited patiently, before she tried again — by a new route.

"Do you like being a minister?"

The Rev. Paul Ford looked up now, very quickly.

"Do I like — Why, what an odd question! Why do you ask that, my dear?"

"Nothing — only the way you looked. It made me think of my father. He used to look like that — sometimes."

"Did he?" The minister's voice was polite, but his eyes had gone back to the dried leaf on the ground.

"Yes, and I used to ask him just as I did you if he was glad he was a minister."

The man under the tree smiled a little sadly.

"Well — what did he say?"

"Oh, he always said he was, of course, but 'most always he said, too, that he wouldn't STAY a minister a minute if 'twasn't for the rejoicing texts."

"The — WHAT?" The Rev. Paul Ford's eyes left the leaf and gazed wonderingly into Pollyanna's merry little face.

"Well, that's what father used to call 'em," she laughed. "Of course the Bible didn't name 'em that. But it's all those that begin 'Be glad in the Lord,' or 'Rejoice greatly,' or 'Shout for joy,' and all that, you know — such a lot of 'em. Once, when father felt specially bad, he counted 'em. There were eight hundred of 'em."

"Eight hundred!"

"Yes — that told you to rejoice and be glad, you know; that's why father named 'em the 'rejoicing texts.'"

"Oh!" There was an odd look on the minister's face. His eyes had fallen to the words on the top paper in his hands — "But woe unto you, scribes and Pharisees, hypocrites!" "And so your father — liked those 'rejoicing texts,'" he murmured.

"Oh, yes," nodded Pollyanna, emphatically. "He said he felt better right away, that first day he thought to count 'em. He said if God took the trouble to tell us eight hundred times to be glad and rejoice, He must want us to do it — SOME. And father felt ashamed that he hadn't done it more. After that, they got to be such a comfort to him, you know, when things went wrong; when the Ladies' Aiders got to fight — I mean, when they DIDN'T AGREE about something," corrected Pollyanna, hastily. "Why, it was those texts, too, father said, that made HIM think of the game — he began with ME on the crutches — but he said 'twas the rejoicing texts that started him on it."

"And what game might that be?" asked the minister.

"About finding something in everything to be glad about, you know. As I said, he began with me on the crutches." And once more Pollyanna told her story — this time to a man who listened with tender eyes and understanding ears.

A little later Pollyanna and the minister descended the hill, hand in hand. Pollyanna's face was radiant. Pollyanna loved to talk, and she had been talking now for some time: there seemed to be so many, many things about the game, her father, and the old home life that the minister wanted to know.

At the foot of the hill their ways parted, and Pollyanna down one road, and the minister down another, walked on alone.

In the Rev. Paul Ford's study that evening the minister sat thinking.

Near him on the desk lay a few loose sheets of paper — his sermon notes. Under the suspended pencil in his fingers lay other sheets of paper, blank — his sermon to be. But the minister was not thinking either of what he had written, or of what he intended to write. In his imagination he was far away in a little Western town with a missionary minister who was poor, sick, worried, and almost alone in the world — but who was poring over the Bible to find how many times his Lord and Master had told him to "rejoice and be glad."

After a time, with a long sigh, the Rev. Paul Ford roused himself, came back from the far Western town, and adjusted the sheets of paper under his hand.

"Matthew twenty-third; 13 — 14 and 23," he wrote; then, with a gesture of impatience, he dropped his pencil and pulled toward him a magazine left on the desk by his wife a few minutes before. Listlessly his tired eyes turned from paragraph to paragraph until these words arrested them:

"A father one day said to his son, Tom, who, he knew, had refused to fill his mother's woodbox that morning: 'Tom, I'm sure you'll be glad to go and bring in some wood for your mother.' And without a word Tom went. Why? Just because his father showed so plainly that he expected him to do the right thing. Suppose he had said: 'Tom, I overheard what you said to your mother this morning, and I'm ashamed of you. Go at once and fill that woodbox!' I'll warrant that woodbox, would be empty yet, so far as Tom was concerned!"

On and on read the minister — a word here, a line there, a paragraph somewhere else:

"What men and women need is encouragement. Their natural resisting powers should be strengthened, not weakened.... Instead of always harping on a man's faults, tell him of his virtues. Try to pull him out of his rut of bad habits. Hold up to him his better self, his REAL self that can dare and do and win out!... The influence of a beautiful, helpful, hopeful character is contagious, and may revolutionize a whole town....

People radiate what is in their minds and in their hearts. If a man feels kindly and obliging, his neighbors will feel that way, too, before long. But if he scolds and scowls and criticizes — his neighbors will return scowl for scowl, and add interest!... When you look for the bad, expecting it, you will get it. When you know you will find the good — you will get that.... Tell your son Tom you KNOW he'll be glad to fill that woodbox — then watch him start, alert and interested!"

The minister dropped the paper and lifted his chin. In a moment he was on his feet, tramping the narrow room back and forth, back and forth. Later, some time later, he drew a long breath, and dropped himself in the chair at his desk.

"God helping me, I'll do it!" he cried softly. "I'll tell all my Toms I KNOW they'll be glad to fill that woodbox! I'll give them work to do, and I'll make them so full of the very joy of doing it that they won't have TIME to look at their neighbors' woodboxes!" And he picked up his sermon notes, tore straight through the sheets, and cast them from him, so that on one side of his chair lay "But woe unto you," and on the other, "scribes and Pharisees, hypocrites!" while across the smooth white paper before him his pencil fairly flew — after first drawing one black line through Matthew twenty-third; 13 — 14 and 23.

Thus it happened that the Rev. Paul Ford's sermon the next Sunday was a veritable bugle-call to the best that was in every man and woman and child that heard it; and its text was one of Pollyanna's shining eight hundred:

"Be glad in the Lord and rejoice, ye righteous, and shout for joy all ye that are upright in heart."

CHAPTER 22
DEVOTIONAL & JOURNAL

"Eight hundred!"

"Yes — that told you to rejoice and be glad, you know; that's why father named 'em the 'rejoicing texts.'"

"Oh!... And so your father — liked those 'rejoicing texts,'" he murmured.

"Oh, yes," nodded Pollyanna, emphatically. "He said he felt better right away, that first day he thought to count 'em. He said if God took the trouble to tell us eight hundred times to be glad and rejoice, He must want us to do it..."

Before he speaks to Pollyanna, Reverend Ford, the town's minister, would probably have said that his congregation didn't deserve joy. But after talking to Pollyanna and reading these lines in a magazine article —"Instead of always harping on a man's faults, tell him of his virtues.... When you look for the bad, expecting it, you will get it. When you know you will find the good — you will get that...."— he tears up his harsh sermon and instead preaches on one of her rejoicing texts, inspired to lift up his church members and encourage rather than criticize them.

Be glad in the Lord, and rejoice, ye righteous: and shout for joy, all ye that are upright in heart.
Psalm 32:11 KJV

The verse he preaches on is the King James Version, but I love the paraphrase below that also takes in part of the previous verse:

...abiding love surrounds those who trust in the Lord. So rejoice in him, all those who are his, and shout for joy, all those who try to obey him.
Psalm 32:10-11 TLB

We can feel we don't deserve to rejoice, because we know our faults too well. At times for all of us, and all of the time for some of us, we feel we don't belong among the righteous or the upright in heart the traditional translations mention. We all fall short of that. Even now we are following God and know we're saved by Jesus's sacrifice for us, we still slip up and do wrong. We aren't the women we want to be.

But that doesn't mean we don't deserve to rejoice. None of us are righteous by ourselves, only in Him. And that is such a blessing. We don't need to struggle to be perfect. We just need to trust in the Lord, have the will to obey Him, let Him work in us enabling us to do His will, and trust Him to do the rest. We *can* know his abiding love and we *can* rejoice!

Relax, everything's going to be all right; rest, everything's coming together;
open your hearts, love is on the way!
Jude 2 MSG

What is getting in the way of you feeling God's love and rejoicing in Him?

Do you know there's something you need to ask His forgiveness for?

Can you trust that He forgives when you ask, and that you *do* deserve joy?

What does living joyfully mean to you? How does it feel to be glad and rejoice?

Lord, thank You for Your abiding love, and the joy You give when our hearts are right with You. Please give me the will to obey You. Please forgive me where I have fallen short and disobeyed. Help me to trust that Your mighty Spirit will work in me to help me obey You better. Help me to gladly accept Your grace, Your blessing of love and joy. Help me to look for the best in others and in myself, to seek to encourage and support rather than criticize and judge. Thank You!

CHAPTER TWENTY-THREE:
AN ACCIDENT

At Mrs. Snow's request, Pollyanna went one day to Dr. Chilton's office to get the name of a medicine which Mrs. Snow had forgotten. As it chanced, Pollyanna had never before seen the inside of Dr. Chilton's office.

"I've never been to your home before! This IS your home, isn't it?" she said, looking interestedly about her.

The doctor smiled a little sadly.

"Yes — such as 'tis," he answered, as he wrote something on the pad of paper in his hand; "but it's a pretty poor apology for a home, Pollyanna. They're just rooms, that's all — not a home."

Pollyanna nodded her head wisely. Her eyes glowed with sympathetic understanding.

"I know. It takes a woman's hand and heart, or a child's presence to make a home," she said.

"Eh?" The doctor wheeled about abruptly.

"Mr. Pendleton told me," nodded Pollyanna, again; "about the woman's hand and heart, or the child's presence, you know. Why don't you get a woman's hand and heart, Dr. Chilton? Or maybe you'd take Jimmy Bean — if Mr. Pendleton doesn't want him."

Dr. Chilton laughed a little constrainedly.

"So Mr. Pendleton says it takes a woman's hand and heart to make a home, does he?" he asked evasively.

"Yes. He says his is just a house, too. Why don't you, Dr. Chilton?"

"Why don't I — what?" The doctor had turned back to his desk.

"Get a woman's hand and heart. Oh — and I forgot." Pollyanna's face showed suddenly a painful color. "I suppose I ought to tell you. It wasn't Aunt Polly that Mr. Pendleton loved long ago; and so we — we aren't going there to live. You see, I told you it was — but I made a mistake. I hope YOU didn't tell any one," she finished anxiously.

"No — I didn't tell any one, Pollyanna," replied the doctor, a little queerly.

"Oh, that's all right, then," sighed Pollyanna in relief. "You see you're the only one I told, and I thought Mr. Pendleton looked sort of funny when I said I'd told YOU."

"Did he?" The doctor's lips twitched.

"Yes. And of course he wouldn't want many people to know it — when 'twasn't true. But why don't you get a woman's hand and heart, Dr. Chilton?"

There was a moment's silence; then very gravely the doctor said:

"They're not always to be had — for the asking, little girl."

Pollyanna frowned thoughtfully.

"But I should think you could get 'em," she argued. The flattering emphasis was unmistakable.

"Thank you," laughed the doctor, with uplifted eyebrows. Then, gravely again: "I'm afraid some of your older sisters would not be quite so — confident. At least, they — they haven't shown themselves to be so — obliging," he observed.

Pollyanna frowned again. Then her eyes widened in surprise.

"Why, Dr. Chilton, you don't mean — you didn't try to get somebody's hand and heart once, like Mr. Pendleton, and — and couldn't, did you?"

The doctor got to his feet a little abruptly.

"There, there, Pollyanna, never mind about that now. Don't let other people's troubles worry your little head. Suppose you run back now to Mrs. Snow. I've written down the name of the medicine, and the directions how she is to take it. Was there anything else?"

Pollyanna shook her head.

"No, Sir; thank you, Sir," she murmured soberly, as she turned toward the door. From the little hallway she called back, her face suddenly alight: "Anyhow, I'm glad 'twasn't my mother's hand and heart that you wanted and couldn't get, Dr. Chilton. Good-by!"

It was on the last day of October that the accident occurred. Pollyanna, hurrying home from school, crossed the road at an apparently safe distance in front of a swiftly approaching motor car.

Just what happened, no one could seem to tell afterward. Neither was there any one found who could tell why it happened or who was to blame that it did happen. Pollyanna, however, at five o'clock, was borne, limp and unconscious, into the little room that was so dear to her. There, by a white-faced Aunt Polly and a weeping Nancy she was undressed tenderly and put to bed, while from the village, hastily summoned by telephone, Dr. Warren was hurrying as fast as another motor car could bring him.

"And ye didn't need ter more'n look at her aunt's face," Nancy was sobbing to Old Tom in the garden, after the doctor had arrived and was closeted in the hushed room; "ye didn't need ter more'n look at her aunt's face ter see that 'twa'n't no duty that was eatin' her. Yer hands don't shake, and yer eyes don't look as if ye was tryin' ter hold back the Angel o' Death himself, when you're jest doin' yer DUTY, Mr. Tom they don't, they don't!"

"Is she hurt — bad?" The old man's voice shook.

"There ain't no tellin'," sobbed Nancy. "She lay back that white an' still she might easy be dead; but Miss Polly said she wa'n't dead — an' Miss Polly had oughter know, if any one would — she kept up such a listenin' an' a feelin' for her heartbeats an' her breath!"

"Couldn't ye tell anythin' what it done to her? — that — that — " Old Tom's face worked convulsively.

Nancy's lips relaxed a little.

"I wish ye WOULD call it somethin', Mr. Tom an' somethin' good an' strong, too. Drat it! Ter think of its runnin' down our little girl! I always hated the evil-smellin' things, anyhow — I did, I did!"

"But where is she hurt?"

"I don't know, I don't know," moaned Nancy. "There's a little cut on her blessed head, but 'tain't bad — that ain't — Miss Polly says. She says she's afraid it's infernally she's hurt."

A faint flicker came into Old Tom's eyes.

"I guess you mean internally, Nancy," he said dryly. "She's hurt infernally, all right — plague take that autymobile! — but I don't guess Miss Polly'd be usin' that word, all the same."

"Eh? Well, I don't know, I don't know," moaned Nancy, with a shake of her head as she turned away. "Seems as if I jest couldn't stand it till that doctor gits out o' there. I wish I had a washin' ter do — the biggest washin' I ever see, I do, I do!" she wailed, wringing her hands helplessly.

Even after the doctor was gone, however, there seemed to be little that Nancy could tell Mr. Tom. There appeared to be no bones broken, and the cut was of slight consequence; but the doctor had looked very grave, had shaken his head slowly, and had said that time alone could tell. After he had gone, Miss Polly had shown a face even whiter and more drawn looking than before. The patient had not fully recovered consciousness, but at present she seemed to be resting as comfortably as could be expected. A trained nurse had been sent for, and would come that night.

That was all. And Nancy turned sobbingly, and went back to her kitchen.

It was sometime during the next forenoon that Pollyanna opened conscious eyes and realized where she was.

"Why, Aunt Polly, what's the matter? Isn't it daytime? Why don't I get up?" she cried. "Why, Aunt Polly, I can't get up," she moaned, falling back on the pillow, after an ineffectual attempt to lift herself.

"No, dear, I wouldn't try — just yet," soothed her aunt quickly, but very quietly.

"But what is the matter? Why can't I get up?"

Miss Polly's eyes asked an agonized question of the white-capped young woman standing in the window, out of the range of Pollyanna's eyes.

The young woman nodded.

"Tell her," the lips said.

Miss Polly cleared her throat, and tried to swallow the lump that would scarcely let her speak.

"You were hurt, dear, by the automobile last night. But never mind that now. Auntie wants you to rest and go to sleep again."

"Hurt? Oh, yes; I — I ran." Pollyanna's eyes were dazed. She lifted her hand to her forehead. "Why, it's — done up, and it — hurts!"

"Yes, dear; but never mind. Just — just rest."

"But, Aunt Polly, I feel so funny, and so bad! My legs feel so — so queer — only they don't FEEL — at all!"

With an imploring look into the nurse's face, Miss Polly struggled to her feet, and turned away. The nurse came forward quickly.

"Suppose you let me talk to you now," she began cheerily. "I'm sure I think it's high time we were getting acquainted, and I'm going to introduce myself. I am Miss Hunt, and I've come to help your aunt take care of you. And the very first thing I'm going to do is to ask you to swallow these little white pills for me."

Pollyanna's eyes grew a bit wild.

"But I don't want to be taken care of — that is, not for long! I want to get up. You know I go to school. Can't I go to school to-morrow?"

From the window where Aunt Polly stood now there came a half-stifled cry.

"To-morrow?" smiled the nurse, brightly. "Well, I may not let you out quite so soon as that, Miss Pollyanna. But just swallow these little pills for me, please, and we'll see what THEY'LL do."

"All right," agreed Pollyanna, somewhat doubtfully; "but I MUST go to school day after to-morrow — there are examinations then, you know."

She spoke again, a minute later. She spoke of school, and of the automobile, and of how her head ached; but very soon her voice trailed into silence under the blessed influence of the little white pills she had swallowed.

CHAPTER 23
DEVOTIONAL & JOURNAL

"I've never been to your home before! This IS your home, isn't it?" she said, looking interestedly about her.

The doctor smiled a little sadly. "Yes — such as 'tis," he answered, as he wrote something on the pad of paper in his hand; "but it's a pretty poor apology for a home, Pollyanna. They're just rooms, that's all — not a home."

Pollyanna nodded her head wisely. Her eyes glowed with sympathetic understanding. "I know. It takes a woman's hand and heart, or a child's presence to make a home," she said.... "But why don't you get a woman's hand and heart, Dr. Chilton?"

There was a moment's silence; then very gravely the doctor said: "They're not always to be had for the asking, little girl."

Dr. Chilton lives a lot less than joyfully, in hired rooms rather than a home, twenty years after the woman he loved refused him. It can be hard to trust that God has a plan and purpose for our good when we don't get something we deeply desire, like a happy marriage. I don't think it was just me feeling like that when all my friends were getting married, and I seemed permanently single!

> *Take delight in the Lord, and he will give you the desires of your heart.*
> Psalm 37:4 NIV

This verse is often used as if God is some sort of fairy godmother, or a cosmic slot machine who will give us the candy we want if we feed in enough devotion pennies! But thinking of it that way can make us feel that if we don't have everything we desire, we're not good enough to be given what we want, or we're somehow failing in our spiritual life.

In the Good News Translation the first part of the verse is translated as *Seek your happiness in the Lord.* If what we most want and what we know with make us most happy is God, we always get our heart's desire — in God, who is always there for us!

There's an Ann Landers joke that goes: "The poor wish to be rich, the rich wish to be happy, the single wish to be married, and the married wish to be dead." Extreme, but honest! If our happiness is based on our circumstance, we'll never be happy. When we're single, we can blame our lack of joy on our singleness. Or married people longing for a more satisfying life can blame their marriage.

Either way, we're giving another person, whether the spouse we're with or the spouse we long for, too much power over our experience of joy. No man or woman, no matter how wonderful, can meet all our emotional needs. Only God can do that.

I came to give life with joy and abundance.
John 10:10 VOICE

Whether you're married or single, how does that affect your ability to live joyfully?

If you're single and the longing to be married is stealing your joy, can you hand that desire over to God and seek Him first? Or if you're married and living less than joyfully, can you stop blaming your spouse and hoping they'll change enough to make you happy, and seek your happiness in God instead?

What changes would seeking happiness in the Lord before anything else create in your life?

Lord, I want to seek my happiness and my delight in You instead of hoping someone else will make me happy. You love me with an unfailing love, deeper and truer than any person could ever love me. If I'm single, please help me to be joyfully single. If I'm married, please help me to be joyfully married. Help me to trust that You have a plan and a purpose for my highest good. Whether I am married or single, help me to live my life to the full, focused on You. Thank You!

CHAPTER TWENTY-FOUR:
JOHN PENDLETON

Pollyanna did not go to school "to-morrow," nor the "day after to-morrow." Pollyanna, however, did not realize this, except momentarily when a brief period of full consciousness sent insistent questions to her lips. Pollyanna did not realize anything, in fact, very clearly until a week had passed; then the fever subsided, the pain lessened somewhat, and her mind awoke to full consciousness. She had then to be told all over again what had occurred.

"And so it's hurt that I am, and not sick," she sighed at last. "Well, I'm glad of that."

"G-glad, Pollyanna?" asked her aunt, who was sitting by the bed.

"Yes. I'd so much rather have broken legs like Mr. Pendleton's than life-long-invalids like Mrs. Snow, you know. Broken legs get well, and lifelong-invalids don't."

Miss Polly — who had said nothing whatever about broken legs — got suddenly to her feet and walked to the little dressing table across the room. She was picking up one object after another now, and putting each down, in an aimless fashion quite unlike her usual decisiveness. Her face was not aimless-looking at all, however; it was white and drawn.

On the bed Pollyanna lay blinking at the dancing band of colors on the ceiling, which came from one of the prisms in the window. "I'm glad it isn't smallpox that ails me, too," she murmured contentedly. "That would be worse than freckles. And I'm glad 'tisn't whooping cough — I've had that, and it's horrid — and I'm glad 'tisn't appendicitis nor measles, 'cause they're catching — measles are, I mean — and they wouldn't let you stay here."

"You seem to — to be glad for a good many things, my dear," faltered Aunt Polly, putting her hand to her throat as if her collar bound.

Pollyanna laughed softly.

"I am. I've been thinking of 'em — lots of 'em — all the time I've been looking up at that rainbow. I love rainbows. I'm so glad Mr. Pendleton gave me those prisms! I'm glad of some things I haven't said yet. I don't know but I'm 'most glad I was hurt."

"Pollyanna!"

Pollyanna laughed softly again. She turned luminous eyes on her aunt. "Well, you see, since I have been hurt, you've called me 'dear' lots of times — and you didn't before. I love to be called 'dear' — by folks that belong to you, I mean. Some of the Ladies' Aiders did call me that; and of course that was pretty nice, but not so nice as if they had belonged to me, like you do. Oh, Aunt Polly, I'm so glad you belong to me!"

Aunt Polly did not answer. Her hand was at her throat again. Her eyes were full of tears. She had turned away and was hurrying from the room through the door by which the nurse had just entered.

It was that afternoon that Nancy ran out to Old Tom, who was cleaning harnesses in the barn. Her eyes were wild.

"Mr. Tom, Mr. Tom, guess what's happened," she panted. "You couldn't guess in a thousand years — you couldn't, you couldn't!"

"Then I cal'late I won't try," retorted the man, grimly, "specially as I hain't got more'n TEN ter live, anyhow, probably. You'd better tell me first off, Nancy."

"Well, listen, then. Who do you s'pose is in the parlor now with the mistress? Who, I say?"

Old Tom shook his head.

"There's no tellin'," he declared.

"Yes, there is. I'm tellin'. It's — John Pendleton!"

"Sho, now! You're jokin', girl."

"Not much I am — an' me a-lettin' him in myself — crutches an' all! An' the team he come in a-waitin' this minute at the door for him, jest as if he wa'n't the cranky old crosspatch he is, what never talks ter no one! jest think, Mr. Tom — HIM a-callin' on HER!"

"Well, why not?" demanded the old man, a little aggressively.

Nancy gave him a scornful glance.

"As if you didn't know better'n me!" she derided.

"Eh?"

"Oh, you needn't be so innercent," she retorted with mock indignation; " — you what led me wild goose chasin' in the first place!"

"What do ye mean?"

Nancy glanced through the open barn door toward the house, and came a step nearer to the old man.

"Listen! 'Twas you that was tellin' me Miss Polly had a lover in the first place, wa'n't it? Well, one day I thinks I finds two and two, and I puts 'em together an' makes four. But it turns out ter be five — an' no four at all, at all!"

With a gesture of indifference Old Tom turned and fell to work.

"If you're goin' ter talk ter me, you've got ter talk plain horse sense," he declared testily. "I never was no hand for figgers."

Nancy laughed.

"Well, it's this," she explained. "I heard somethin' that made me think him an' Miss Polly was lovers."

"MR. PENDLETON!" Old Tom straightened up.

"Yes. Oh, I know now; he wasn't. It was that blessed child's mother he was in love with, and that's why he wanted — but never mind that part," she added hastily, remembering just in time her promise to Pollyanna not to tell that Mr. Pendleton had wished her to come and live with him. "Well, I've been askin' folks about him some, since, and I've found out that him an' Miss Polly hain't been friends for years, an' that she's been hatin' him like pizen owin' ter the silly gossip that coupled their names tergether when she was eighteen or twenty."

"Yes, I remember," nodded Old Tom. "It was three or four years after Miss Jennie give him the mitten and went off with the other chap. Miss Polly knew about it, of course, and was sorry for him. So she tried ter be nice to him. Maybe she overdid it a little — she hated that minister chap so who had took off her sister. At any rate, somebody begun ter make trouble. They said she was runnin' after him."

"Runnin' after any man — her!" interjected Nancy.

"I know it; but they did," declared Old Tom, "and of course no gal of any spunk'll stand that. Then about that time come her own lover an' the trouble with HIM. After that she shut up like an oyster an' wouldn't have nothin' ter do with nobody fur a spell. Her heart jest seemed to turn bitter at the core."

"Yes, I know. I've heard about that now," rejoined Nancy; "an' that's why you could 'a' knocked me down with a feather when I see HIM at the door — him, what she hain't spoke to for years! But I let him in an' went an' told her."

"What did she say?" Old Tom held his breath suspended.

"Nothin' — at first. She was so still I thought she hadn't heard; and I was jest goin' ter say it over when she speaks up quiet like: 'Tell Mr. Pendleton I will be down at once.' An' I come an' told him. Then I come out here an' told you," finished Nancy, casting another backward glance toward the house.

"Humph!" grunted Old Tom; and fell to work again.

In the ceremonious "parlor" of the Harrington homestead, Mr. John Pendleton did not have to wait long before a swift step warned him of Miss Polly's coming. As he attempted to rise, she made a gesture of remonstrance. She did not offer her hand, however, and her face was coldly reserved.

"I called to ask for — Pollyanna," he began at once, a little brusquely.

"Thank you. She is about the same," said Miss Polly.

"And that is — won't you tell me HOW she is?" His voice was not quite steady this time.

A quick spasm of pain crossed the woman's face.

"I can't, I wish I could!"

"You mean — you don't know?"

"Yes."

"But — the doctor?"

"Dr. Warren himself seems — at sea. He is in correspondence now with a New York specialist. They have arranged for a consultation at once."

"But — but what WERE her injuries that you do know?"

"A slight cut on the head, one or two bruises, and — and an injury to the spine which has seemed to cause — paralysis from the hips down."

A low cry came from the man. There was a brief silence; then, huskily, he asked:

"And Pollyanna — how does she — take it?"

"She doesn't understand — at all — how things really are. And I CAN'T tell her."

"But she must know — something!"

Miss Polly lifted her hand to the collar at her throat in the gesture that had become so common to her of late.

"Oh, yes. She knows she can't — move; but she thinks her legs are — broken. She says she's glad it's broken legs like yours rather than 'lifelong-invalids' like Mrs. Snow's; because broken legs get well, and the other — doesn't. She talks like that all the time, until it — it seems as if I should — die!"

Through the blur of tears in his own eyes, the man saw the drawn face opposite, twisted with emotion. Involuntarily his thoughts went back to what Pollyanna had said when he had made his final plea for her presence: "Oh, I couldn't leave Aunt Polly — now!"

It was this thought that made him ask very gently, as soon as he could control his voice:

"I wonder if you know, Miss Harrington, how hard I tried to get Pollyanna to come and live with me."

"With YOU! — Pollyanna!"

The man winced a little at the tone of her voice; but his own voice was still impersonally cool when he spoke again.

"Yes. I wanted to adopt her — legally, you understand; making her my heir, of course."

The woman in the opposite chair relaxed a little. It came to her, suddenly, what a brilliant future it would have meant for Pollyanna — this adoption; and she wondered if Pollyanna were old enough and mercenary enough — to be tempted by this man's money and position.

"I am very fond of Pollyanna," the man was continuing. "I am fond of her both for her own sake, and for — her mother's. I stood ready to give Pollyanna the love that had been twenty-five years in storage."

"LOVE." Miss Polly remembered suddenly why SHE had taken this child in the first place — and with the recollection came the remembrance of Pollyanna's own words uttered that very morning: "I love to be called 'dear' by folks that belong to you!" And it was this love-hungry little girl that had been offered the stored-up affection of twenty-five years: — and she was old enough to be tempted by love! With a sinking heart Miss Polly realized that. With a sinking heart, too, she realized something else: the dreariness of her own future now without Pollyanna.

"Well?" she said.

And the man, recognizing the self-control that vibrated through the harshness of the tone, smiled sadly.

"She would not come," he answered.

"Why?"

"She would not leave you. She said you had been so good to her. She wanted to stay with you — and she said she THOUGHT you wanted her to stay," he finished, as he pulled himself to his feet.

He did not look toward Miss Polly. He turned his face resolutely toward the door. But instantly he heard a swift step at his side, and found a shaking hand thrust toward him.

"When the specialist comes, and I know anything — definite about Pollyanna, I will let you hear from me," said a trembling voice. "Good-by — and thank you for coming. Pollyanna will be pleased."

CHAPTER 24
DEVOTIONAL & JOURNAL

"After that she shut up like an oyster an' wouldn't have nothin' ter do with nobody fur a spell. Her heart jest seemed to turn bitter at the core."

Miss Polly has lived most of her life with a hardened bitter heart, after being hurt by loss. Injuries can leave scars, on our spirits and emotions as much as on our bodies. The hearts that start out being most tender can end with the hardest scars.

Many of us are better at hiding our scars than Miss Polly is. For too many years, I had a damaged and bitter heart, without even realizing it. Signs might be relationships that don't last, whether that's short-lived friendships, romantic relationships that fizzle after a few dates, or estrangement from family. Persistent lack of joy and being angry with God may also be signs.

When we've been hurt, holding onto bitterness and resentment can seem reasonable to our human logic. It feels natural to want to defend ourselves from future heartbreak. It's someone else who has a bitterness issue. We have righteous anger. Or so we can think, to justify holding onto it.

Thankfully, God uses a different logic! Because bitterness, resentment and hardness of heart kill our joy and block us from feeling His love, He seeks to transform them.

And I will give them singleness of heart and put a new spirit within them.
I will take away their stony, stubborn heart and give them a tender, responsive heart.
Ezekiel 11:19 NLT

First, we need to be willing to admit to it. If ask God's forgiveness, He will help. We need to be kind and compassionate, both to ourselves, and to anyone who hurt us. We need to forgive ourselves, and them. We need to trust that God will take care of it. He heals hurting hearts, and makes them new.

Make a list of everyone you feel any anger or resentment toward (you may want to use scrap paper for this one, so you can destroy it afterwards). Add to the list anyone who has hurt you in any way, and who you know in your heart you haven't quite forgiven. Be completely honest. No one but you will see this list. You may find God is on the list. You may find your own name is on the list!

Ask God to soften your heart and give you compassion for everyone whose name is on the list. Even Him. And even you! *Especially* you. We can't forgive others until we accept God's loving forgiveness for ourselves. So open your heart to His forgiveness first. Then pray for every name on the list. It's not easy to pray for those we feel angry with, but once we do pray for them, it becomes impossible to hold onto unforgiveness. What did you feel as you prayed?

Destroy the list. Trust that God will work in your heart and mind. Trust that as bitterness is rooted out, joy can grow in its place. Trust that God will protect your newly softened heart. Be ready to feel again!

Lord, please show me if there's anger, resentment, or bitterness I've refused to let go of, hidden in my heart and mind. I know and trust that You can heal those hurts and soften any hardness in my heart. Help me to release the hurt and the anger to You, knowing You are big enough to handle it. Give me a tender and responsive heart of compassion and forgiveness, toward You, toward myself, and toward anyone else who has hurt me. As I let go of bitterness, please fill that space with joy and love.
Thank you!

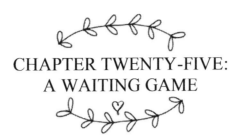

CHAPTER TWENTY-FIVE:
A WAITING GAME

On the day after John Pendleton's call at the Harrington homestead, Miss Polly set herself to the task of preparing Pollyanna for the visit of the specialist.

"Pollyanna, my dear," she began gently, "we have decided that we want another doctor besides Dr. Warren to see you. Another one might tell us something new to do — to help you get well faster, you know."

A joyous light came to Pollyanna's face.

"Dr. Chilton! Oh, Aunt Polly, I'd so love to have Dr. Chilton! I've wanted him all the time, but I was afraid you didn't, on account of his seeing you in the sun parlor that day, you know; so I didn't like to say anything. But I'm so glad you do want him!"

Aunt Polly's face had turned white, then red, then back to white again. But when she answered, she showed very plainly that she was trying to speak lightly and cheerfully.

"Oh, no, dear! It wasn't Dr. Chilton at all that I meant. It is a new doctor — a very famous doctor from New York, who — who knows a great deal about — about hurts like yours."

Pollyanna's face fell.

"I don't believe he knows half so much as Dr. Chilton."

"Oh, yes, he does, I'm sure, dear."

"But it was Dr. Chilton who doctored Mr. Pendleton's broken leg, Aunt Polly. If — if you don't mind VERY much, I WOULD LIKE to have Dr. Chilton — truly I would!"

A distressed color suffused Miss Polly's face. For a moment she did not speak at all; then she said gently — though yet with a touch of her old stern decisiveness:

"But I do mind, Pollyanna. I mind very much. I would do anything — almost anything for you, my dear; but I — for reasons which I do not care to speak of now, I don't wish Dr. Chilton called in on — on this case. And believe me, he can NOT know so much about — about your trouble, as this great doctor does, who will come from New York to-morrow."

Pollyanna still looked unconvinced.

"But, Aunt Polly, if you LOVED Dr. Chilton — "

"WHAT, Pollyanna?" Aunt Polly's voice was very sharp now. Her cheeks were very red, too.

"I say, if you loved Dr. Chilton, and didn't love the other one," sighed Pollyanna, "seems to me that would make some difference in the good he would do; and I love Dr. Chilton."

The nurse entered the room at that moment, and Aunt Polly rose to her feet abruptly, a look of relief on her face.

"I am very sorry, Pollyanna," she said, a little stiffly; "but I'm afraid you'll have to let me be the judge, this time. Besides, it's already arranged. The New York doctor is coming to-morrow."

As it happened, however, the New York doctor did not come "to-morrow." At the last moment a telegram told of an unavoidable delay owing to the sudden illness of the specialist himself. This led Pollyanna into a renewed pleading for the substitution of Dr. Chilton — "which would be so easy now, you know."

But as before, Aunt Polly shook her head and said "no, dear," very decisively, yet with a still more anxious assurance that she would do anything — anything but that — to please her dear Pollyanna.

As the days of waiting passed, one by one, it did indeed, seem that Aunt Polly was doing everything (but that) that she could do to please her niece.

"I wouldn't 'a' believed it — you couldn't 'a' made me believe it," Nancy said to Old Tom one morning. "There don't seem ter be a minute in the day that Miss Polly ain't jest hangin' 'round waitin' ter do somethin' for that blessed lamb if 'tain't more than ter let in the cat — an' her what wouldn't let Fluff nor Buff up-stairs for love nor money a week ago; an' now she lets 'em tumble all over the bed jest 'cause it pleases Miss Pollyanna!

"An' when she ain't doin' nothin' else, she's movin' them little glass danglers 'round ter diff'rent winders in the room so the sun'll make the 'rainbows dance,' as that blessed child calls it. She's sent Timothy down ter Cobb's greenhouse three times for fresh flowers — an' that besides all the posies fetched in ter her, too. An' the other day, if I didn't find her sittin' 'fore the bed with the nurse actually doin' her hair, an' Miss Pollyanna lookin' on an' bossin' from the bed, her eyes all shinin' an' happy. An' I declare ter goodness, if Miss Polly hain't wore her hair like that every day now — jest ter please that blessed child!"

Old Tom chuckled.

"Well, it strikes me Miss Polly herself ain't lookin' none the worse — for wearin' them 'ere curls 'round her forehead," he observed dryly.

"Course she ain't," retorted Nancy, indignantly. "She looks like FOLKS, now. She's actually almost — "

"Keerful, now, Nancy!" interrupted the old man, with a slow grin. "You know what you said when I told ye she was handsome once."

Nancy shrugged her shoulders.

"Oh, she ain't handsome, of course; but I will own up she don't look like the same woman, what with the ribbons an' lace jiggers Miss Pollyanna makes her wear 'round her neck."

"I told ye so," nodded the man. "I told ye she wa'n't — old."

Nancy laughed.

"Well, I'll own up she HAIN'T got quite so good an imitation of it — as she did have, 'fore Miss Pollyanna come. Say, Mr. Tom, who WAS her lover? I hain't found that out, yet; I hain't, I hain't!"

"Hain't ye?" asked the old man, with an odd look on his face. "Well, I guess ye won't then from me."

"Oh, Mr. Tom, come on, now," wheedled the girl. "Ye see, there ain't many folks here that I CAN ask."

"Maybe not. But there's one, anyhow, that ain't answerin'," grinned Old Tom. Then, abruptly, the light died from his eyes. "How is she, ter-day — the little gal?"

Nancy shook her head. Her face, too, had sobered.

"Just the same, Mr. Tom. There ain't no special diff'rence, as I can see — or anybody, I guess. She jest lays there an' sleeps an' talks some, an' tries ter smile an' be 'glad' 'cause the sun sets or the moon rises, or some other such thing, till it's enough ter make yer heart break with achin'."

"I know; it's the 'game' — bless her sweet heart!" nodded Old Tom, blinking a little.

"She told YOU, then, too, about that 'ere — game?"

"Oh, yes. She told me long ago." The old man hesitated, then went on, his lips twitching a little. "I was growlin' one day 'cause I was so bent up and crooked; an' what do ye s'pose the little thing said?"

"I couldn't guess. I wouldn't think she could find ANYTHIN' about THAT ter be glad about!"

"She did. She said I could be glad, anyhow, that I didn't have ter STOOP SO FAR TER DO MY WEEDIN' 'cause I was already bent part way over."

Nancy gave a wistful laugh.

"Well, I ain't surprised, after all. You might know she'd find somethin'. We've been playin' it — that game — since almost the first, 'cause there wa'n't no one else she could play it with — though she did speak of — her aunt."

"MISS POLLY!"

Nancy chuckled.

"I guess you hain't got such an awful diff'rent opinion o' the mistress than I have," she bridled.

Old Tom stiffened.

"I was only thinkin' 'twould be — some of a surprise — to her," he explained with dignity.

"Well, yes, I guess 'twould be — THEN," retorted Nancy. "I ain't sayin' what 'twould be NOW. I'd believe anythin' o' the mistress now — even that she'd take ter playin' it herself!"

"But hain't the little gal told her — ever? She's told ev'ry one else, I guess. I'm hearin' of it ev'rywhere, now, since she was hurted," said Tom.

"Well, she didn't tell Miss Polly," rejoined Nancy. "Miss Pollyanna told me long ago that she couldn't tell her, 'cause her aunt didn't like ter have her talk about her father; an' 'twas her father's game, an' she'd have ter talk about him if she did tell it. So she never told her."

"Oh, I see, I see." The old man nodded his head slowly. "They was always bitter against the minister chap — all of 'em, 'cause he took Miss Jennie away from 'em. An' Miss Polly — young as she was — couldn't never forgive him; she was that fond of Miss Jennie — in them days. I see, I see. 'Twas a bad mess," he sighed, as he turned away.

"Yes, 'twas — all 'round, all 'round," sighed Nancy in her turn, as she went back to her kitchen.

For no one were those days of waiting easy. The nurse tried to look cheerful, but her eyes were troubled. The doctor was openly nervous and impatient. Miss Polly said little; but even the softening waves of hair about her face, and the becoming laces at her throat, could not hide the fact that she was growing thin and pale. As to Pollyanna — Pollyanna petted the dog, smoothed the cat's sleek head, admired the flowers and ate the fruits and jellies that were sent in to her; and returned innumerable cheery answers to the many messages of love and inquiry that were brought to her bedside. But she, too, grew pale and thin; and the nervous activity of the poor little hands and arms only emphasized the pitiful motionlessness of the once active little feet and legs now lying so woefully quiet under the blankets.

As to the game — Pollyanna told Nancy these days how glad she was going to be when she could go to school again, go to see Mrs. Snow, go to call on Mr. Pendleton, and go to ride with Dr. Chilton, nor did she seem to realize that all this "gladness" was in the future, not the present.

Nancy, however, did realize it — and cry about it, when she was alone.

CHAPTER 25
DEVOTIONAL & JOURNAL

"As to the game — Pollyanna told Nancy these days how glad she was going to be when she could go to school again, go to see Mrs. Snow, go to call on Mr. Pendleton, and go to ride with Dr. Chilton: nor did she seem to realize that all this "gladness" was in the future, not the present."

After an injury confines Pollyanna to bed, she can't find gladness in what's happening in the present, only in her hopes for the future. It's such a very human thing to pin our happiness on something we hope will happen in the future. Thankfully, God promises Christians an amazing future! We have so much to hope for.

I heard a loud voice from the throne.
It said, "Now God's home is with people. He will live with them. They will be his people. God
himself will be with them and will be their God.
He will wipe away every tear from their eyes. There will be no more death, sadness, crying, or pain.
All the old ways are gone."
Revelation 21:3-4 ERV

Though it's wonderful to know God has a glorious future planned for believers, by itself, I don't find hope of a better future enough to give me true joy in the present, where there *is* sadness, crying, and pain still!

God has freed us from the power of darkness,
and he brought us into the kingdom of his dear Son.
Colossians 1:13 NCV

What I'm only beginning to realize is that we don't have to wait till the future to live with God. His Kingdom starts here and now, in the heart of every believer. He is with us always, through Jesus's loving presence and through His Spirit. He wants us to feel His joy today, not sometime far off in the future.

May the God of hope fill you with all joy and peace as you trust in him,
so that you may overflow with hope by the power of the Holy Spirit.
Romans 15:13 NIV

I love this definition of joy by Kay Warren: "the settled assurance that God is in control of all the details of my life, the quiet confidence that ultimately everything is going to be alright, and the determined choice to praise God in every situation."

Even when things hurt and feel painful to get through, God is with us, willing to carry us through. I'm learning to let go of needing to be in control, and surrender my life completely to God. All I need to do is trust Him, thank Him, and praise Him. He takes care of the rest.

What future event are you waiting for that you hope will make you happier?

Does the hope of future happiness truly sustain you when times are tough?

What hard thing in your life is God asking you to trust Him with right now? Are you willing to hand control over to Him?

What blessings already present in your life do you need to thank God for?

Lord, thank You for the hope you give us of a wonderful future with You. Help me to trust You, not only with my hope of eternal life in You, but with my life right now. Trusting You in this present moment is the only way to real peace and joy, as I rest in You and let You take control. Help me to choose to praise You and to give thanks to You, no matter what my current situation is. Thank You!

CHAPTER TWENTY-SIX:
A DOOR AJAR

Just a week from the time Dr. Mead, the specialist, was first expected, he came. He was a tall, broad-shouldered man with kind gray eyes, and a cheerful smile. Pollyanna liked him at once, and told him so.

"You look quite a lot like MY doctor, you see," she added engagingly.

"YOUR doctor?" Dr. Mead glanced in evident surprise at Dr. Warren, talking with the nurse a few feet away. Dr. Warren was a small, brown-eyed man with a pointed brown beard.

"Oh, THAT isn't my doctor," smiled Pollyanna, divining his thought. "Dr. Warren is Aunt Polly's doctor. My doctor is Dr. Chilton."

"Oh-h!" said Dr. Mead, a little oddly, his eyes resting on Miss Polly, who, with a vivid blush, had turned hastily away.

"Yes." Pollyanna hesitated, then continued with her usual truthfulness. "You see, *I* wanted Dr. Chilton all the time, but Aunt Polly wanted you. She said you knew more than Dr. Chilton, anyway about — about broken legs like mine. And of course if you do, I can be glad for that. Do you?"

A swift something crossed the doctor's face that Pollyanna could not quite translate.

"Only time can tell that, little girl," he said gently; then he turned a grave face toward Dr. Warren, who had just come to the bedside.

Every one said afterward that it was the cat that did it. Certainly, if Fluffy had not poked an insistent paw and nose against Pollyanna's unlatched door, the door would not have swung noiselessly open on its hinges until it stood perhaps a foot ajar; and if the door had not been open, Pollyanna would not have heard her aunt's words.

In the hall the two doctors, the nurse, and Miss Polly stood talking. In Pollyanna's room Fluffy had just jumped to the bed with a little purring "meow" of joy when through the open door sounded clearly and sharply Aunt Polly's agonized exclamation.

"Not that! Doctor, not that! You don't mean — the child — will NEVER WALK again!"

It was all confusion then. First, from the bedroom came Pollyanna's terrified "Aunt Polly Aunt Polly!" Then Miss Polly, seeing the open door and realizing that her words had been heard, gave a low little moan and — for the first time in her life — fainted dead away.

The nurse, with a choking "She heard!" stumbled toward the open door. The two doctors stayed with Miss Polly. Dr. Mead had to stay — he had caught Miss Polly as she fell.

Dr. Warren stood by, helplessly. It was not until Pollyanna cried out again sharply and the nurse closed the door, that the two men, with a despairing glance into each other's eyes, awoke to the immediate duty of bringing the woman in Dr. Mead's arms back to unhappy consciousness.

In Pollyanna's room, the nurse had found a purring gray cat on the bed vainly trying to attract the attention of a white-faced, wild-eyed little girl. "Miss Hunt, please, I want Aunt Polly. I want her right away, quick, please!"

The nurse closed the door and came forward hurriedly. Her face was very pale. She — she can't come just this minute, dear. She will — a little later. What is it? Can't I — get it?"

Pollyanna shook her head. "But I want to know what she said — just now. Did you hear her? I want Aunt Polly — she said something. I want her to tell me 'tisn't true — 'tisn't true!"

The nurse tried to speak, but no words came. Something in her face sent an added terror to Pollyanna's eyes.

"Miss Hunt, you DID hear her! It is true! Oh, it isn't true! You don't mean I can't ever — walk again?"

"There, there, dear — don't, don't!" choked the nurse. "Perhaps he didn't know. Perhaps he was mistaken. There's lots of things that could happen, you know."

"But Aunt Polly said he did know! She said he knew more than anybody else about — about broken legs like mine!"

"Yes, yes, I know, dear; but all doctors make mistakes sometimes. Just — just don't think any more about it now — please don't, dear."

Pollyanna flung out her arms wildly. "But I can't help thinking about it," she sobbed. "It's all there is now to think about. Why, Miss Hunt, how am I going to school, or to see Mr. Pendleton, or Mrs. Snow, or — or anybody?" She caught her breath and sobbed wildly for a moment. Suddenly she stopped and looked up, a new terror in her eyes. "Why, Miss Hunt, if I can't walk, how am I ever going to be glad for — ANYTHING?"

Miss Hunt did not know "the game;" but she did know that her patient must be quieted, and that at once. In spite of her own perturbation and heartache, her hands had not been idle, and she stood now at the bedside with the quieting powder ready. "There, there, dear, just take this," she soothed; "and by and by we'll be more rested, and we'll see what can be done then. Things aren't half as bad as they seem, dear, lots of times, you know."

Obediently Pollyanna took the medicine, and sipped the water from the glass in Miss Hunt's hand. "I know; that sounds like things father used to say," faltered Pollyanna, blinking off the tears. "He said there was always something about everything that might be worse; but I reckon he'd never just heard he couldn't ever walk again. I don't see how there CAN be anything about that, that could be worse — do you?"

Miss Hunt did not reply. She could not trust herself to speak just then.

CHAPTER 26
DEVOTIONAL & JOURNAL

"That sounds like things father used to say," faltered Pollyanna, blinking off the tears. "He said there was always something about everything that might be worse; but I reckon he'd never just heard he couldn't ever walk again. I don't see how there CAN be anything about that, that could be worse — do you?"

Pollyanna overhears the doctors telling Miss Polly they don't think she will walk again, and is devastated. Playing the Glad Game doesn't mean pretending everything is fine when it isn't. Grief is a healing necessity when we're dealing with a loss of any kind, whether death of a loved one, a job loss, loss of something hoped for, loss of health, loss of a relationship, pregnancy loss, financial losses, loss of a beloved pet, or any other loss.

Blessed are those who mourn, for they will be comforted.
Matthew 5:4 NIV

Grieving is hard, and it hurts. Though sometimes in the middle of grief is when He feels furthest away, Jesus is there with us, too, offering comfort, love, and hope. Just like he cried with Mary and Martha when they grieved the death of their brother Lazarus (then raised Lazarus back to life!). Just like He walked out on the sea to comfort the apostles in the middle of the storm.

It is possible to still feel a kind of joy when we grieve. Joy can be wild and exuberant and overwhelming, shouting praise to God with our arms in the air. Oh, how I love that joy! But joy can also be quiet and stubborn and persistent, a candle flame in the dark that can't be extinguished. When we give thanks for His presence with us, in the middle of the storm of grief, we will feel that quiet but deep and true joy.

He doesn't make everything instantly better. But He helps, with a deep and real comfort that speaks to our hearts and souls.

Does telling yourself things could be worse help a situation?

How have you felt when you've experienced losses in your life?

Where have you found comfort when you grieve?

Have you ever felt that still quiet joy, even in the middle of an emotional storm?

Lord, it's hard to accept loss as a part of life. It's hard to trust You have a plan and a purpose when I'm hurting. Please help me to truly mourn my loss. Help me to feel Your comfort, Your loving presence with me. And help me to know You don't expect me to grieve alone. Give me willingness to reach out for help from other people. Help me to trust You will bring me through this storm. Thank You!

CHAPTER TWENTY-SEVEN:
TWO VISITS

It was Nancy who was sent to tell Mr. John Pendleton of Dr. Mead's verdict. Miss Polly had remembered her promise to let him have direct information from the house. To go herself, or to write a letter, she felt to be almost equally out of the question. It occurred to her then to send Nancy.

There had been a time when Nancy would have rejoiced greatly at this extraordinary opportunity to see something of the House of Mystery and its master. But to-day her heart was too heavy to, rejoice at anything. She scarcely even looked about her at all, indeed, during the few minutes, she waited for Mr. John Pendleton to appear.

"I'm Nancy, sir," she said respectfully, in response to the surprised questioning of his eyes, when he came into the room. "Miss Harrington sent me to tell you about — Miss Pollyanna."

"Well?"

In spite of the curt terseness of the word, Nancy quite understood the anxiety that lay behind that short "well?"

"It ain't well, Mr. Pendleton," she choked.

"You don't mean — " He paused, and she bowed her head miserably.

"Yes, sir. He says — she can't walk again — never."

For a moment there was absolute silence in the room; then the man spoke, in a voice shaken with emotion.

"Poor — little — girl! Poor — little — girl!"

Nancy glanced at him, but dropped her eyes at once. She had not supposed that sour, cross, stern John Pendleton could look like that.

In a moment he spoke again, still in the low, unsteady voice.

"It seems cruel — never to dance in the sunshine again! My little prism girl!"

There was another silence; then, abruptly, the man asked:

"She herself doesn't know yet — of course — does she?"

"But she does, sir." sobbed Nancy, "an' that's what makes it all the harder. She found out — drat that cat! I begs yer pardon," apologized the girl, hurriedly. "It's only that the cat pushed open the door an' Miss Pollyanna overheard 'em talkin'. She found out — that way."

"Poor — little — girl!" sighed the man again.

"Yes, sir. You'd say so, sir, if you could see her," choked Nancy. "I hain't seen her but twice since she knew about it, an' it done me up both times. Ye see it's all so fresh an' new to her, an' she keeps thinkin' all the time of new things she can't do — NOW. It worries her, too, 'cause she can't seem ter be glad — maybe you don't know about her game, though," broke off Nancy, apologetically.

"The 'glad game'?" asked the man. "Oh, yes; she told me of that."

"Oh, she did! Well, I guess she has told it generally ter most folks. But ye see, now she — she can't play it herself, an' it worries her. She says she can't think of a thing — not a thing about this not walkin' again, ter be glad about."

"Well, why should she?" retorted the man, almost savagely.

Nancy shifted her feet uneasily.

"That's the way I felt, too — till I happened ter think — it WOULD be easier if she could find somethin', ye know. So I tried to — to remind her."

"To remind her! Of what?" John Pendleton's voice was still angrily impatient.

"Of — of how she told others ter play it Mis' Snow, and the rest, ye know — and what she said for them ter do. But the poor little lamb just cries, an' says it don't seem the same, somehow. She says it's easy ter TELL lifelong invalids how ter be glad, but 'tain't the same thing when you're the lifelong invalid yerself, an' have ter try ter do it. She says she's told herself over an' over again how glad she is that other folks ain't like her; but that all the time she's sayin' it, she ain't really THINKIN' of anythin' only how she can't ever walk again."

Nancy paused, but the man did not speak. He sat with his hand over his eyes.

"Then I tried ter remind her how she used ter say the game was all the nicer ter play when — when it was hard," resumed Nancy, in a dull voice. "But she says that, too, is diff'rent — when it really IS hard. An' I must be goin', now, sir," she broke off abruptly.

At the door she hesitated, turned, and asked timidly:

"I couldn't be tellin' Miss Pollyanna that — that you'd seen Jimmy Bean again, I s'pose, sir, could I?"

"I don't see how you could — as I haven't seen him," observed the man a little shortly. "Why?"

"Nothin', sir, only — well, ye see, that's one of the things that she was feelin' bad about, that she couldn't take him ter see you, now. She said she'd taken him once, but she didn't think he showed off very well that day, and that she was afraid you didn't think he would make a very nice child's presence, after all. Maybe you know what she means by that; but I didn't, sir."

"Yes, I know — what she means."

"All right, sir. It was only that she was wantin' ter take him again, she said, so's ter show ye he really was a lovely child's presence. And now she — can't — drat that autymobile! I begs yer pardon, sir. Good-by!" And Nancy fled precipitately.

It did not take long for the entire town of Beldingsville to learn that the great New York doctor had said Pollyanna Whittier would never walk again; and certainly never before had the town been so stirred. Everybody knew by sight now the piquant little freckled face that had always a smile of greeting; and almost everybody knew of the "game" that Pollyanna was playing. To think that now never again would that smiling face be seen on their streets — never again would that cheery little voice proclaim the gladness of some everyday experience! It seemed unbelievable, impossible, cruel.

In kitchens and sitting rooms, and over back-yard fences women talked of it, and wept openly. On street corners and in store lounging-places the men talked, too, and wept — though not so openly. And neither the talking nor the weeping grew less when fast on the heels of the news itself, came Nancy's pitiful story that Pollyanna, face to face with what had come to her, was bemoaning most of all the fact that she could not play the game; that she could not now be glad over — anything.

It was then that the same thought must have, in some way, come to Pollyanna's friends. At all events, almost at once, the mistress of the Harrington homestead, greatly to her surprise, began to receive calls: calls from people she knew, and people she did not know; calls from men, women, and children — many of whom Miss Polly had not supposed that her niece knew at all.

Some came in and sat down for a stiff five or ten minutes. Some stood awkwardly on the porch steps, fumbling with hats or hand-bags, according to their sex. Some brought a book, a bunch of flowers, or a dainty to tempt the palate. Some cried frankly. Some turned their backs and blew their noses furiously. But all inquired very anxiously for the little injured girl; and all sent to her some message — and it was these messages which, after a time, stirred Miss Polly to action.

First came Mr. John Pendleton. He came without his crutches to-day.

"I don't need to tell you how shocked I am," he began almost harshly. "But can — nothing be done?"

Miss Polly gave a gesture of despair.

"Oh, we're 'doing,' of course, all the time. Dr. Mead prescribed certain treatments and medicines that might help, and Dr. Warren is carrying them out to the letter, of course. But — Dr. Mead held out almost no hope."

John Pendleton rose abruptly — though he had but just come. His face was white, and his mouth was set into stern lines. Miss Polly, looking at him, knew very well why he felt that he could not stay longer in her presence. At the door he turned.

"I have a message for Pollyanna," he said. "Will you tell her, please, that I have seen Jimmy Bean and — that he's going to be my boy hereafter. Tell her I thought she would be — GLAD to know. I shall adopt him, probably."

For a brief moment Miss Polly lost her usual well-bred self-control.

"You will adopt Jimmy Bean!" she gasped.

The man lifted his chin a little.

"Yes. I think Pollyanna will understand. You will tell her I thought she would be — GLAD!"

"Why, of — of course," faltered Miss Polly.

"Thank you," bowed John Pendleton, as he turned to go.

In the middle of the floor Miss Polly stood, silent and amazed, still looking after the man who had just left her. Even yet she could scarcely believe what her ears had heard. John Pendleton ADOPT Jimmy Bean? John Pendleton, wealthy, independent, morose, reputed to be miserly and supremely selfish, to adopt a little boy — and such a little boy?

With a somewhat dazed face Miss Polly went up-stairs to Pollyanna's room. "Pollyanna, I have a message for you from Mr. John Pendleton. He has just been here. He says to tell you he has taken Jimmy Bean for his little boy. He said he thought you'd be glad to know it."

Pollyanna's wistful little face flamed into sudden joy.

"Glad? GLAD? Well, I reckon I am glad! Oh, Aunt Polly, I've so wanted to find a place for Jimmy — and that's such a lovely place! Besides, I'm so glad for Mr. Pendleton, too. You see, now he'll have the child's presence."

"The — what?"

Pollyanna colored painfully. She had forgotten that she had never told her aunt of Mr. Pendleton's desire to adopt her — and certainly she would not wish to tell her now that she had ever thought for a minute of leaving her — this dear Aunt Polly!

"The child's presence," stammered Pollyanna, hastily. "Mr. Pendleton told me once, you see, that only a woman's hand and heart or a child's presence could make a — a home. And now he's got it — the child's presence."

"Oh, I — see," said Miss Polly very gently; and she did see — more than Pollyanna realized. She saw something of the pressure that was probably brought to bear on Pollyanna herself at the time John Pendleton was asking HER to be the "child's presence," which was to transform his great pile of gray stone into a home. "I see," she finished, her eyes stinging with sudden tears.

Pollyanna, fearful that her aunt might ask further embarrassing questions, hastened to lead the conversation away from the Pendleton house and its master.

"Dr. Chilton says so, too — that it takes a woman's hand and heart, or a child's presence, to make a home, you know," she remarked.

Miss Polly turned with a start.

"DR. CHILTON! How do you know — that?"

"He told me so. 'Twas when he said he lived in just rooms, you know — not a home."

Miss Polly did not answer. Her eyes were out the window.

"So I asked him why he didn't get 'em — a woman's hand and heart, and have a home."

"Pollyanna!" Miss Polly had turned sharply. Her cheeks showed a sudden color.

"Well, I did. He looked so — so sorrowful."

"What did he — say?" Miss Polly asked the question as if in spite of some force within her that was urging her not to ask it.

"He didn't say anything for a minute; then he said very low that you couldn't always get 'em for the asking."

There was a brief silence. Miss Polly's eyes had turned again to the window. Her cheeks were still unnaturally pink.

Pollyanna sighed.

"He wants one, anyhow, I know, and I wish he could have one."

"Why, Pollyanna, HOW do you know?"

"Because, afterwards, on another day, he said something else. He said that low, too, but I heard him. He said that he'd give all the world if he did have one woman's hand and heart. Why, Aunt Polly, what's the matter?"

Aunt Polly had risen hurriedly and gone to the window.

"Nothing, dear. I was changing the position of this prism," said Aunt Polly, whose whole face now was aflame.

CHAPTER 27
DEVOTIONAL & JOURNAL

"The poor little lamb just cries, an' says it don't seem the same, somehow. She says it's easy ter TELL lifelong invalids how ter be glad, but 'tain't the same thing when you're the lifelong invalid yerself, an' have ter try ter do it. She says she's told herself over an' over again how glad she is that other folks ain't like her; but that all the time she's sayin' it, she ain't really THINKIN' of anythin' only how she can't ever walk again."

Grief can be made so much harder when we or other people expect ourselves to be happier after a certain length of time has passed, or to grieve a certain way. We might have judged some emotions as unacceptable, like anger with God or with a loved one. We may have feared others would judge the emotions. We may think what has happened doesn't justify the sense of loss we feel. Or we might have hidden the intensity of how we felt in an effort to protect other people, feeling we had to stay strong for their sake.

There is a right time for everything, and everything on earth will happen at the right time...
There is a time to cry and a time to laugh. There is a time to be sad and a time to dance with joy.
Ecclesiastes 3:1, 4 ERV

Especially for Christians, there can be a pressure to deny our grief. But faking it isn't what God wants from us, and it's not playing the Glad Game, either. Feeling sorrow and anger, even anger with God, isn't a sign of weak faith. It's part of being human, the emotional and feeling beings God created us to be.

He meets us where we are, no matter how messy that is. We don't need to pretend to have it all together for Him. He still loves and accepts us, even when we're angry with Him. True joy and gladness isn't about sticking a smiley-face Band-Aid over our hurts. Trying to make ourselves feel happy or closing off our feelings can make the pain of the loss and the intensity of the emotions even worse. We can be real with God.

Whether what's real for you is telling jokes in the ER to deal with concern for a sick child, or needing to cry weeks after a loss when people are trying to jolly you out of it and saying you "should" feel better now, He understands.

The people around Pollyanna seem to expect she should respond differently. What do you think?

Have you ever felt you had to fake "being fine" when really you felt sad or angry?

If that's happened to you, do you feel you've let yourself truly grieve for those losses?

Can you express to God how you feel about any losses you've experienced, knowing He will accept You no matter what you feel?

Lord, please help me to be honest with You about my feelings. It might not always be appropriate to show others every single bit of how I feel, but it's always right to be honest with You. Even when I'm angry with You over things I feel are unfair and wrong, You are my safe place. You will understand and still love me. Help me to bring all my feelings to You, so they don't come between us and wall me off from feeling the joy of Your presence. Thank You!

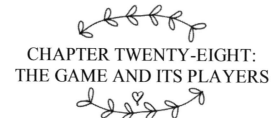

CHAPTER TWENTY-EIGHT:
THE GAME AND ITS PLAYERS

It was not long after John Pendleton's second visit that Milly Snow called one afternoon. Milly Snow had never before been to the Harrington homestead. She blushed and looked very embarrassed when Miss Polly entered the room.

"I — I came to inquire for the little girl," she stammered.

"You are very kind. She is about the same. How is your mother?" rejoined Miss Polly, wearily.

"That is what I came to tell you — that is, to ask you to tell Miss Pollyanna," hurried on the girl, breathlessly and incoherently. "We think it's — so awful — so perfectly awful that the little thing can't ever walk again; and after all she's done for us, too — for mother, you know, teaching her to play the game, and all that. And when we heard how now she couldn't play it herself — poor little dear! I'm sure I don't see how she CAN, either, in her condition! — but when we remembered all the things she'd said to us, we thought if she could only know what she HAD done for us, that it would HELP, you know, in her own case, about the game, because she could be glad — that is, a little glad — " Milly stopped helplessly, and seemed to be waiting for Miss Polly to speak.

Miss Polly had sat politely listening, but with a puzzled questioning in her eyes. Only about half of what had been said, had she understood. She was thinking now that she always had known that Milly Snow was "queer," but she had not supposed she was crazy. In no other way, however, could she account for this incoherent, illogical, unmeaning rush of words.

When the pause came she filled it with a quiet:

"I don't think I quite understand, Milly. Just what is it that you want me to tell my niece?"

"Yes, that's it; I want you to tell her," answered the girl, feverishly. "Make her see what she's done for us. Of course she's SEEN some things, because she's been there, and she's known mother is different; but I want her to know HOW different she is — and me, too. I'm different. I've been trying to play it — the game — a little."

Miss Polly frowned. She would have asked what Milly meant by this "game," but there was no opportunity.

Milly was rushing on again with nervous volubility.

"You know nothing was ever right before — for mother. She was always wanting 'em different. And, really, I don't know as one could blame her much — under the circumstances. But now she lets me keep the shades up, and she takes interest in things — how she looks, and her nightdress, and all that. And she's actually begun to knit little things

— reins and baby blankets for fairs and hospitals. And she's so interested, and so GLAD to think she can do it! — and that was all Miss Pollyanna's doings, you know, 'cause she told mother she could be glad she'd got her hands and arms, anyway; and that made mother wonder right away why she didn't DO something with her hands and arms. And so she began to do something — to knit, you know. And you can't think what a different room it is now, what with the red and blue and yellow worsteds, and the prisms in the window that SHE gave her — why, it actually makes you feel BETTER just to go in there now; and before I used to dread it awfully, it was so dark and gloomy, and mother was so — so unhappy, you know.

"And so we want you to please tell Miss Pollyanna that we understand it's all because of her. And please say we're so glad we know her, that we thought, maybe if she knew it, it would make her a little glad that she knew us. And — and that's all," sighed Milly, rising hurriedly to her feet. "You'll tell her?"

"Why, of course," murmured Miss Polly, wondering just how much of this remarkable discourse she could remember to tell.

These visits of John Pendleton and Milly Snow were only the first of many; and always there were the messages — the messages which were in some ways so curious that they caused Miss Polly more and more to puzzle over them.

One day there was the little Widow Benton. Miss Polly knew her well, though they had never called upon each other. By reputation she knew her as the saddest little woman in town — one who was always in black. To-day, however, Mrs. Benton wore a knot of pale blue at the throat, though there were tears in her eyes. She spoke of her grief and horror at the accident; then she asked diffidently if she might see Pollyanna.

Miss Polly shook her head.

"I am sorry, but she sees no one yet. A little later — perhaps."

Mrs. Benton wiped her eyes, rose, and turned to go. But after she had almost reached the hall door she came back hurriedly.

"Miss Harrington, perhaps you'd give her — a message," she stammered.

"Certainly, Mrs. Benton; I shall be very glad to."

Still the little woman hesitated; then she spoke.

"Will you tell her, please, that — that I've put on THIS," she said, just touching the blue bow at her throat. Then, at Miss Polly's ill-concealed look of surprise, she added: "The little girl has been trying for so long to make me wear — some color, that I thought she'd be — glad to know I'd begun. She said that Freddy would be so glad to see it, if I would. You know Freddy's ALL I have now. The others have all — " Mrs. Benton shook her head and turned away. "If you'll just tell Pollyanna — SHE'LL understand." And the door closed after her.

A little later, that same day, there was the other widow — at least, she wore widow's garments. Miss Polly did not know her at all. She wondered vaguely how Pollyanna could have known her. The lady gave her name as "Mrs. Tarbell."

"I'm a stranger to you, of course," she began at once. "But I'm not a stranger to your little niece, Pollyanna. I've been at the hotel all summer, and every day I've had to take long walks for my health. It was on these walks that I've met your niece — she's such a dear little girl! I wish I could make you understand what she's been to me. I was very sad when I came up here; and her bright face and cheery ways reminded me of — my own little girl that I lost years ago. I was so shocked to hear of the accident; and then when I learned that the poor child would never walk again, and that she was so unhappy because she couldn't be glad any longer — the dear child! — I just had to come to you."

"You are very kind," murmured Miss Polly.

"But it is you who are to be kind," demurred the other. "I — I want you to give her a message from me. Will you?"

"Certainly."

"Will you just tell her, then, that Mrs. Tarbell is glad now. Yes, I know it sounds odd, and you don't understand. But — if you'll pardon me I'd rather not explain." Sad lines came to the lady's mouth, and the smile left her eyes. "Your niece will know just what I mean; and I felt that I must tell — her. Thank you; and pardon me, please, for any seeming rudeness in my call," she begged, as she took her leave.

Thoroughly mystified now, Miss Polly hurried up-stairs to Pollyanna's room.

"Pollyanna, do you know a Mrs. Tarbell?"

"Oh, yes. I love Mrs. Tarbell. She's sick, and awfully sad; and she's at the hotel, and takes long walks. We go together. I mean — we used to." Pollyanna's voice broke, and two big tears rolled down her cheeks.

Miss Polly cleared her throat hurriedly.

"We'll, she's just been here, dear. She left a message for you — but she wouldn't tell me what it meant. She said to tell you that Mrs. Tarbell is glad now."

Pollyanna clapped her hands softly.

"Did she say that — really? Oh, I'm so glad!"

"But, Pollyanna, what did she mean?"

"Why, it's the game, and — " Pollyanna stopped short, her fingers to her lips.

"What game?"

"N-nothing much, Aunt Polly; that is — I can't tell it unless I tell other things that — that I'm not to speak of."

It was on Miss Polly's tongue to question her niece further; but the obvious distress on the little girl's face stayed the words before they were uttered.

Not long after Mrs. Tarbell's visit, the climax came. It came in the shape of a call from a certain young woman with unnaturally pink cheeks and abnormally yellow hair; a young woman who wore high heels and cheap jewelry; a young woman whom Miss Polly knew very well by reputation — but whom she was angrily amazed to meet beneath the roof of the Harrington homestead.

Miss Polly did not offer her hand. She drew back, indeed, as she entered the room.

The woman rose at once. Her eyes were very red, as if she had been crying. Half defiantly she asked if she might, for a moment, see the little girl, Pollyanna.

Miss Polly said no. She began to say it very sternly; but something in the woman's pleading eyes made her add the civil explanation that no one was allowed yet to see Pollyanna.

The woman hesitated; then a little brusquely she spoke. Her chin was still at a slightly defiant tilt.

"My name is Mrs. Payson — Mrs. Tom Payson. I presume you've heard of me — most of the good people in the town have — and maybe some of the things you've heard ain't true. But never mind that. It's about the little girl I came. I heard about the accident, and — and it broke me all up. Last week I heard how she couldn't ever walk again, and — and I wished I could give up my two uselessly well legs for hers. She'd do more good trotting around on 'em one hour than I could in a hundred years. But never mind that. Legs ain't always given to the one who can make the best use of 'em, I notice."

She paused, and cleared her throat; but when she resumed her voice was still husky.

"Maybe you don't know it, but I've seen a good deal of that little girl of yours. We live on the Pendleton Hill road, and she used to go by often — only she didn't always GO BY. She came in and played with the kids and talked to me — and my man, when he was home. She seemed to like it, and to like us. She didn't know, I suspect, that her kind of folks don't generally call on my kind. Maybe if they DID call more, Miss Harrington, there wouldn't be so many — of my kind," she added, with sudden bitterness.

"Be that as it may, she came; and she didn't do herself no harm, and she did do us good — a lot o' good. How much she won't know — nor can't know, I hope; 'cause if she did, she'd know other things — that I don't want her to know.

"But it's just this. It's been hard times with us this year, in more ways than one. We've been blue and discouraged — my man and me, and ready for — 'most anything. We was reckoning on getting a divorce about now, and letting the kids well, we didn't know what we would do with the kids. Then came the accident, and what we heard about the little girl's never walking again. And we got to thinking how she used to come and sit on our doorstep and train with the kids, and laugh, and — and just be glad. She was always being glad about something; and then, one day, she told us why, and about the game, you know; and tried to coax us to play it.

"Well, we've heard now that she's fretting her poor little life out of her, because she can't play it no more — that there's nothing to be glad about. And that's what I came to tell her to-day — that maybe she can be a little glad for us, 'cause we've decided to stick to each other, and play the game ourselves. I knew she would be glad, because she used to feel kind of bad — at things we said, sometimes. Just how the game is going to help us, I can't say that I exactly see, yet; but maybe 'twill. Anyhow, we're going to try — 'cause she wanted us to. Will you tell her?"

"Yes, I will tell her," promised Miss Polly, a little faintly. Then, with sudden impulse, she stepped forward and held out her hand. "And thank you for coming, Mrs. Payson," she said simply.

The defiant chin fell. The lips above it trembled visibly. With an incoherently mumbled something, Mrs. Payson blindly clutched at the outstretched hand, turned, and fled.

The door had scarcely closed behind her before Miss Polly was confronting Nancy in the kitchen.

"Nancy!"

Miss Polly spoke sharply. The series of puzzling, disconcerting visits of the last few days, culminating as they had in the extraordinary experience of the afternoon, had strained her nerves to the snapping point. Not since Miss Pollyanna's accident had Nancy heard her mistress speak so sternly.

"Nancy, WILL you tell me what this absurd 'game' is that the whole town seems to be babbling about? And what, please, has my niece to do with it? WHY does everybody, from Milly Snow to Mrs. Tom Payson, send word to her that they're 'playing it'? As near as I can judge, half the town are putting on blue ribbons, or stopping family quarrels, or learning to like something they never liked before, and all because of Pollyanna. I tried to ask the child herself about it, but I can't seem to make much headway, and of course I don't like to worry her — now. But from something I heard her say to you last night, I should judge you were one of them, too. Now WILL you tell me what it all means?"

To Miss Polly's surprise and dismay, Nancy burst into tears.

"It means that ever since last June that blessed child has jest been makin' the whole town glad, an' now they're turnin' 'round an' tryin' ter make her a little glad, too."

"Glad of what?"

"Just glad! That's the game."

Miss Polly actually stamped her foot.

"There you go like all the rest, Nancy. What game?"

Nancy lifted her chin. She faced her mistress and looked her squarely in the eye.

"I'll tell ye, ma'am. It's a game Miss Pollyanna's father learned her ter play. She got a pair of crutches once in a missionary barrel when she was wantin' a doll; an' she cried, of course, like any child would. It seems 'twas then her father told her that there wasn't ever anythin' but what there was somethin' about it that you could be glad about; an' that she could be glad about them crutches."

"Glad for — CRUTCHES!" Miss Polly choked back a sob — she was thinking of the helpless little legs on the bed up-stairs.

"Yes'm. That's what I said, an' Miss Pollyanna said that's what she said, too. But he told her she COULD be glad — 'cause she DIDN'T NEED 'EM."

"Oh-h!" cried Miss Polly.

"And after that she said he made a regular game of it — findin' somethin' in everythin' ter be glad about. An' she said she could do it, too, and that she didn't seem ter mind not havin' the doll so much, 'cause she was so glad she DIDN'T need the crutches. An' they called it the 'jest bein' glad' game. That's the game, ma'am. She's played it ever since."

"But, how — how — " Miss Polly came to a helpless pause.

"An' you'd be surprised ter find how cute it works, ma'am, too," maintained Nancy, with almost the eagerness of Pollyanna herself. "I wish I could tell ye what a lot she's done for mother an' the folks out home. She's been ter see 'em, ye know, twice, with me. She's made me glad, too, on such a lot o' things — little things, an' big things; an' it's made 'em so much easier. For instance, I don't mind 'Nancy' for a name half as much since she told me I could be glad 'twa'n't 'Hephzibah.' An' there's Monday mornin's, too, that I used ter hate so. She's actually made me glad for Monday mornin's."

"Glad — for Monday mornings!"

Nancy laughed.

"I know it does sound nutty, ma'am. But let me tell ye. That blessed lamb found out I hated Monday mornin's somethin' awful; an' what does she up an' tell me one day but this: 'Well, anyhow, Nancy, I should think you could be gladder on Monday mornin' than on any other day in the week, because 'twould be a whole WEEK before you'd have another one!' An' I'm blest if I hain't thought of it ev'ry Monday mornin' since — an' it HAS helped, ma'am. It made me laugh, anyhow, ev'ry time I thought of it; an' laughin' helps, ye know — it does, it does!"

"But why hasn't — she told me — the game?" faltered Miss Polly. "Why has she made such a mystery of it, when I asked her?"

Nancy hesitated.

"Beggin' yer pardon, ma'am, you told her not ter speak of — her father; so she couldn't tell ye. 'Twas her father's game, ye see."

Miss Polly bit her lip.

"She wanted ter tell ye, first off," continued Nancy, a little unsteadily. "She wanted somebody ter play it with, ye know. That's why I begun it, so she could have some one."

"And — and — these others?" Miss Polly's voice shook now.

"Oh, ev'rybody, 'most, knows it now, I guess. Anyhow, I should think they did from the way I'm hearin' of it ev'rywhere I go. Of course she told a lot, and they told the rest. Them things go, ye know, when they gets started. An' she was always so smilin' an' pleasant ter ev'ry one, an' so — so jest glad herself all the time, that they couldn't help knowin' it, anyhow. Now, since she's hurt, ev'rybody feels so bad — specially when they heard how bad SHE feels 'cause she can't find anythin' ter be glad about. An' so they've been comin' ev'ry day ter tell her how glad she's made THEM, hopin' that'll help some. Ye see, she's always wanted ev'rybody ter play the game with her."

"Well, I know somebody who'll play it — now," choked Miss Polly, as she turned and sped through the kitchen doorway.

Behind her, Nancy stood staring amazedly.

"Well, I'll believe anythin' — anythin' now," she muttered to herself. "Ye can't stump me with anythin' I wouldn't believe, now — o' Miss Polly!"

A little later, in Pollyanna's room, the nurse left Miss Polly and Pollyanna alone together.

"And you've had still another caller to-day, my dear," announced Miss Polly, in a voice she vainly tried to steady. "Do you remember Mrs. Payson?"

"Mrs. Payson? Why, I reckon I do! She lives on the way to Mr. Pendleton's, and she's got the prettiest little girl baby three years old, and a boy 'most five. She's awfully nice, and so's her husband — only they don't seem to know how nice each other is. Sometimes they fight — I mean, they don't quite agree. They're poor, too, they say, and of course they don't ever have barrels, 'cause he isn't a missionary minister, you know, like — well, he isn't."

A faint color stole into Pollyanna's cheeks which was duplicated suddenly in those of her aunt.

"But she wears real pretty clothes, sometimes, in spite of their being so poor," resumed Pollyanna, in some haste. "And she's got perfectly beautiful rings with diamonds and rubies and emeralds in them; but she says she's got one ring too many, and that she's going to throw it away and get a divorce instead. What is a divorce, Aunt Polly? I'm afraid it isn't very nice, because she didn't look happy when she talked about it. And she said if she did get it, they wouldn't live there any more, and that Mr. Payson would go 'way off, and maybe the children, too. But I should think they'd rather keep the ring, even if they did have so many more. Shouldn't you? Aunt Polly, what is a divorce?"

"But they aren't going 'way off, dear," evaded Aunt Polly, hurriedly. "They're going to stay right there together."

"Oh, I'm so glad! Then they'll be there when I go up to see — O dear!" broke off the little girl, miserably. "Aunt Polly, why CAN'T I remember that my legs don't go any more, and that I won't ever, ever go up to see Mr. Pendleton again?"

"There, there, don't," choked her aunt. "Perhaps you'll drive up sometime. But listen! I haven't told you, yet, all that Mrs. Payson said. She wanted me to tell you that they — they were going to stay together and to play the game, just as you wanted them to."

Pollyanna smiled through tear-wet eyes.

"Did they? Did they, really? Oh, I am glad of that!"

"Yes, she said she hoped you'd be. That's why she told you, to make you — GLAD, Pollyanna."

Pollyanna looked up quickly.

"Why, Aunt Polly, you — you spoke just as if you knew — DO you know about the game, Aunt Polly?"

"Yes, dear." Miss Polly sternly forced her voice to be cheerfully matter-of-fact. "Nancy told me. I think it's a beautiful game. I'm going to play it now — with you."

"Oh, Aunt Polly — YOU? I'm so glad! You see, I've really wanted you most of anybody, all the time."

Aunt Polly caught her breath a little sharply. It was even harder this time to keep her voice steady; but she did it.

"Yes, dear; and there are all those others, too. Why, Pollyanna, I think all the town is playing that game now with you — even to the minister! I haven't had a chance to tell you, yet, but this morning I met Mr. Ford when I was down to the village, and he told me to say to you that just as soon as you could see him, he was coming to tell you that he hadn't stopped being glad over those eight hundred rejoicing texts that you told him about. So you see, dear, it's just you that have done it. The whole town is playing the game, and the whole town is wonderfully happier — and all because of one little girl who taught the people a new game, and how to play it."

Pollyanna clapped her hands.

"Oh, I'm so glad," she cried. Then, suddenly, a wonderful light illumined her face. "Why, Aunt Polly, there IS something I can be glad about, after all. I can be glad I've HAD my legs, anyway — else I couldn't have done — that!"

CHAPTER 28
DEVOTIONAL & JOURNAL

"The whole town is playing the game, and the whole town is wonderfully happier — and all because of one little girl who taught the people a new game, and how to play it."

As Pollyanna battles to accept her inability to walk, most of the townsfolk come forward to tell her aunt how she's made a difference in their lives.

Pollyanna didn't hide her joy and her God-given light, but shared it and multiplied it by sharing it! She doesn't only share it with church people, but with everyone she meets. And she shares not only with her words, but with the way she lives. She accepts others and treats them all the same without judging them, from the richest man in town to a woman with a bad reputation, shunned by most "respectable" folk.

> *"You're here to be light, bringing out the God-colors in the world.*
> *God is not a secret to be kept. We're going public with this, as public as a city on a hill.*
> *If I make you light-bearers, you don't think I'm going to hide you under a bucket, do you?*
> *I'm putting you on a light stand. Now that I've put you there on a hilltop, on a light stand—shine!*
> *Keep open house; be generous with your lives.*
> *By opening up to others, you'll prompt people to open up with God, this generous Father in heaven."*
> Matthew 5:14-16 MSG

I've been learning these past few years what God means when He asks us to be generous with our lives. He's made it clear to me that I'm to have an attitude of service and love. He wants everything I do to be either serving Him, or serving others, with love. This is a 180 for me, because though on the surface I looked to be giving, I often gave resentfully. But the biggest way we can change the world around us is with love.

God's love shining through us changes everything, starting with us!

If people came forward to thank you for bringing a positive change to their lives, what would you like them to say about you?

Is there anything you'd need to do differently for that to happen?

How does your life share His light and love?

What would help you feel God's light shining and His rainbow colors glowing more strongly in your life?

Lord, help me to open my heart and mind to Your light, Your bright rainbow colors and Your love, to let them be seen by everyone I meet. We all can carry and shine Your light, it's not limited to the special few. Show me how You want me to make a difference for You, today and every day. Thank You!

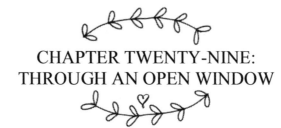

CHAPTER TWENTY-NINE:
THROUGH AN OPEN WINDOW

One by one the short winter days came and went — but they were not short to Pollyanna. They were long, and sometimes full of pain. Very resolutely, these days, however, Pollyanna was turning a cheerful face toward whatever came. Was she not specially bound to play the game, now that Aunt Polly was playing it, too? And Aunt Polly found so many things to be glad about! It was Aunt Polly, too, who discovered the story one day about the two poor little waifs in a snow-storm who found a blown-down door to crawl under, and who wondered what poor folks did that didn't have any door! And it was Aunt Polly who brought home the other story that she had heard about the poor old lady who had only two teeth, but who was so glad that those two teeth "hit"!

Pollyanna now, like Mrs. Snow, was knitting wonderful things out of bright colored worsteds that trailed their cheery lengths across the white spread, and made Pollyanna — again like Mrs. Snow — so glad she had her hands and arms, anyway.

Pollyanna saw people now, occasionally, and always there were the loving messages from those she could not see; and always they brought her something new to think about — and Pollyanna needed new things to think about.

Once she had seen John Pendleton, and twice she had seen Jimmy Bean. John Pendleton had told her what a fine boy Jimmy was getting to be, and how well he was doing. Jimmy had told her what a first-rate home he had, and what bang-up "folks" Mr. Pendleton made; and both had said that it was all owing to her.

"Which makes me all the gladder, you know, that I HAVE had my legs," Pollyanna confided to her aunt afterwards.

The winter passed, and spring came. The anxious watchers over Pollyanna's condition could see little change wrought by the prescribed treatment. There seemed every reason to believe, indeed, that Dr. Mead's worst fears would be realized — that Pollyanna would never walk again.

Beldingsville, of course, kept itself informed concerning Pollyanna; and of Beldingsville, one man in particular fumed and fretted himself into a fever of anxiety over the daily bulletins which he managed in some way to procure from the bed of suffering. As the days passed, however, and the news came to be no better, but rather worse, something besides anxiety began to show in the man's face: despair, and a very dogged determination, each fighting for the mastery. In the end, the dogged determination won; and it was then that Mr. John Pendleton, somewhat to his surprise, received one Saturday morning a call from Dr. Thomas Chilton.

"Pendleton," began the doctor, abruptly, "I've come to you because you, better than any one else in town, know something of my relations with Miss Polly Harrington."

John Pendleton was conscious that he must have started visibly — he did know something of the affair between Polly Harrington and Thomas Chilton, but the matter had not been mentioned between them for fifteen years, or more.

"Yes," he said, trying to make his voice sound concerned enough for sympathy, and not eager enough for curiosity. In a moment he saw that he need not have worried, however: the doctor was quite too intent on his errand to notice how that errand was received.

"Pendleton, I want to see that child. I want to make an examination. I MUST make an examination."

"Well — can't you?"

"CAN'T I! Pendleton, you know very well I haven't been inside that door for more than fifteen years. You don't know — but I will tell you — that the mistress of that house told me that the NEXT time she ASKED me to enter it, I might take it that she was begging my pardon, and that all would be as before — which meant that she'd marry me. Perhaps you see her summoning me now — but I don't!"

"But couldn't you go — without a summons?"

The doctor frowned.

"Well, hardly. I have some pride, you know."

"But if you're so anxious — couldn't you swallow your pride and forget the quarrel — "

"Forget the quarrel!" interrupted the doctor, savagely. "I'm not talking of that kind of pride. So far as THAT is concerned, I'd go from here there on my knees — or on my head — if that would do any good. It's PROFESSIONAL pride I'm talking about. It's a case of sickness, and I'm a doctor. I can't butt in and say, 'Here, take me! can I?'"

"Chilton, what was the quarrel?" demanded Pendleton.

The doctor made an impatient gesture, and got to his feet.

"What was it? What's any lovers' quarrel after it's over?" he snarled, pacing the room angrily. "A silly wrangle over the size of the moon or the depth of a river, maybe — it might as well be, so far as its having any real significance compared to the years of misery that follow them! Never mind the quarrel! So far as I am concerned, I am willing to say there was no quarrel. Pendleton, I must see that child. It may mean life or death. It will mean — I honestly believe — nine chances out of ten that Pollyanna Whittier will walk again!"

The words were spoken clearly, impressively; and they were spoken just as the one who uttered them had almost reached the open window near John Pendleton's chair. Thus it happened that very distinctly they reached the ears of a small boy kneeling beneath the window on the ground outside.

Jimmy Bean, at his Saturday morning task of pulling up the first little green weeds of the flowerbeds, sat up with ears and eyes wide open.

"Walk! Pollyanna!" John Pendleton was saying. "What do you mean?"

"I mean that from what I can hear and learn — a mile from her bedside — that her case is very much like one that a college friend of mine has just helped. For years he's been making this sort of thing a special study. I've kept in touch with him, and studied, too, in a way. And from what I hear — but I want to SEE the girl!"

John Pendleton came erect in his chair.

"You must see her, man! Couldn't you — say, through Dr. Warren?"

The other shook his head.

"I'm afraid not. Warren has been very decent, though. He told me himself that he suggested consultation with me at the first, but — Miss Harrington said no so decisively that he didn't dare venture it again, even though he knew of my desire to see the child. Lately, some of his best patients have come over to me — so of course that ties my hands still more effectually. But, Pendleton, I've got to see that child! Think of what it may mean to her — if I do!"

"Yes, and think of what it will mean — if you don't!" retorted Pendleton.

"But how can I — without a direct request from her aunt? — which I'll never get!"

"She must be made to ask you!"

"How?"

"I don't know."

"No, I guess you don't — nor anybody else. She's too proud and too angry to ask me — after what she said years ago it would mean if she did ask me. But when I think of that child, doomed to lifelong misery, and when I think that maybe in my hands lies a chance of escape, but for that confounded nonsense we call pride and professional etiquette, I — " He did not finish his sentence, but with his hands thrust deep into his pockets, he turned and began to tramp up and down the room again, angrily.

"But if she could be made to see — to understand," urged John Pendleton.

"Yes; and who's going to do it?" demanded the doctor, with a savage turn.

"I don't know, I don't know," groaned the other, miserably.

Outside the window Jimmy Bean stirred suddenly. Up to now he had scarcely breathed, so intently had he listened to every word.

"Well, by Jinks, I know!" he whispered, exultingly. "I'M a-goin' ter do it!" And forthwith he rose to his feet, crept stealthily around the corner of the house, and ran with all his might down Pendleton Hill.

CHAPTER 29
DEVOTIONAL & JOURNAL

Very resolutely, these days, however, Pollyanna was turning a cheerful face toward whatever came. Was she not specially bound to play the game, now that Aunt Polly was playing it, too. And Aunt Polly found so many things to be glad about! It was Aunt Polly, too, who discovered the story one day about the two poor little waifs in a snow-storm who found a blown-down door to crawl under, and who wondered what poor folks did that didn't have any door! And it was Aunt Polly who brought home the other story that she had heard about the poor old lady who had only two teeth, but who was so glad that those two teeth "hit"!

Though Pollyanna tries to play the Glad Game again, do you think she is truly accepting her changed circumstances?

Aunt Polly's examples seem more like using other people's misfortunes as a reason to be glad. Is that playing the Glad Game the best way? Does telling yourself other people are worse off help?

Pollyanna is "determined to be cheerful". Like trying to keep New Year's Resolutions, trying to make ourselves do as we know we should sometimes works for a while, but doesn't usually create any lasting changes.

Why am I so sad? Why am I so troubled? I will put my hope in God, and once again I will praise him, my savior and my God.
Psalm 43:5 GNT

The Message paraphrases "put my hope in God" as "fix my eyes on God". Focusing on Him is what carries us through sadness and trouble and brings us through to hope and praise.

I've never succeeded in changing myself by willpower. I can give the illusion of it, but I've learned that isn't real. For example, when I decide I really want to. I can work at losing weight. On three separate occasions, I've halved my dress size. The problem is, I've still spent most of my adult life overweight. Because I haven't made a lasting change to my core attitudes about food and what I eat, after a while the weight has always come back (and brought buddies along to hang out on my hips, too!).

Yes, it is God who is working in you.
He helps you want to do what pleases him, and he gives you the power to do it.
Philippians 2:13

This New Year, I did something different. I didn't make my usual lose weight/ be nicer/ work harder resolutions. Not one. Instead, I asked God to help me to keep surrendering myself to Him, to help me to let go my own plans and flow with whatever His will for me is.

God's power working within us makes the real difference. He works in us from the inside out, creating true and lasting change. I hope!

What could you do today to focus more on God, even in difficult circumstances?

How might that change things?

What would it mean to stop trying so hard and trust God to work in you and through you?

Lord, please help me to stop trying so hard, and look to You instead. Work in me, Lord. Change me from the inside out so I can feel Your joy no matter what is happening in my life. Give me hope again. Help me to give thanks to You and praise You. Whatever feels huge now in my life will be as nothing in eternity. Carry me through any difficulties today Lord, trusting that You will bring me safely home. Thank You!

CHAPTER THIRTY:
JIMMY TAKES THE HELM

"It's Jimmy Bean. He wants ter see ye, ma'am," announced Nancy in the doorway.

"Me?" rejoined Miss Polly, plainly surprised. "Are you sure he did not mean Miss Pollyanna? He may see her a few minutes to-day, if he likes."

"Yes'm. I told him. But he said it was you he wanted."

"Very well, I'll come down." And Miss Polly arose from her chair a little wearily.

In the sitting room she found waiting for her a round-eyed, flushed-faced boy, who began to speak at once.

"Ma'am, I s'pose it's dreadful — what I'm doin', an' what I'm sayin'; but I can't help it. It's for Pollyanna, and I'd walk over hot coals for her, or face you, or — or anythin' like that, any time. An' I think you would, too, if you thought there was a chance for her ter walk again. An' so that's why I come ter tell ye that as long as it's only pride an' et — et-somethin' that's keepin' Pollyanna from walkin', why I knew you WOULD ask Dr. Chilton here if you understood — "

"Wh-at?" interrupted Miss Polly, the look of stupefaction on her face changing to one of angry indignation.

Jimmy sighed despairingly.

"There, I didn't mean ter make ye mad. That's why I begun by tellin' ye about her walkin' again. I thought you'd listen ter that."

"Jimmy, what are you talking about?"

Jimmy sighed again.

"That's what I'm tryin' ter tell ye."

"Well, then tell me. But begin at the beginning, and be sure I understand each thing as you go. Don't plunge into the middle of it as you did before — and mix everything all up!"

Jimmy wet his lips determinedly.

"Well, ter begin with, Dr. Chilton come ter see Mr. Pendleton, an' they talked in the library. Do you understand that?"

"Yes, Jimmy." Miss Polly's voice was rather faint.

"Well, the window was open, and I was weedin' the flower-bed under it; an' I heard 'em talk."

"Oh, Jimmy! LISTENING?"

"'Twa'n't about me, an' 'twa'n't sneak listenin'," bridled Jimmy. "And I'm glad I listened. You will be when I tell ye. Why, it may make Pollyanna — walk!"

"Jimmy, what do you mean?" Miss Polly was leaning forward eagerly.

"There, I told ye so," nodded Jimmy, contentedly. "Well, Dr. Chilton knows some doctor somewhere that can cure Pollyanna, he thinks — make her walk, ye know; but he can't tell sure till he SEES her. And he wants ter see her somethin' awful, but he told Mr. Pendleton that you wouldn't let him."

Miss Polly's face turned very red.

"But, Jimmy, I — I can't — I couldn't! That is, I didn't know!" Miss Polly was twisting her fingers together helplessly.

"Yes, an' that's what I come ter tell ye, so you WOULD know," asserted Jimmy, eagerly. "They said that for some reason — I didn't rightly catch what — you wouldn't let Dr. Chilton come, an' you told Dr. Warren so; an' Dr. Chilton couldn't come himself, without you asked him, on account of pride an' professional et — et — well, et-somethin anyway. An' they was wishin' somebody could make you understand, only they didn't know who could; an' I was outside the winder, an' I says ter myself right away, 'By Jinks, I'll do it!' An' I come — an' have I made ye understand?"

"Yes; but, Jimmy, about that doctor," implored Miss Polly, feverishly. "Who was he? What did he do? Are they SURE he could make Pollyanna walk?"

"I don't know who he was. They didn't say. Dr. Chilton knows him, an' he's just cured somebody just like her, Dr. Chilton thinks. Anyhow, they didn't seem ter be doin' no worryin' about HIM. 'Twas YOU they was worryin' about, 'cause you wouldn't let Dr. Chilton see her. An' say — you will let him come, won't you? — now you understand?"

Miss Polly turned her head from side to side. Her breath was coming in little uneven, rapid gasps. Jimmy, watching her with anxious eyes, thought she was going to cry. But she did not cry. After a minute she said brokenly:

"Yes — I'll let — Dr. Chilton — see her. Now run home, Jimmy — quick! I've got to speak to Dr. Warren. He's up-stairs now. I saw him drive in a few minutes ago."

A little later Dr. Warren was surprised to meet an agitated, flushed-faced Miss Polly in the hall. He was still more surprised to hear the lady say, a little breathlessly:

"Dr. Warren, you asked me once to allow Dr. Chilton to be called in consultation, and — I refused. Since then I have reconsidered. I very much desire that you SHOULD call in Dr. Chilton. Will you not ask him at once — please? Thank you."

CHAPTER 30
DEVOTIONAL & JOURNAL

"An' so that's why I come ter tell ye that as long as it's only pride an' et — et-somethin' that's keepin' Pollyanna from walkin', why I knew you WOULD ask Dr. Chilton here if you understood — "

"Wh-at?" interrupted Miss Polly, the look of stupefaction on her face changing to one of angry indignation.

Miss Polly's refusal to allow Dr. Chilton to see Pollyanna as a patient comes from hurt pride, and conflicts with her love for Pollyanna when Jimmy Bean tells her the doctor may be able to cure Pollyanna.

I learned God-worship when my pride was shattered.
Heart-shattered lives ready for love don't for a moment escape God's notice.
Psalm 61:16-17 MSG

While pride rules us, we can't truly love. Pride is the source of many relationship issues. Pride stops us from hearing and following God. And pride can be one of the hardest sins to see in ourselves.

It's not just the obvious – showing excessive self-esteem and self-importance. Thinking our way of doing things is best and insisting on our own way, holding onto resentment and grudges, having feelings that are easily hurt, getting irritated over little things, stubbornness – all these can be signs of pride.

Hmm, ask my husband, he'll tell you I show all of that last group! And I'm not proud of it, because it's caused so many arguments and unhappiness between us. But I hope he won't have seen it quite so much lately. I want to choose surrender to God, not pride. I want to choose following His will, not pride. I want to choose love, not pride.

How do you feel when people around you behave pridefully?

Which indications of pride are you aware of in yourself?

How does it affect you?

Are you willing to let God take your pride?

Lord, it's hard for me to admit to having sinful pride. Yet if it's there, I'm willing to let go of it, because pride gets in the way of me truly loving other people and loving You. Please help me to see it in myself, and to bring it to You for forgiveness. Heal my pride, give me a healthy sense of myself, bring me into right relationship with You. I want to choose love, not pride. Thank You!

CHAPTER THIRTY-ONE:
A NEW UNCLE

The next time Dr. Warren entered the chamber where Pollyanna lay watching the dancing shimmer of color on the ceiling, a tall, broad-shouldered man followed close behind him.

"Dr. Chilton! — oh, Dr. Chilton, how glad I am to see YOU!" cried Pollyanna. And at the joyous rapture of the voice, more than one pair of eyes in the room brimmed hot with sudden tears. "But, of course, if Aunt Polly doesn't want — "

"It is all right, my dear; don't worry," soothed Miss Polly, agitatedly, hurrying forward. "I have told Dr. Chilton that — that I want him to look you over — with Dr. Warren, this morning."

"Oh, then you asked him to come," murmured Pollyanna, contentedly.

"Yes, dear, I asked him. That is — " But it was too late. The adoring happiness that had leaped to Dr. Chilton's eyes was unmistakable and Miss Polly had seen it. With very pink cheeks she turned and left the room hurriedly.

Over in the window the nurse and Dr. Warren were talking earnestly. Dr. Chilton held out both his hands to Pollyanna.

"Little girl, I'm thinking that one of the very gladdest jobs you ever did has been done to-day," he said in a voice shaken with emotion.

At twilight a wonderfully tremulous, wonderfully different Aunt Polly crept to Pollyanna's bedside. The nurse was at supper. They had the room to themselves.

"Pollyanna, dear, I'm going to tell you — the very first one of all. Some day I'm going to give Dr. Chilton to you for your — uncle. And it's you that have done it all. Oh, Pollyanna, I'm so — happy! And so — glad! — darling!"

Pollyanna began to clap her hands; but even as she brought her small palms together the first time, she stopped, and held them suspended.

"Aunt Polly, Aunt Polly, WERE you the woman's hand and heart he wanted so long ago? You were — I know you were! And that's what he meant by saying I'd done the gladdest job of all — to-day. I'm so glad! Why, Aunt Polly, I don't know but I'm so glad that I don't mind — even my legs, now!"

Aunt Polly swallowed a sob.

"Perhaps, some day, dear — " But Aunt Polly did not finish. Aunt Polly did not dare to tell, yet, the great hope that Dr. Chilton had put into her heart. But she did say this — and surely this was quite wonderful enough — to Pollyanna's mind:

"Pollyanna, next week you're going to take a journey. On a nice comfortable little bed you're going to be carried in cars and carriages to a great doctor who has a big house many miles from here made on purpose for just such people as you are. He's a dear friend of Dr. Chilton's, and we're going to see what he can do for you!"

CHAPTER 31
DEVOTIONAL & JOURNAL

"Pollyanna, dear, I'm going to tell you — the very first one of all. Some day I'm going to give Dr. Chilton to you for your uncle."

Miss Polly finds happiness and gives Pollyanna great joy when she lets go of her pride and stubbornness after twenty years and agrees to marry Dr. Chilton. When she was finally willing to do what she'd resisted, seeing it as weakness, Miss Polly allowed God's grace and power to operate in the situation.

But the Lord said, "My grace is all you need.
Only when you are weak can everything be done completely by my power."
2 Corinthians 12:9 ERV

It's human to resist our weakness and our broken places, to want to be strong and to focus on our strengths. But God's ways are not our ways. Since I became ill, I've had to accept that I'd lost the strength I previously prided myself on. But my weakness has made me more dependent on God, and drawn me closer to Him.

"For I know the plans I have for you, says the Lord.
They are plans for good and not for evil, to give you a future and a hope."
Jeremiah 29:11 TLB

I do now have a future and a hope. I do now have a peace and joy I didn't have. God has taken something I wouldn't have chosen, and used it to create something good. I just need to admit my weakness, and hand it over to Him.

I can do all things through Christ, because he gives me strength.
Philippians 4:13 NCV

C. S. Lewis wrote, "The more we get what we now call "ourselves" out of the way and let Him take us over, the more truly ourselves we become." Only through our surrendering to God can He make us all He created us to be.

Is God whispering to you of anything you've stubbornly held on to that gets in the way of you living a joyful abundant life? Could you let it go now?

Where do you feel weak? Can you accept your weaknesses and ask God to show you the blessing in them, and let Him use them for His purposes? What might be stopping you?

What is God asking You to allow Him to do in your life?
Today? This week? This month? This year?

Lord, please show me where I'm weak and broken, so I can bring those places to You to be healed. Help me to be willing to let Your purposes to be worked out in my life, even if that means I need to admit to my weakness. Help me to be thankful for Your strength, and to trust that if You ask me to do something, You will give me the strength I need. I'm so grateful to know that! Thank you.

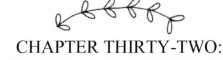

CHAPTER THIRTY-TWO:
A LETTER FROM POLLYANNA

"Dear Aunt Polly and Uncle Tom: — Oh, I can — I can — I CAN walk! I did today all the way from my bed to the window! It was six steps. My, how good it was to be on legs again!

"All the doctors stood around and smiled, and all the nurses stood beside of them and cried. A lady in the next ward who walked last week first, peeked into the door, and another one who hopes she can walk next month, was invited in to the party, and she laid on my nurse's bed and clapped her hands. Even Black Tilly who washes the floor, looked through the piazza window and called me 'Honey, child' when she wasn't crying too much to call me anything.

"I don't see why they cried. *I* wanted to sing and shout and yell! Oh — oh — oh! just think, I can walk — walk — WALK! Now I don't mind being here almost ten months, and I didn't miss the wedding, anyhow. Wasn't that just like you, Aunt Polly, to come on here and get married right beside my bed, so I could see you. You always do think of the gladdest things!

"Pretty soon, they say, I shall go home. I wish I could walk all the way there. I do. I don't think I shall ever want to ride anywhere any more. It will be so good just to walk. Oh, I'm so glad! I'm glad for everything. Why, I'm glad now I lost my legs for a while, for you never, never know how perfectly lovely legs are till you haven't got them — that go, I mean. I'm going to walk eight steps to-morrow.

"With heaps of love to everybody,

"POLLYANNA."

THE END

CHAPTER 32
DEVOTIONAL & JOURNAL

"I don't see why they cried. *I* wanted to sing and shout and yell! Oh — oh — oh! just think, I can walk — walk — WALK! Now I don't mind being here almost ten months..."

For many months after I became ill, I felt despairing and angry with God. Why had He done this to me? Why hadn't He healed me when I prayed? How could this be for my good?

He heals the brokenhearted and binds up their wounds.
Psalm 147: 3

It's taken over a year to realize the truth of how this applies in my life: God does heal us, but the healing may not always take the exact form we expect. It may happen on a spiritual level, rather than a physical one; or like Pollyanna's healing it may need time and hard work, and the effects may not show immediately.

I still want to be physically well again, but God has used this illness to give me a far greater gift than that. Trusting Him more, being more content, feeling His peace, surrendering to Him, being able to feel joy despite the circumstances — these are a powerful healing. These mean far more than simply having my physical health back.

Friends, when life gets really difficult, don't jump to the conclusion that God isn't on the job.
Instead, be glad that you are in the very thick of what Christ experienced.
This is a spiritual refining process, with glory just around the corner.
1 Peter 4:12-13 MSG

Oddly, maybe I'm not the least likely person to write a book on joy, after all! If God can use someone as flawed and imperfect as me to write this book, you can trust that He can help you to experience more of His joy, peace, and love.

Wherever you are, He will meet you there.

What wounds do you need to bring to God to be healed? Can you trust that He will heal you?

What do you think your healing will look like?

Lord, help me to trust You no matter what, and to keep my focus on You. Help me to open my heart, mind and body to Your healing power and love. Fill me with Your joy and peace while You work Your purposes for good in my life. Thank You!

Weeping may endure for a night, but joy comes in the morning.
Psalm 30:5 NKJV

CONCLUSION

No, in all these things we have complete victory through him who loved us!
For I am certain that nothing can separate us from his love: neither death nor life, neither angels nor
other heavenly rulers or powers, neither the present nor the future, neither the world above nor the
world below—there is nothing in all creation that will ever be able to separate us from the love of
God which is ours through Christ Jesus our Lord.
Romans 8:37-39 GNT

I hope that you've found reading the devotionals and journaling each chapter a blessing, and that You've found the Glad Game has helped you to appreciate the good that exists in your life, give more thanks to God, grow spiritually, and know more joy. My prayer for you is that your life be filled to overflowing with God's love, peace, and indescribable joy.

Working on the Pollyanna project has definitely blessed me. I've learned so much from the process of writing this book over the past six weeks. I've surrendered more of myself and my life to God. I've experienced how God's love transforms relationships. I've experienced great joy and peace.

But as is so often the case when we choose to draw nearer to God and surrender more to Him, I've also experienced ups and downs. A day of feeling amazing faith and joy is often followed by a day of feeling despair. I've learned to identify the feelings of despair as enemy attack. We do have an enemy who tries to oppose every onward step of our soul's progress, and all doubt and discouragement comes from him.

So be prepared – you may find you also experience doubt and discouragement. It's actually a positive sign of progress, and another lesson to be learned!

We put feeling first and faith second. but God puts it the other way around, faith first and feeling second. We ask God to help, and we surrender ourselves to Him, yet we don't always feel different straight away, or the feelings ebb and flow, and we start to doubt Him, or wonder if we did it right.

The answer is to hold onto faith, no matter what we feel. Believe God is working in your life, and the feelings will follow. God's love, joy, and peace are there for us, our birthright when we accept Jesus's sacrifice for us and are reborn as God's beloved children.

Take it one day at a time, trusting Him. We aren't yet perfect. We will stumble and fall at times. But we have a God who is always there, ready to catch us in loving arms.

So I beg you, brothers and sisters, because of the great mercy God has shown us, offer your lives as a living sacrifice to him—an offering that is only for God and pleasing to him. Considering what he has done, it is only right that you should worship him in this way.
Romans 12:1 ERV

How has God brought you nearer him as you've journaled through Pollyanna?

Lord, I am Yours. I surrender myself and my whole life to You, and I believe and trust You accept me as I am. I lay myself and all my burdens before You, trusting that You intend only good for me, and You will carry me. Please work Your will in my life, and teach me to trust You like a little child, resting securely from now on in Your love, peace and joy. Thank You!

Let us hold on firmly to the hope we profess, because we can trust God to keep his promise.
Hebrews 10:23 GNT

HOW TO PLAY THE GLAD GAME

Pollyanna explains the Glad Game as, "To just find something about everything to be glad about — no matter what it was."

That's easy with the obviously good things in our life, but with some things it can feel almost impossible. So those things are mainly what I'm talking about here.

WHAT THE GAME IS NOT!

It's definitely NOT ignoring reality, and especially not telling other people or ourselves we should buck up or be glad of things if we don't feel it! Pollyanna cried and grieved over many things in the course of the story, and couldn't play the game for months after losing the ability to walk. And she didn't dish out unwanted advice to "look on the bright side", not usually telling people what she saw as a thing to be glad over in their situation unless they asked her to. We cry with those who grieve and laugh with those who celebrate. That includes giving ourselves permission to mourn appropriately. God is close to the brokenhearted. It's okay to be sad or angry for a while, as long as we lean on God and hand our grief to Him rather than try to struggle with it alone.

> *Rejoice with those who rejoice; mourn with those who mourn.*
> Romans 12:15 NIV

WHAT THE GAME *IS*!

Though we need to grieve, it's also important that when bad things happen, we don't stay stuck in sorrow, anger, or whatever our first reaction is. If we trust that God has a plan and a purpose for us, and that He intends only good for us, then we need to look for the good in every situation, even the hard and terrible ones. We choose to trust God and look for the joy. We won't want to do a victory punch and sing and dance and shout our praise and gratitude for all things, no. Though at times that wonderfully exuberant elation fountains up in us, sometimes the best we can manage is a quiet gently faithful steadfastness, a glowing candle against the darkness, a trust that God *does* have a plan and a purpose, and it *is* for our good.

> *Weeping may endure for a night, but joy comes in the morning*
> Psalm 30:5 (NKJV)

HOW TO PLAY THE GLAD GAME BY OURSELVES

Let your roots grow down into him and draw up nourishment from him.
See that you go on growing in the Lord, and become strong and vigorous in the truth you were taught.
Let your lives overflow with joy and thanksgiving for all he has done.
Colossians 2:7 TLB

Giving thanks. Journaling. Prayer. These three can make such a difference to how we play the Glad Game. When things are good, keeping a gratitude journal, writing down the things we're glad about and give thanks for, is easy, and amplifies our joy. But even when it feels there's little to be thankful for in our lives, keeping a gratitude journal helps. Maybe *especially* when we feel we have little to be thankful for! I have a space on my daily journal sheets, and at the end of the day I write down the three things I'm most grateful for. Some days, even coming up with three is tough. I roll my eyes at myself when I write oh-so-obvious things like, "I'm breathing", "I can write", "We have electric light", "God still loves me even though I don't feel it." But doing that, and specifically thanking God for those three things, whatever they are that day, does make a difference to my attitude. Even a seed of faith is enough. The time to really make sure we play the game is when we're feeling discontented. When we don't seem to have enough. When it feels like *we* aren't enough, we're being given more than we can handle. That's when we need to know God is there for us and we can lean on Him, let Him nourish us.

HOW TO PLAY THE GAME WITH OTHERS

Get together regularly with friends to support and encourage each other in seeing the best in all our circumstances, holding each other while grieving the hurts, celebrating with each other over the successes. Or join a Glad Club, like this Facebook group started especially for readers of this book - https://www.facebook.com/groups/LessonsfromPollyanna/

Agree to check in at least once a week. Be real about what you're finding challenging, but stay positive. Resolve to take a difficult situation to God rather than dwelling on what is wrong with it.

Always give thanks to God the Father for everything in the name of our Lord Jesus Christ.
Ephesians 5:20 ERV

DISCUSSION QUESTIONS FOR BOOK GROUPS

Did you find reading the book for the first time or reading it again after a long time the same or different from your expectations? In what ways?

Calling someone a Pollyanna implies they are unrealistic and overly optimistic. Would you agree?

What do you see as the difference between "living" and simply breathing, as Pollyanna puts it? What makes you feel alive?

Which character in the book is most like you? What made you feel that connection?

What would you think about differently in your life right now if you looked for the blessing in everything, the things to be glad about?

Reverend Ford intended to give a harshly judgmental sermon, but changed it to an encouraging supportive one after he talked to Pollyanna. How can you use that principle in your relationships? Not just with other people, but with God, and with yourself?

Which part of the book did you like the most? Why?

What so you see as the difference between "playing the Glad Game" and having faith and hope in God?

If Pollyanna hadn't been able to walk again, would that have changed your view of the story? How and why?

Did reading the book change you and how you view life in any way?

HOW TO HAVE A PERSONAL RELATIONSHIP WITH JESUS

This is the core of what I believe as a Christian:

I believe in one God, creator of everything that exists, both seen and unseen. God created the universe and it was originally perfect.

God saw all that he had made, and it was very good.
Genesis 1:31

I believe that God isn't distant and impersonal, but wants to be in relationship with every person. He gave humans the gift of free will, and like disobedient children humanity chose to turn away from God to do whatever we wanted. Because of that, death and suffering came into the world. Every single one of us, even the best of us, has thought or done wrong, unloving things (sinned). In our broken imperfect state, having chosen to do wrong, we aren't able to be in relationship with God.

All have sinned and fallen short of the glory of God.
Romans 3:23

I believe that God didn't leave it there! He cares for us, no matter what we've done, and wants each one of us to live as His beloved child. He knows us personally. He feels our hurts, He sees each tear we cry, and He has a plan and a purpose for each of us. In His mercy and grace, to save us from spiritual death, He sent His son Jesus Christ, fully human and fully God, to redeem us and make us right with Him again.

God demonstrates His own love toward us, in that while we were yet sinners, Christ died for us.
Romans 5:8

I believe Jesus took the penalty for the wrongdoing of all humanity when He died on the cross. His life and death rebuilt that broken bridge between God and humanity, and makes it possible for us to know God again. But it didn't end with Him dying. He rose again, and still lives! Jesus defeated death, so that we can have life in Him.

God so loved the world that He gave His one and only Son, Jesus Christ, that whoever believes in Him shall not perish, but have eternal life.
John 3:16

I believe that to be forgiven for the wrongs we've done, we each need to ask God's forgiveness for turning away from Him, and accept Jesus as Lord of our life. No matter what we do or how we try, we can't save ourselves. We can't make ourselves right with God again by our own power. No matter how "good" we try to be, it's not enough. We're still prisoners of our past mistakes, and will still slip up and do wrong. The only way to be in a good relationship with God is by His gift of grace – reaching out to us and forgiving us for all we've done wrong. We need to admit that we've sinned (done wrong). We need to be willing to stop living life the way we have done, and choose to follow Jesus instead.

You were separate from Christ...without hope and without God in the world. But now in Christ Jesus you who once were far away have been brought near by the blood of Christ.
Ephesians 2:12,13

I believe that once we choose to accept Jesus as Lord, we're given a full pardon for the things we've done wrong in the past. God forgives us, fully and completely. He gives us peace with ourselves and with Him, and blesses us with new life. He is with us at all times through His Holy Spirit, who helps us to live God's way. He changes us, helps us, guides and supports us. He works in our lives as we believe and trust in God, and sets us free to accept ourselves and to truly love God and others.

But the Comforter, the Holy Spirit, whom the Father will send in my name, will teach you all things and will remind you of everything I have said to you.
Jesus speaking in John 14:26

I believe that if we want to choose life and accept Jesus as Lord, it starts by telling Him that! There are no right or wrong words to use with God. Jesus knows and loves each one of us. We can come to Him in total honesty. It's okay to tell Him everything—even if we feel confused, or angry, or tempted to do the wrong thing.

This is an example of a prayer you might use if you want to start again with God:

"Dear Lord,

I know I've done wrong in my life, and I ask for Your forgiveness.

I believe You died for my sins and rose from the dead.

I trust You and want to follow You as my Lord and Savior.

Guide my life and help me to be the person You created me to be.

Thank you.

In Your name, Jesus, Amen."

If you've decided to accept God's love and follow Jesus, welcome to God's family!

Just like any relationship, in order to grow closer to Him and experience a fuller relationship with Him, it's important to follow up on your commitment:

♥ Spend time with God each day. It doesn't have to be a long chunk of time, but take some time out daily to pray to Him and read His Word. Ask God to increase your faith and your understanding of the Bible. If you don't have a Bible, there are plenty of apps and websites (Bible Gateway is one example) where you can read the Bible in different translations for free.

♥ When you pray, you don't need to use special words. You can talk to God like you would to a friend, any time you want. And don't just talk, listen too.

♥ Seek fellowship and friendship with other followers of Jesus and find a church where you can worship God in the company of others.

♥ Keep making the choice to follow Jesus every time you want to do anything wrong or unloving. If you do wrong, and we all do at times, admit it, and ask forgiveness. Seek God's help to do better next time.

♥ Know that God loves you. Even if you don't feel it, He does! The more you practice believing that He does, the more you'll feel it!

MORE BIBLE VERSES ABOUT JOY

Everything on earth, shout with joy to God!
Psalm 66:1 NCV

You make known to me the path of life;
you will fill me with joy in your presence, with eternal pleasures at your right hand.
Psalm 16:11 NIV

Since God cares for you, let Him carry all your burdens and worries.
1 Peter 5:7 VOICE

"The Lord your God in your midst, The Mighty One, will save;
He will rejoice over you with gladness, He will quiet you with His love,
He will rejoice over you with singing."
Zephaniah 3:17 NKJV

"Count it all joy, my brothers, when you meet trials of various kinds,
for you know that the testing of your faith produces steadfastness."
James 1:2-3

And now, my brothers and sisters, be filled with joy in the Lord....
I know that I still have a long way to go. But there is one thing I do:
I forget what is in the past and try as hard as I can to reach the goal before me.
Philippians 3:1, 13

We pray that you'll have the strength to stick it out over the long haul — not the grim strength of
gritting your teeth but the glory-strength God gives. It is strength that endures the unendurable and
spills over into joy, thanking the Father who makes us strong enough to take part in everything bright
and beautiful that he has for us.
Colossians 1:11-12

THANK YOU FOR READING...

I hope you enjoyed reading and journaling through *Lessons from Pollyanna!* My prayer for you is that you experience more of God's love peace and joy in your life.

If you found this book helpful, please consider telling other readers about books you enjoyed by posting a short review on Amazon, Goodreads, or anywhere else readers discuss books. Word of mouth is an author's best friend and it helps people find the books they want to read. Your opinion counts! Thank you so much!

If you're interested in my other books, check my Books page on my website at www.autumnmacarthur.com

SUBSCRIBE

You can download free printables (and a free Christian romance, if you'd like!), be among the first to know when my new books are published and get news of special offers and subscriber only contests, by signing up for my newsletter at:

https://www.subscribepage.com/LFPsubscribers

Emails will arrive no more than weekly, your email address will never be shared, and you can unsubscribe at any time. You'll receive the download link as soon as you confirm your subscription.

Or use the QR code below which will take you directly to my sign-up page.

Made in the USA
San Bernardino, CA
09 May 2020